FEEDING THE DRAGON

Inside the Trillion Dollar Dilemma
Facing Hollywood, the NBA, & American Business

CHRIS FENTON

Post Hill
PRESS

A POST HILL PRESS BOOK
ISBN: 978-1-64293-586-8
ISBN (eBook): 978-1-64293-587-5

Post Hill Press
New York • Nashville
posthillpress.com

Published in the United States of America

~

Self-reflection is an extremely powerful force. When I started writing, I felt passionate as a voice of dissent. By the end, I learned I was also complicit. Though my thoughts have altered, my mission has remained steady: we either continue to coexist through the bond formed by the exchange of culture and commerce, or we consciously start a cold war between the world's two superpowers.

~

In Memory of J.C. Spink...

Dedicated to my wife, Jennifer, and my children, Kaylie and Dylan.

Special thanks to my parents for giving me the foundation for success and purpose.

Thanks to my amazing in-laws, brother, extended family, and friends for inspiration and support.

Thanks to the US-Asia Institute for including me in your vital mission of bilateral diplomacy.

Thanks to my former colleagues for providing a platform to utilize my skills, network, drive, experience, and persistence. Parts of my story detail our work from the turn of this century through 2013. Those activities were both colorful and historic. I portray those days with absolute reverence and adoration for each of you. We shared a wonderful journey together!

Thanks to all others involved in my memoirs...you made them educational and entertaining.

And finally, thanks to filmmaker Kevin Feige and his amazing colleagues at Marvel. You proved bilateral success can be achieved while also being true to your brand, movies, fans, and, most importantly, your nation...our nation...the United States of America....

The views expressed in this book are mine and do not necessarily reflect the stances of the US-Asia Institute.

Though I used extensive notes and other source materials to detail events from long ago, certain creative freedoms did come into play, possibly resulting in some inaccuracies.

My career has focused largely in the movie business, where "showing" rather than "telling" is the norm. The quoted dialogue from real people throughout the book was inspired by my recollection of each event and should not be taken as verbatim. That said, my goal was to handle the words of each character with great sensitivity and deep respect, since this book's mission is to entertain with great constructiveness towards a larger purpose. Its intent and content are not of a tell-all work of gossip and sensationalism.

Table of Contents

1.

THE COLD OPEN

APRIL 6, 2013, FIVE HOURS BEFORE THE RED CARPET
BEIJING, CHINA

"CAN YOU BELIEVE this shit?" Andy Anderson, one of DMG's Beijing-based VPs, peered through the fog of brownish haze across the courtyard of Taimiao, the Imperial Ancestral Temple. It was here at the temple, the holy shrine behind the heavenly gates that lead to the Forbidden City, where we would premiere *Iron Man 3*. I was on my early afternoon check-in. A sea of workers hustled around us in the freezing gloom, hammering nails, smoking, spitting, and taping the red carpet to the ground. The whole thing hummed with activity, but at this point, it all seemed more random and precarious than productive.

"Is it cloudy today?" I asked, slipping on a pair of gloves. "Feels like it's going to snow."

Andy laughed nervously. "Gonna be cold as a motherfucker tonight, but no worries about snow." He craned his head back and squinted, trying to see the Beijing sky hidden behind the covering of smog. "Believe it or not. It's actually sunny today. Above the toxic haze."

Tens of thousands of feet above where we stood on the eastern edge of China, a cold front descended from the Arctic. The front crossed the Asian continent west to east, the cold dense air squeezing the warmer air in the lower atmosphere and pushing it east. This weather effect caused fresh winds to howl across the Mongolian steppes, and

1

thunderclouds of clay-colored dust to tumble through the Gobi Desert. Here in China, the easterly winds effectively swept a winter's worth of automobile exhaust, the puke from industrial activity, methane from animal production, and pollution from the booming nation's coal-burning power plants east, straight through the Black Triangle toward Beijing. That's where mountains slowed the breeze of blended toxins and trapped the poisonous concoction from blowing out to sea. As the cold air continued to roll down from the Arctic, it formed a layer over the city that compressed the smog, sealing the capital and its citizens in their own gaseous waste.

"What's the PM2.5 count?" I asked Andy. PM2.5 is an air pollutant that damages the heart and lungs and is linked to cancer. PM2.5 was the principal toxic agent in the Chinese smog swirling around us. According to the Environmental Protection Agency, a good level of PM2.5 would fall between 0–50 PPM (parts per million) on the Air Quality Index. A reading of 150–200 PPM is considered unhealthy. I was hoping the number would fall in this range.

Andy shot me a look. "Sure you wanna know?" He clicked his radio and began talking in Mandarin.

Of course, I wanted to know. I wanted to gauge the air quality and safety for the hundreds of people working outdoors. I also had other concerns on my mind, and they were as pervasive as the smog.

Andy pinched the receiver in his ear and listened to a garbled response. His Mandarin was much better than mine, but he was still shaky. However, with something like an air quality reading, it was pretty basic. "PPM is approaching six hundred," he translated, "and climbing. It'll get worse throughout the day."

Jesus, I thought. *Gotta be a Karmic lesson in all of this.* It's as if Maoist China, long underfed and mostly agrarian for thousands of years, finally got to gorge on the mass-produced factory food of their Industrial Revolution. And, when indigestion set in and China farted, Mother Earth gave her a Dutch oven. If there's a lesson, it's one I did not have the perspective to appreciate.

Not only was the air quality an issue that day, so was the safety of one of America's most valuable assets. As part of our launch strategy, we were bringing a national treasure and diplomatic tool. More valuable than the Hope Diamond, the Crown Jewels, or any gem sitting in a vault or art hanging on a museum wall. This asset, which needed to be safeguarded against climate, theft, and physical harm, had generated tens of billions of dollars, brought joy to countless citizens around the world, and had the unique power to make men, women, and children of all colors and creeds rise up from couches, movie theaters, subways, and seats on airplanes to cheer, laugh, and cry. I'm not talking about our former NBA client Kobe Bryant or our past marketing ambassador and Olympic champion Michael Phelps, either. That day, the asset was known to us on the ground as RDJ. To the world, he's Robert Downey Jr.

"What the hell is this?" I asked Andy, pointing to the swelling crowd. "Who are all these people?" There must have been five to six hundred of them, milling around the red carpet's entrance.

"Some are workers taking a break. Others are fans. Who the fuck knows, really?"

"Anybody can just walk in here?" I asked, taking in the landscape, knowing that, in roughly five hours, Robert Downey Jr. would arrive at the very spot where I was standing. "Has anything been done since Downey's security detail came through last night? Doesn't seem like it." I walked over to a flimsy barricade being hastily assembled by a Chinese man, his cigarette jangling in his lips as he hammered wood. "Take a look at these." I put my hand on the top and pushed gently. The barricade teetered. "These will all collapse on to the red carpet the moment crowds push against them. Robert could easily get mobbed."

Andy pressed his hands to his forehead thinking about what to do. "We'll fix it. We'll figure it out. We always do."

"I know," I said, and it was true. Somehow in China, you just figured it out.

On April 6, 2013, I was serving as President of DMG Entertainment Motion Picture Group and General Manager of DMG North America. Only a short time before my introduction to DMG in 2000, DMG had been worth roughly $25 million, but it quickly became one of China's fastest-growing private companies. By 2013 its value soared to around $600 million. And, if things went well with *Iron Man 3*, the company aimed to go public on the Shenzhen Stock Exchange. Such a move would turn DMG into a multi-billion-dollar behemoth.

On the day of the *Iron Man 3* Chinese premiere, I wore many hats. I was the acting link between Hollywood and China, charged with keeping things copacetic amongst the standard chaos. Or perhaps more accurately, I was the captain of a pirate ship cutting through the smog, my crew battening down the hatches before the oncoming media storm. Some may have expected a standard-issue Los Angeles asshole pacing a red carpet, yelling into his cell phone. But that wasn't my style. I was definitely a proud son and tour guide to my parents that day, who traveled from New York just for the event, and most importantly, I was a cultural diplomat and ambassador to China, working at the very delicate tip of an economic and political spear penetrating the heart of China.

For the past ten years, DMG's three founding partners, my colleagues, and I have been steadily and carefully building ties within China's people and government, winning the respect of both parties, and — most crucially — drawing China into the very fabric of the work. Our success was the direct result of putting Chinese culture, creativity, locations, and people on screen in a respectful and meaningful way. It's *this* work, the work of the cultural diplomat, that, more than anything else, helped DMG climb to the point where we could make history. We were not just premiering a movie that day in 2013, we were opening what would become the biggest market for Hollywood — period. Our business was not only to follow the NBA's template for success by making China's 1.4 billion consumers love American movies but to bring China to the table as a partner in these blockbusters. We were essentially opening the Middle Kingdom but in a whole new way. That is, if we didn't screw it up.

Movie launches can create domino effects that generally go one of two ways. A well-orchestrated debut can turn a hit film into an unstoppable juggernaut that makes billions of dollars. A poorly orchestrated opening, or one that suffers from a bad press hit, can go in the exact opposite direction—straight to mega-flop status. Given the number of films released each year, and the many complicated moving parts of successfully producing, distributing, and marketing, movies are far more likely to bomb than to become massive hits.

This is especially true in China, where the government can pull a film for any reason. When Quentin Tarantino's *Django Unchained* surprised the Chinese film industry by garnering both censorship approval and a coveted Chinese release, there was no shock at all when the film was abruptly pulled from theaters, hardly into its very first showings. Why? Because it was discovered that the approvals for the film were given while many officials of the film regulatory bodies were on holiday. It was no wonder that when, as the story goes, a senior official looked out the window of his black, stretch Audi A6 and saw a large line around the block, he asked his driver why. When he found it was for *Django Unchained*, he called down to his subordinate and asked about the movie. After hearing the plot and tone, he asked why it got through. His subordinate stumbled with giving an answer, so the kill-switch was activated. Spent marketing dollars vaporized and heads rolled. All it took was one bureaucrat Tarantino fan without a good reason for his boss, and that was all she wrote.

Nike commercials in 2004 found a similar fate, and that was more than a decade after the GOAT (Greatest of All Time) himself, Michael Jordan, first brought both his iconic brand and the NBA to China in a massively impactful way. Even though those Nike spots starred the legendary LeBron James, the State Administration of Radio, Film, and Television (SARFT) didn't like the use of dragons and loathed that China's prized mythological animals lost to LeBron. "The ads were an insult to the country's national dignity," stated SARFT officials. That was enough to pull it from television within hours. Millions in content production and media spending were lost. Even worse, it set Nike, LeBron, and the NBA backwards in a market they coveted.

Both anecdotes played into my anxiety. Photos as simple as Robert Downey Jr. wearing a smog mask—incredibly insulting to China—on the red carpet, or worse, being a no-show at his own premiere because of safety issues cited by his security detail would kill us and the movie's returns in China. The bad press could torpedo everything we were trying to do in China. And to top it off, it could decimate returns on DMG's hefty financial investment in *Iron Man 3*.

Like most ambassadors, I had developed a love and loyalty to my adoptive country. I felt a sense of mission that went far beyond box-office numbers. US-China relations were on the line. We all knew it. We had to make it work. But as an American, something bigger was at stake. We were pulling a rival country's culture into our own. We were doing more than opening a market or making nice with China. We were bridging a cultural gap, making the world smaller, more stable, less contentious, and much safer. Failure would surely result in the opposite effect.

I see the bilateral relationship connected like a cell phone connects to a cell tower. In a perfect scenario, there are five bars—Fenton's Five Forces—of service connecting the two. Let's compare those five bars to that of five diplomacy forces that either connect countries or distance them: politics, national security, human rights, culture, and commerce. In the case of the US and China, three of those forces share no common ground—politics, national security, and human rights. The best we can hope for is both countries agree to disagree on each. And even that, we haven't gotten to bilaterally. For the other two—culture and commerce—bilaterally we have a real chance to connect and bond even further. And we are. Michael Jordan and the NBA represent one example. Marvel and Hollywood are another. In forging the bilateral exchange of culture and commerce, there will always be connective tissue between the superpowers. The cell service will work, at least with two bars, if you will. However, if bilateral collaboration stops with those two forces, the final two bars of cell service go blank. The connection between cell phone and cell tower ends. The world's two superpowers stop communicating. A new and mighty cold war begins. Ever escalating. With no end in sight.

Dramatic, but that was the significance of *Iron Man 3*. If it works, the two forces become enhanced. If it fails…

"When does RDJ's security get here for their walkthrough?" I asked Andy.

Andy glanced at his clipboard then checked his watch. "Oh shit. They'll be here in five minutes."

"Where's Kirby?" I asked.

"This way." Andy led me over to the soundboard area, where Jason Kirby, the events director and jack-of-all-trades stood hunched over the board, simultaneously shouting orders while flicking buttons on and off in the lighting panel. Guys like Kirby and Andy never spoke Mandarin calmly into their headsets. They barked or shouted orders instead.

Kirby pushed a few buttons, and the massive floodlights shot colored beams of light through the smog towards the majestic temple. Even though it was mid-afternoon, the thick, polluted air allowed us to preview how the stage and backdrop would look that night. It was magnificent: a vintage Chinese scene, reflecting exactly how one would imagine the Forbidden City—that is, if Hollywood took over. Using Tinseltown magic, the projection of those lights magnified the ancient relic of Chinese history, reminding me why we were there. We'd come to make history at the intersection of Hollywood and Beijing. For a moment, I took it all in. It felt good, really good.

"Wow! That's badass!" I said, coughing up a mixture of smoke and smog. "Well done, my friend. Tonight's going to be one for the books."

"Hope so." Kirby allowed himself a smile. "And in the right way too." He turned his red-rimmed eyes towards me. He looked stressed and exhausted. It was well below freezing, but his forehead glistened with sweat. I wondered how long it had been since he'd taken a break, the hours and days of scrambling to coordinate the first-ever premiere of a Hollywood film in China, featuring one of the biggest global superstars in the world. "Have you seen the barricades?"

"Yeah, that's why I'm over here. Can we do better?"

Kirby took a deep breath, removed his headset, and mopped his forehead with his sleeve. "The kind of barricades Downey's team requested don't fucking exist in China. We had to build this shit from scratch. And the security personnel numbers they requested are unrealistic too. Beijing doesn't have qualified-yet-polished crowd control in the private sector. We've got plenty of soldiers and police in this country, but the government simply won't throw them our way. They don't need to. They don't want to."

"That's insane! When Jordan's here, they shut down half of Beijing. Full military and police protection at all times! When we had Kobe in Shanghai, it was wall-to-wall police! Even the Strongman Competition had half of Chengdu's police force on security detail for those big boys! Remember that scene in downtown? It was chaos, but the police kept it in check," I exclaimed. "This makes absolutely no sense."

"Seriously, Kirby. Even here in the Forbidden City for that '"Battle of the Nine Gates"' basketball event we did with Nike and the CBA [Chinese Basketball Association], soldiers and police outnumbered the audience. They were fucking everywhere," Andy added, starring at Kirby. "There must be some real 'uniforms' available. Downey is possibly the biggest movie star in the world. He's easily the equivalent of the most famous NBA stars. Probably even bigger!"

Kirby barked something into his headset. He waited for a beat, then wiped his brow.

"Times have changed, guys. Remember when you would arrive at Beijing airport? All the pageantry of the ramp down the plane to the tarmac with soldiers saluting and shit?" Kirby asked. "Doesn't happen anymore."

And boy, was Kirby right. By 2013, the Chinese government didn't need to kiss ass anymore like that with Hollywood. The roles had completely reversed. It was so obvious when I stopped a moment and thought about it too. Robert Downey Jr. was coming to China. That was something that would've never happened five years ago. The difference now versus then was the government hadn't begged him to come. They would've had to in 2008. However, now, they expected him to come. They expected it because Robert wanted his movie to do well in the second-largest market on Earth. And they also expected it because he was looking to grow his fanbase in China for movies down the road. China had leverage. No one had to move mountains to get Robert to make the trip or to accommodate him while in China. That was all on us now. And since the leverage dynamic had changed in the favor of China, it was never going to change back.

"They do love their basketball though," Andy grinned. "If LeBron showed up today, I'd bet soldiers would be lined up. Only a matter of time before they do that with movie stars."

"LeBron, yes. But movie stars…that's wishful thinking." Kirby handed a thumb drive to a production assistant.

Kirby didn't mince words, and he was right. However, we didn't have time to debate it either. We needed bodies. We had to find American-quality security to protect Robert. That was the priority, and Kirby was super stressed and desperate to find a solution.

"It's okay, Kirby." I patted him on the back. "We'll figure this out. We always do."

"Not at this level! We're screwed." He threw his hands in the air.

Kirby was right, the event could go sideways. However, in China, thinking about failure ensured it would happen. Like walking a tightrope, you can't think about falling to your death. You must focus on your next step. Do that, and you'll get across. That's what we had to do. One step at a time.

A worker with a headset ran up to us, speaking rapidly in Mandarin. I picked up a word or two but waited for Kirby to translate the rest.

"RDJ's security just got here," Kirby said. He looked panicked. Running large-scale marketing and televised events in China can harden a person. Kirby's panic button was as calloused as the fingertips of a heavy metal guitarist on a world tour. If he got anxious, you knew it was bad.

"Andy, come with me." I briskly walked the quarter mile of red carpet, approaching the gates. Through the haze, we saw Dave, Downey's head of security. Dave was British and some sort of former special-operative Bond-esque badass who could break your neck just by looking at you. I could see him inside the gates, already shaking his head, pissed.

"Guys, what the bloody hell have you been doing all night?" he shouted as we approached. "How many additional security people did you get? Did you find any?"

Andy checked his clipboard, improvising. "Think we found another fifty or so."

"Fifty? Where are they? Do they know what the heck they're doing?" Dave paused and then nodded, acknowledging me. "Hey, Chris. Good to see you." He shook my hand.

"Good press conference this morning, right?" I asked, trying to bring some positivity to the conversation. "Downey was a pro."

"Yeah, no kidding. What the fuck was that shit he ate though? Looked terrible," Dave asked, head swiveling like an owl as he spoke. His constant observation and evaluation were reminiscent of an operative on a patrol behind enemy lines. Quite frankly, most Westerners who were new to China found the country so distant and strange they wore a similar look. It was just that Dave was always on the watch for trouble. That was his job. Everyone else had more of a deer-in-headlights look that stemmed from fascination, anxiety, curiosity, and, at times, plain shock.

"They call it Tanghulu. It's a bitter Chinese fruit that's sugarcoated to make it more appetizing. They're sometimes called Chinese hawberries," I explained, talking nervously, fearful of what else his trained eye might catch. "Regardless, Downey was a trooper. The crowd and press absolutely loved him."

"Christ, look at these things!" Dave took a few quick steps over to a barricade. He nudged it gently, and it toppled to the ground. "Imagine hundreds of people behind me, all pushing towards Robert. Know what I'm saying? This all falls over and everyone gets trampled. And guess what happens to Robert?"

"Yeah, I get it. We're working on a fix," I said, feigning confidence. Even though we typically found a solution, the scale of this event was bigger and the stakes much higher. That truly did scare me. And even if we were fortunate enough to solve the problem, I knew it would happen at the last second. Daunting stress and chaos would definitely precede that moment of well-earned relief. After all, this was China. That's just how it goes.

"Guys, I need a couple hundred more crowd control specialists and security detail before I can let Robert even *think* about doing this red carpet. Especially one this long!" He gazed towards the temple's gate where the long red tongue of carpet unfurled to a stop. "I mean, look at this thing. It goes on for miles." He paused, staring at the massive, thirty-foot-tall gate and the temple's elaborate interior, just visible through the passage. Kirby was still tinkering with the lighting, so everything danced with colors. First purple, then green, then yellow, and then in various mixtures. It truly was spectacular, even in daylight's smoggy haze. "By the way, that looks fucking awesome," Dave added. "I'll admit that. Robert will love it."

"Thank you." Andy nodded, taking the compliment, knowing it could be the last for a while. His lungs bucked in a spasmic coughing fit, known as the "Beijing Cough."

Dave scowled. "Don't even get me started on the air. It's downright toxic. Felt like I had strep throat when I went to bed last night, and now I'm getting that feeling again." He paused. "Robert will have to wear a smog mask tonight. I hope you know that."

Andy and I rolled our eyes at each other. The smog mask threat was beyond worrisome. While wearing a mask might seem like a reasonable way to protect one's health, here in China, it was the ultimate sign of disrespect. The Chinese were well aware of the filth in their air, but they surely didn't need a foreigner to point that out for them.

"That feeling in your throat will go away as you sleep. Your hotel filters the air," I said. "The smog is supposed to blow out of town tomorrow and maybe even tonight. As you know, the mask situation is a concern."

"Tonight is all I care about right now. Please get what I need, or I have to kill the red carpet. And clear out the bloody smog, if you want to kill the mask." He turned to go, then stopped to give one last gaze across the area. "I'll be back one hour before Robert's scheduled arrival to check on everything," he shouted above the construction noise. "If it's not right—" He paused, frowning. "Just make sure it's right!"

"We'll get it done!" Andy shouted back. Dave's driver shut the door of the Mercedes sedan, and they drove off.

"Will we really?" I asked quietly, knowing this challenge was in a class by itself.

Andy gave me a worried look. "Don't fucking know." He turned to a colleague and shouted something in Mandarin, then called Kirby on the radio.

"I'm getting Kirby out here," Andy said to me. "The government can barricade crowds from a distance. The PLA and PAP can suppress unrest, large crowds, and protests better than anyone. They can megaphone orders to the masses, making everyone comply. They can herd thousands into bullpens in only a few minutes. But no, if you got something to do in the private sector, there's no one that can handle this kind of stuff. It's so fucked!"

I nodded. He was right. The PLA (People's Liberation Army) and the PAP (People's Armed Police) were the best, but unfortunately, government resources weren't an option. We had to find some private-sector solutions.

"China just ain't used to putting a massive international movie star on a red carpet. NBA star, yes. Hollywood star, not yet." Andy coughed, then continued, "Shaking hands with thousands of fans, autographs, and selfies, talking to reporters and posing for pictures…doing everything up close and personal without it turning into a massive shit show. This Hollywood shit is new."

"What's up?" Kirby trotted up with five assistant event directors behind him.

"We need more security," I said, "and barricades that actually barricade."

"Well, as far as additional security personnel, I did discover a plan of last resort. Not going to be pretty, though." Kirby turned and shouted some Mandarin orders into his headset, balancing two conversations in two languages simultaneously. He had bilingual multitasking down to an art form. "We can call in farmers."

"Farmers?" I raised my eyebrows.

"I got a connection to a guy who can get us farmers—*one thousand* of them. Just need a little bit of notice and a big wad of yuan."

"Sorry, Kirby," Andy said, "I'm still not following. What are we going to do with a thousand farmers?"

"This guy, my contact, is hooked in with the local villages beyond the ring roads. Remember, beyond the fourth or fifth ring, it gets pretty rank with old-school China shit. Go beyond that, and you start hitting farmland and little backwards villages. Millions of farmers out there and this cold weather sucks ass for farming. They got nothing going on."

"Makes sense. Go on." I said, excitement mounting.

"This guy just takes buses with loudspeakers out there and shouts out a potential gig in the city. Tells them to jump on the bus. Rounds them all up. He's got some other guy in the city who he can grab a thousand cheap black suits from. He gets all these farmers to wear them.

They love it too. They get to go into the big city wearing fancy clothes," Kirby explained. "Oh yeah, and since it's for security purposes, he'll make sure they're all six feet at minimum."

"Shit, let's do that!" Andy chimed in.

Kirby glanced at his watch. "He needs three hours' notice, so if we're going to do this, we need to know now."

"Three hours?" I looked out, the crowd milling around the arrival area and red carpet swelled. Less than five hours until showtime.

"Yes, three fuckin' hours," Kirby said. "And that's miracle-speed. You know how hard it is to round up a thousand six-foot-plus farmers from the outskirts of Beijing and fight traffic to get them here? There's no fucking phones or internet out there." Veins popped in Kirby's neck. "If we're going to do it, we need to jump on this shit yesterday!"

"Please call your guy immediately," I said, snapping into decision mode. "Now what about the barricades?"

Kirby again barked into his headset, then thought for a moment. "We can put in the steel gates and quad them up like we did during production," he offered, referring to the process of taking two steel gates in parallel and connecting them to two others perpendicularly, thereby creating a fenced area of open space that could separate the red carpet from the crowds on the opposite side. We used a similar process in an attempt to keep Chinese lookie-loos from spying on the outdoor filming of *Iron Man 3* in Beijing.

"No way," I said, "Downey will want to interact with fans. That's his thing." I started to take a deep breath and then stopped, remembering the toxic smog would not help my anxiety. "We need to enhance what we have, make these barricades more secure. That's the only option."

Kirby nodded, again speaking Mandarin into the headset. "Done."

"Thank you." I had no confidence that the plan would work, but we had no alternative.

"Just tell me one thing, were you planning on wearing something different for tonight's event?"

"Yeah, of course." I looked down at my jeans and untucked button-down. I'd dressed casually, knowing I could go back to the hotel to change. "We have government officials attending tonight. Disney and Marvel executives will be there. I need to suit it up," I explained. "Why do you ask?"

"Because if we want to pull this off," Kirby said, motioning to the brigade of construction workers approaching with armloads of plywood and tools, "you're gonna have to pitch in."

"All hands on deck!" Andy shouted, grabbing a nail gun.

Oh, China...I sighed. That kind of last-minute, do-what-it-takes situation was so damn typical.

Kirby took a drill from a box and slapped it into my palm.

I smiled.

"Let's get this done."

APRIL 6, 2013, ONE HOUR BEFORE THE RED CARPET BEIJING, CHINA

"Look at all those buses." Andy pointed beyond the reinforced barri-cades we'd been working on as a long line of buses rolled to a stop amid an ever-growing crowd at the red carpet's entrance. Must have been a few thousand strong by that point. The energy level over the past four hours had amplified tenfold. The buzz of the fans was deafening, the sensory overload only enhanced by Kirby's perfected light show, which strobed and danced just as much around the arrival area as it did around the stage inside the temple. The sights and sounds didn't just fuel the crowd with excitement, it energized our crew. Everyone knew the importance and enormity of what was about to happen. We may have been scared as to whether we'd pull it off, but that fear was, at least partially, offset by the euphoria that overtook us all.

From the buses, serious-looking Chinese men dressed in ultra-cheap *Men in Black*-style suits streamed out in an organized, almost-disciplined fashion. Picture hundreds of Yao Ming-sized farmers, dazed and confused from what was likely their first time in Beijing proper, stepping into a sea of overwhelming celebrity-crazed insanity. If we needed a calm, collected, confident security force, this wasn't it.

Their leader walked toward me and Andy, who was, as usual, yelling endless instructions in Mandarin into his headset. Kirby raced over to meet us, also screaming into his headset. We all shook hands, and the leader now started shouting instructions to the confused farmers. They responded, frantically lining both sides of the red carpet, spacing themselves evenly along the vast stretch to the temple's gates.

Once they were in position, I observed the fake security guards. At first glance, the quarter-mile line was impressive. Hulking, stone-faced men in suits created an awesome display of force. However, upon closer inspection, the façade became obvious. Their faces bore signs of confusion and fear. These guys had been taken from their familiar countryside, dropped into an urban world of sensory chaos and asked to stand in neat rows. Not one of them looked comfortable. And they surely didn't look like they knew what the hell to do if something went wrong. They were strong and able-bodied, but the celebrity-crazed threats to RDJ would be much more intense than an unruly mule or goat. Yes, they looked foreboding from a distance, but beyond that, they were an impediment.

"Is this buddy of yours going to be able to direct all these farmers if something goes wrong?" I asked Kirby.

"Ha." Kirby cackled. He hacked off a Beijing wet, phlegm-filled cough. "My guy's not even here. He had to run off to some other event in Sanlitun. He'll be back to load 'em on the buses when it's over. That's it."

"Seriously?" I asked, shocked. Then something grabbed my attention. Out of the corner of my eye, I noticed Dave slicing through the crowd toward me. I worked up a smile. "Hi, Dave, how are you?"

"Looks like you brought in the cavalry," he said, laughing sarcastically. "What's the deal with these guys?" He pointed, noting the fake security almost instantly. "I have a suspicion you raided a fireworks factory looking for some burly men. Have these guys ever even seen a suit before today?"

"You wanted more security, so we got your more security," I said, feeling ill-equipped to lie.

"Who can translate for me?" he asked. "I need to ask a few questions."

Kirby yelled into his headset and a translator appeared. Apparently, Kirby's Beijing form of Mandarin differed from the dialect spoken by these farmers. To the peasant farmers, the vernacular of the city might as well have been another language altogether.

With the help of a translator, Dave performed a few interviews with the farmers. I stood just out of earshot, holding my breath. He simultaneously inspected the newly improved barricades, putting all his weight into them, pushing and pulling.

"This isn't going to go well, is it?" I muttered to Kirby as we both looked on. "And what is up with these guys?" I pointed to the trees throughout the courtyard that surrounded the red carpet. They were filled with fans. On every climbable branch sat a person, some of them twenty feet up.

Just then, the crowd began to push against one of the barricades, excited by something. I saw heads turning towards it at first, and then the commotion made sense. They had mistaken Dave, the handsome, athletic, white guy in a nice suit, to be a celebrity. And Dave, sensing the impending stampede that was soon to trample him, yelled to the translator who shouted at the nearby farmers.

"This is bad. Really bad!" I said to Kirby, as farmers looked at each other dumbfounded. Some of them even backed away from the ruckus, fearful.

I ran over to help, and the crowd, sensing a weakness in order, grew more aggressive. The farmers looked around for someone else to do their job. Dave continued to yell with no effect, getting right in his translator's face, demanding action. The translator, seeing his orders ignored, even turned a farmer toward the crowd and like a puppet, tried desperately to move the farmer's arms into a position of authority. But it was futile. Dave threw up his hands, screamed something at a guy in a tree, and then stormed towards us, red-faced and completely pissed.

Kirby prepared for a berating.

"Yep, it's fucked," he whispered deadpan, "and to answer your other question, I have no fucking idea what those people are doing up in the trees."

I tensed up as Dave approached. *Oh, shit...*

"Guys, this isn't going to fucking work. What the bloody fuck is this fucking shit?" Dave yelled, directing his question to us, to the surroundings, to the heavens, to the freaking ancestors, and to anyone and anything that would listen. He was angry as all hell, but he was also concerned. His boss, his prized gravy train and prime responsibility, Robert Downey Jr., was minutes away from arrival, and we'd prepared what amounted to a deathtrap. "China needs to figure out how to do this right. Like Hollywood expects. When will this country get their shit together?"

"Never. China has no intention of doing things like us." I said, knowing that wasn't what Dave wanted to hear. But it was the truth. "They don't need to."

"Fuck!" Dave was steaming mad. He was also gravely concerned.

Dave pulled out his phone just as a portion of the crowd flipped over a barricade. A throng of people spilled onto the red carpet like dominos falling. Yelling, screaming, pushing, shoving—thank God it all happened just gently enough that no one got hurt, but the symbolism and timing were undeniably bad, really bad.

"No way am I letting Robert down this red carpet. It's done. Canceled. No fucking way!" He pointed to a row of farmers. "Someone tell those guys to help those people up. Seriously! And for heaven's sake, get those damn people out of the trees."

Of course, the farmers were no help. If they moved at all, it was to get out of the way. They simply wanted to go home.

"Where the fuck did you find those guys?" Dave began dialing.

I looked at Andy, who just shook his head. Dave put his finger in one ear and spoke into the receiver. "Yeah, it's me. Let Robert know the red carpet won't happen. Just too risky. I'm making the call. We're going to delay arrival by one hour. He'll do the stage event only. I'll figure out a secure drop-off point and let the driver know."

And that was that. The call was over, and so was our dream of the myriad of Chinese journalists lining the red carpet to cover one of Hollywood's biggest stars engaging with Chinese fans. It was an enormous lost opportunity, and it was crushing.

Dave didn't miss a beat, though. He simply transitioned his attention to a new problem. "Okay, guys," he said. He inhaled deeply to calm himself a bit, looking at me, Andy, and Kirby. "Let's figure out a new, secure drop-off area now that Robert can't be dropped off here." He then hurled a deep, loud Beijing Cough into his hand, suddenly regretting his relaxation technique.

Kirby muttered some choice language under his breath and walked away, barking new orders into his headset. Change of plans—stat. That's the Chinese way. Nothing new to Kirby or any of us, but still always frustrating. Cruise control simply wasn't a thing.

I took in a dirty breath of air, turning to Andy. "Dude, this is going to be one heck of a stressful evening. Guaranteed!" I ran my fingers through my wet hair, realizing for the first time that I too was sweating. I stared at the ground, shaking my head.

I then looked at Dave. "I get it, I'm not upset at you, but damn. There were so many promised interviews with red-carpet reporters. Journalists are going to shit when they hear we're canceling. Not to mention all these fans who have one shot—just one—to actually see this guy up close and personal."

"Guys, I told you what had to be done, and it wasn't done," his tone had softened. "I understand it's China, and this event security stuff isn't a developed practice here, but my job is to guarantee Robert's safety. This whole setup is too damn risky."

I have to admit that his English accent did soften the disappointing news. He definitely had practice at it too. Surely it wasn't the first time he'd had to reject a situation on behalf of a client.

For the next few minutes, we debated the pros and cons of various ingress and egress spots for RDJ, and we picked the best one. As Dave walked off to ready the area, Andy, Kirby, and I turned our attention to peacefully dispersing the crowd. After which we'd have to get our farmers back to their homeland in an orderly fashion. Then, of course, there were the journalists who had been promised interviews. We had to avoid setting off a riot or enraging the press and influencers who had come and waited patiently (for the most part) in the freezing cold. The press was aggressive in China. They had to be. Alerting them of this change was not going to be pleasant. They expected one-on-ones with one of the world's biggest stars, and if that wasn't delivered, who knows what they'd write in light of their disappointment. It could kill our film. Even worse, it could kill our company.

"Huddle up, guys. Please," I said to Andy and Kirby. "We need to figure out how to deliver the bad news without causing a riot. We don't want journalists and camera crews pissed off. If they go rogue and complain on the internet about this, we're toast. The movie is toast. And this whole thing could become a tainted effort, not just opening this movie, but any Hollywood movie. The Politburo could yank the film and there goes every single thing we have worked for over the past ten years. Shit, DMG could lose its ability to distribute films over this, if we play it wrong."

"Okay, okay," Andy said, looking pale and walking briskly with us through the gates. "Let's get the sign-off from Dave on the new drop-off spot first. Then we'll get with Mike and the PR team and discuss how to give these journalists the news."

We walked into the courtyard. Seats were getting full. VIP guests and government officials had started to arrive. Everything looked to be running smoothly with lots of buzz and excitement. Any layman would've thought things were going swell, but all I could see was a public relations disaster waiting to happen.

My China phone buzzed in my pocket—not a good sign. Generally, when my phone rang on nights like tonight, it was because of a problem, and usually, a big problem like a politician calling with a threat, a panicked staffer in over his head, a Panavision camera falling off a tripod, a reporter tipped on a negative story, a studio executive pissed about a weeks-worth of production footage, or a VIP missing a flight.... *What else could go wrong?*

Annoyed and extremely fearful, I yanked the phone from my pocket and checked the number. It was RDJ's publicist. Surely, she was calling to complain. And why not? Her client had flown halfway across the world to promote his film, only to find out that he wouldn't be able to complete one of the most important parts of the agenda. Not because of him, but because of us. An absolute disaster! We blew our shot and wasted his valuable time. Not only that, but as soon as the journalists learned we were canceling the red-carpet interviews and fan interaction, Robert's reputation would be tarnished almost as much as ours. He'd be completely screwed too. And so would the movie.

"What a shit show," I said out loud as I answered my phone. "Hello." I braced for an earful.

"Is this Chris?" a man's familiar voice asked on the other end.

"Yes." I squeezed my ear against the phone. The roar throughout the Forbidden City around me was deafening by that point. The crowd's energy was peaking and so was the noise.

"This is Robert," he continued. "Robert Downey."

"Robert." I waved frantically, trying to quiet my colleagues around me. "Hey, how are you?" I grabbed a translator and mouthed, "It's Robert!"

The translator turned to the group and mouthed the same in Mandarin.

"I'm good," Robert replied, "I'm excited. Ready to shake some hands and meet my fans...my fans in China."

"Fantastic. They're excited to see you too. I'm so sorry about the red-carpet situation."

"There is no red-carpet situation," he said in his cool-as-ice movie-star voice. The same we've all heard in a hundred movies.

Still, I struggled to understand what he meant.

"I'm going to do it," he added matter-of-factly.

"Wait...what? Dave told you about the security situation, right?"

Andy and Kirby and a few of my Chinese colleagues were now staring at me in silence, watching my reaction closely. The surprised look on my face told them a change in plans was occurring, and likely a good one.

"Of course he did," Robert responded. "I don't care, though. You guys told me about the importance of this movie as a form of cultural diplomacy. The importance of me coming to China, making the Chinese people feel they are a priority. Meeting the people. Shaking their hands. Having direct conversations. Being respectful. Listening. Learning. Showing interest in the culture." He paused. "I want to make sure the Chinese people know I *want* to be here. Not that I *need* to be here."

"Love to hear that, Robert."

"Well, I didn't come all this way not to do exactly that."

"Wow. Yeah, all that's really important. I'm so happy you're on board," I said excitedly, feeling suddenly in that moment like the only person in the world truly grasping the enormity of what we were doing.

"You guys said what we are all doing was bigger than simply making a movie. We were bettering the world. Enhancing a bond—the necessary bond between the world's two most powerful countries who are often at odds with each other, right?"

"Yes. Yes, we did."

"Well then, let's do that. Let's bring China and the United States closer together."

"Yeah, Robert. Game on." The energy that had rushed out of me only moments prior suddenly poured back into the depths of my soul. "What's your ETA?"

He paused to ask. It sounded like he was already in the car.

"Five minutes 'til touchdown," he responded. "Time to change the world, Chris. Let's do this."

In a daze of gleeful shock, I was about to hang up when he stopped me. "Chris, one more thing…you still there?"

"Yes," I said, snapping out of my fog of disbelief. "Of course."

"Just wanted to add that I will *not* be wearing a smog mask."

"Sounds good," I said, grinning ear to ear.

A euphoric, out-of-body feeling overtook me. I hung up the phone and looked around, staring into the faces of my team as they waited for me to speak.

"Well, get the red carpet ready," I said. "Robert will be here in five minutes. It's game time."

2.

THE FIRST ACT: CLIFFSNOTES VERSION OF MODERN CHINA

BEFORE ANYONE CAN even think about putting the US and China together to collaborate on one of Hollywood's biggest blockbusters, a historical understanding of the complicated bilateral relationship is needed. It's super important to run through that before continuing to tell this story.

There is no way to discuss US-China policy with respect to trade without each side looking closely in the mirror. In the most basic terms, I think of China having started their own Industrial Revolution in the late 1980s. Yes, that recently, and I think most experts would agree with that assessment.

The US started theirs, as many would argue, as far back as the 1790s. That's quite a head start! And, the challenge to catch up to the US drives the decisions of China's Central Planning Committee.

What's unfair is exactly how the US kickstarted its Industrial Revolution—unfair both to Europe back in those early days as well as to China, today, in how we accuse them of unethical and protectionist practices.

Why? Because China is simply using much of the US playbook from the 1790s.

PIRACY/INTELLECTUAL PROPERTY THEFT:

Samuel Slater opened the first US-based industrial mill in the late 1700s. Many refer to Slater as the "founding father of the US Industrial Revolution." How did he construct such a mill? He used a stolen British design and pirated technology from Europe!

PROTECTIONISM:

The US also used tariffs and other protectionist policies to give US industries the ability to catch up to their European counterparts. In fact, it was the great Alexander Hamilton who labeled these as "Infant Industries." To help these companies grow and flourish, Hamilton constructed many protectionist trade policies, beginning with tariff acts passed through Congress as early as 1789.

YESTERDAY'S EXCESS VS. TODAY'S CHALLENGES:

The United States was just as guilty of the same accusations we make of China today. What's even worse is that if we take a look at the challenges the US faced back then, there are some pretty startling facts that lead to a shocking comparison.

For one, the population of the US in 1790 was not even 4 million. In the late 1980s, China had almost 1.2 billion people. Secondly, the cost of energy was extremely cheap back when the US started to really consume it, fueling economic growth. Let's use 1861 as a reference. A barrel of oil was 49 cents, or the equivalent of roughly $12 today. Now that barrel is roughly $60 and can be much higher. The cost of coal has similarly gotten more expensive. Third, all input resources for fueling manufacturing and technology advances have both increased dramatically in costs, as well as become more and more scarce. And lastly, China is facing a global environmental challenge that was nonexistent during the US Industrial Revolution. The US had no issues billowing smoke into the sky, releasing waste into rivers, tearing apart mountains in the Appalachians, or clear-cutting forests across the country. However, cut to today; the world has awoken to the sensitivities of global ecological balance, and we are the first to blame China for making things worse. Even though China only started its contribution to environmental rot hardly thirty years ago.

Adding to today's challenges, China started its race to become a developed country two centuries after most of the West. China feels a need to accelerate into a modern-day economy at a speed that eclipses anything the world has witnessed before. And they need to do that with a population that dwarfs that of any other developed nation.

To keep things simple historically, I'm going to say China remained a "sleeping giant" for most of the 1800s. Then, the story of modern China begins with the birth of Mao Zedong in 1893 amid dappled willows between the Shao and Shishi Rivers in the rural village of Shaoshan. Coincidentally, this was roughly around the same time that YMCA missionaries first brought the game of basketball to China — in other words, Western influence. Mao, born to a wealthy farmer who was part of the peasant class, was given tremendous advantages in his youth, unlike most of his peasant peers. With a university-level education and access to books (which he read voraciously), he was able to enrich his mind, rather than toil to feed his body. China, at the time of Mao's birth, was largely a Confucian society, classist, dynastic, ruled by the Qing dynasty and a loose federation of provincial governors. This dynastic order, which had been in place for two thousand years, fell apart in 1912 when the last of the emperors, a nine-year-old boy, fled China after being overthrown in a revolution.

Mao joined the revolutionary army, and although he did not fight initially, he would see plenty of war in his future. Over the next forty-plus years, Mao became an increasingly important leader when China was embroiled in alternating wars — one with Japan and one within its borders, resulting in the deaths of ten million people including Mao's second wife. Both she and her sister were beheaded.

From 1911 to 1949, the country also saw the consolidation of power under Mao's Communist Party. It culminated in the formation of the People's Republic of China (PRC), the Republic we commonly refer to as "China," which seventy years since its founding, is still ruled by Mao's Communist Party.

Mao had been greatly influenced by the Soviet Union, particularly the study of Marxism-Leninism which he read as a student around the time of the revolution. The Soviets provided guidance and material support to Mao and China during its forty years of war. Such resources were again provided during the Cold War that existed between the US and USSR. In 1953, following the death of Joseph Stalin, Mao and Nikita Khrushchev (who was far more moderate than Stalin) disagreed on ideological issues, causing Mao to cut off diplomatic ties with the USSR. As a result, China further isolated itself globally.

Over the next couple of decades, Mao completely restructured Chinese society through two initiatives that transitioned the country culturally and industrially but at the expense of twenty-five to thirty million Chinese who starved from the enormous social disruption. The first of those victims died during the Great Cultural Revolution, which effectively inverted the power structure by forcibly removing the highest class of traditional society: the city-dwelling, intellectual elites. Those leaders were imprisoned in work camps and replaced with the lowest rung of Chinese society (rural peasant farmers—our future red-carpet security staff). Suicide rates, often by leaping to death, were so high during this time that in certain cities it was unsafe to walk outside. Being crushed by a falling body was a common fate of the unlucky.

Due to mismanagement and fear of conveying information that might displease Mao and the new leadership, crop yields were consistently overreported. Food was taken away from starving farmers to feed the military and urban populations. The butcher's bill for the

Cultural Revolution alone was twenty million, and more tragedy was to come.

Around the time bodies were dropping out of the sky in the East, some ten thousand miles away in New York City, Stanley Lieber, a descendant of exiled Romanian immigrants, was fighting his own war. This war was galactic in nature and waged first in his head, then on paper with pen and ink. Soon, it resulted in the title *The Fantastic Four*, penned under the pseudonym Stan Lee. Stanley, urged by his wife to write stories that appealed to him, produced a comic book that would revolutionize the industry. It featured heroes who were powerful yet flawed. The uniqueness of the characters instantly struck a chord with comic book readers in the US, and the Marvel Universe was born. It wasn't long before Marvel's universe drew an international following, forming the basis for a global cultural exchange through its universally relevant storylines and characters.

At the same moment back in China, the foundation of another source of cultural exchange occurred—sports. China started to fall in love with the games of basketball and ping pong. First, Mao made clear that his love for basketball trumped many hardcore views taken during the Cultural Revolution, allowing the sport to be played even though all other athletic endeavors with Western roots were banned. Soon after, Mao decreed ping pong as the national sport of China and placed vast resources towards building a world-class team to represent the nation on a global basis.

As for Mao's industrial project, it began something called the Great Leap Forward, propelling the country to become the powerhouse it is today. His industrialization initiative, to a large degree, succeeded but at the cost of five to ten million Chinese citizens. Additionally, as this program wound down, the US-Chinese relations were nonexistent, and public sentiment was mutually negative. China backed North Korea in the Korean War as well as the communist North Vietnamese during the Vietnam War. To the US, Mao and his six hundred million citizens were a reason not to sleep easy at night. It was obvious the country would be a real threat to the US at some point in the very near future. For the Chinese, the same was true. The US was a phony democracy, spreading colonialism throughout the world through secret wars, alliances, and trade agreements.

By April of 1971, it's hard to imagine two nations less knowledgeable and less trusting of one another than China and the United States. But then, fate intervened in a very fortunate way — a quirk of cultural happenstance changed the diplomatic and economic relations between the US and China overnight. It was far more powerful than any bomb, act of terrorism, covert war, or propaganda narrative.

What happened? In a plot twist that feels like it was ripped from a stoner comedy like a *Bill & Ted's Excellent Adventure* remake, the relationship between the US and China (and thus the paradigm of power in the world) changed entirely when an American kid, a ping pong player no less, missed a bus.

3.

PING PONG
BROKE THE ICE

THE US TABLE Tennis team was in Japan in April 1971 for the World Table Tennis Championships. At the time, China dominated the sport, and the US was marginal at best and probably not even deserving of a spot.

A US player by the name of Glenn Cowan missed the team bus in Japan after spending some time with a Chinese player named Zhuang Zedong. Zedong had been teaching Cowan a few tricks, and they had lost track of time. When the facility manager told them he was closing up, the two realized Cowan had missed his ride. Zedong asked his coach if they could give Cowan a lift back to the hotel on the China team bus. The request was granted, and through an interpreter, Cowan and Zedong conversed on the drive. The players bonded so much, Zedong gave Cowan one of the beautiful silk-screen paintings stored on the bus for special gifts to dignitaries, and Cowan, in return, gave the only thing he could find in his bag—a comb, promising the next day to give him something more special.

When they got off the bus, Chinese reporters were there, documenting the journey of the Chinese players. When they caught the unusual sight of a US player coming off the Chinese bus, it created quite a stir. A Chinese reporter who spoke English asked Cowan if he'd like to visit China.

"I'd like to see any country I haven't been to before," Cowan answered matter-of-factly. "Of course."

The next day, Cowan gave Zedong the gift he promised: a t-shirt with the peace symbol and the Beatles quote "Let It Be" underneath. Zedong, a kid who grew up chanting "Down with the American Imperialism!" and believed that the US was the enemy, had been won over by an unlikely friend. Journalists from around the world caught the moment in photos.

Zedong went to the Chinese government asking for approval to invite the US team to China to compete in a series of exhibition matches. Chairman Mao apparently approved the invitation, saying, "Zhuang Zedong not only plays table tennis well, but he is good at foreign affairs and has a mind for politics." I'd imagine his last name didn't hurt either.

Cowan asked the US government if he and eight of his teammates could go to China to play ping pong. The approval was given, and the exhibition matches between the two teams took place in China from April 11 to April 17, 1971.

Both Chairman Mao and President Richard Nixon observed their respective teams enjoying the experience, entertaining crowds, and providing uplifting stories for the journalists covering the event. Chairman Mao then signaled to President Nixon that he was welcome to visit China too.

When Cowan and his teammates finally returned home, journalists rushed the bus, attempting to get the initial, exclusive interview. As the story goes, the first member of the team to detail life behind the Great Wall said famously:

The people are just like us. They are real, they're genuine, they got feeling. I made friends, I made genuine friends, you see. The country is similar to America, but still very different. It's beautiful.

They got the Great Wall, they got plains over there. They got an ancient palace, the parks, there's streams, and they got ghosts that haunt; there's all kinds of, you know, animals. The country changes from the south to the north. The people, they have a unity. They really believe in their Maoism.

President Nixon took note and saw an opportunity to improve the bilateral freeze. His first step, rather than to engage directly with the Chinese, was to end the US embargo on China on June 10, 1971. The iced-over diplomacy and trade between the two nations had finally started to thaw.

Then came the real diplomatic action. President Nixon decided to go all-in, opening direct and personal relations with Chairman Mao and the People's Republic of China. On February 21, 1972, President Nixon and Henry Kissinger accomplished that goal by making the first visit of a sitting US President to China. It officially ended the twenty-three-year freeze of bilateral diplomatic relations and created a new beginning moving forward for what would be the world's two great superpowers.

What happened afterwards? From President Nixon's visit in 1972 until 1989, there seemed to be a consistent, albeit slow, build of diplomacy between the two countries. The ping pong bilateral exchange continued and slowly morphed to encompass a sport more embraced in the US, basketball. Shortly thereafter, the NBA started its early stages of outreach to China, which led to some reliable gains for bilateral commerce and steadied relations. *But...*

4.

JUNE 4, 1989: TIANANMEN SQUARE MASSACRE

T**HERE ISN'T A** Chinese citizen who has lived their whole life in China, born around or after June 4, 1989, who has seen the famous photo of the Chinese man staring down a PLA tank in the heart of Beijing. One doesn't have to live in China to test this theory either. Any freshman at a college in the States can walk up to one of their mainland Chinese class-mates, show them the picture, and ask, "Have you seen this before?" As shocking as it seems, I promise the answer will be, "No."

This tells anyone trying to understand China quite a lot. That moment in history, as well as the revolutionary events surrounding it, have been eradicated from China's memory. Why? The reason is simple. Since the days of Mao, the goal of China is, and has always been, *keep the population, now a whopping 1.4 billion people, just happy enough so that they don't revolt.*

Anyone who wants to do business or exchange culture in China should understand that basic, yet super-macro concept. You cannot do anything that makes either the Chinese government look bad or the people unhappy. Once you understand this concept, it makes every-thing else much clearer.

5.

FIRED

WHEN ASKED HOW I initially got involved with China, my response is, "I got lucky. I was fired." This always gets a slightly uncomfortable laugh. It sounds like a cocktail party quip. But it's true.

Before I could get fired, I needed to get hired, which wasn't easy. After graduating from Cornell in 1993, most of my friends wanted to stay east, in finance in New York City or pursuing degrees in law or medicine. At the time, LA was in turmoil. The Rodney King beatings and a series of riots had rocked the city, not to mention the smog problem, fires, floods, earthquakes, O.J. Simpson, and dirty cops. The list was endless. And my friends, who liked to wear boat shoes and whale belts in the summer and silk scarves with pea coats or pilot jackets in the winter, considered LA a dangerous, second-rate city. "Why would anyone live there?" they'd ask. I thought the same.

However, when I actually visited, I saw something different: a diverse, vibrant city, glorious sunsets, fast cars, beautiful women, and a chance to work in the business of films, television, or music. It was the heartbeat of pop culture. And while I only came to visit LA, when I got there I never wanted to leave.

Back then, the way into Hollywood was the same as it is now. Get a job on the ground floor in one of the top talent agencies, management companies, or studios, and work your way up. The ground floor in Tinseltown most literally and figuratively means a mailroom, where promising hires, including everyone from Harvard grads, MBAs, newly crowned Ivy League lawyers, the children of Hollywood elite, and scrappy hustlers, sort and distribute inbound, outbound, and interoffice correspondence. These jobs, such as one in a talent agency mailroom, pay little, are boring, require grueling hours, and have almost nothing to do with the actual job of being an agent, which involves developing talent so they can produce great work, pitching the work/talent, and then negotiating compensation and hundreds of other important facets of an agreement. What the mailroom jobs do offer is a good dose of humility, a view into how an agency works at its most basic level, and the chance to decide if being an agent is the life they really, *really* want.

But it's a gauntlet. The benefit of this gauntlet is that if you could make it out of the mailroom, you become an assistant. Then, if you work hard enough, play the shark-infested politics perfectly, create the essential industry network, and get some luck to fall your way, you become an agent—a "made" person.

Back then, the unspoken rule of the big agencies was that they took care of their own, forever. If you became an agent at a place like William Morris, you would have a job until you died. Literally, this was true. I remember vividly some unfortunate mailroom staff who were in charge of delivering stool samples from the oldest agents in the building to their respective doctors (I, fortunately, found a way to get promoted out of the mailroom before I inherited that role!). There were stories of agents who died of old age while still working in their cozy offices, three martinis deep from an earlier lunch, gumming their way through nosh.

This kind of certainty appealed to me. It would be hard, sure, but all I knew was that if I got that coveted mailroom job, which didn't seem that hard to get, I'd claw my way to the top or die trying. This was a foregone conclusion. Not only did I have connections from my Cornell network to help get me in the door, but I also had a track record of considerable success. Though green for the business world, I did possess an Ivy League degree, I had founded and led a fraternity on campus, I interviewed well, I had a good head on my shoulders, I was kind, ambitious, outgoing, and I was not afraid to work my ass off.

But I also had a secret weapon that my dad taught me. It perfectly complemented my acute interest and curiosity in others too. He revealed a little family secret that involves the back of a Rolodex card. He recommended that whenever I met someone new, I write down everything I learned about that person and put it on the back of a Rolodex card:

J.C. Spink: brothers are Dan and Brian, Bucknell University, dog lover — to the point where he adopts ones he shouldn't (like stray Pit Bulls), Philadelphia area native, reveres Hollywood moguls Bernie Brillstein and Bob Evans, not a fan of working out, started as assistant for Zide/Perry Productions with buddy Chris Bender, loves 80s music and is a savant about it.

"You have a fascination about other people that's unique. Use it," he said.

"What makes you say that?"

"I remember on a cruise to Alaska. You were nine. Maybe younger. A woman was sitting by herself along the rails close to where we were all playing monopoly or something. You kept looking at her. You started to get concerned. After a while you said to mom and me, 'That woman looks sad and lonely.' We said it's sometimes hard to tell, but yes, she could be. And you responded, 'I'm going to ask her. I don't want her feeling that way.' And with the blink of an eye, there you were, sitting closely, chatting away with her. She suddenly had a big smile on her face. We let you both talk for a long while, and then you came back to the game. You told us every little detail about her. It was incredible. You dug deep, and she told you so much. A short while later, she walked over to us, still smiling. She said, 'Your son is something special. He took a cloudy day for me and made it sunny. Thank you.'"

"I vaguely remember that."

"As a parent, you never forget those moments," he said. "Continue that curiosity. It's an amazing attribute. But now, write it all down. It will serve you well professionally. I promise."

The idea was that, in a pre-Facebook and LinkedIn era when you can research everything about someone online, if I ever needed to contact Bob later in life, I could rattle off insider facts about Bob that were super meaningful to him. They were super interesting to me too. So many people come through one's life, it's hard to remember everything. If I took the time to write it all down, then I could show Bob how much our first encounter impacted me. As a result, whatever time passed would suddenly become irrelevant and the bond rekindled instantly.

"You'd be surprised how many doors open when you impress someone that way," my father explained. "It shows you care. You listened to their story, and you took the time to archive it. That kind of focus on others will take you a long, long way."

I applied his sage instruction immediately upon graduation. I have followed it to this day, even with social media allowing those with much more apathy to cheat their way into my hard Rolodexing work. I simply have to dig a bit deeper now to stay ahead of the pack.

Those original giant Rolodexes remain a fixture in my office today. They consistently help me. The notes penciled onto the back of each card are just as relevant and shocking to the names on the front today, assuming at some point I get the chance to dazzle those people with the knowledge I learned from them. Of course, now I put new information from my most recent relationships into a digital format, but those original Rolodexes are still the model.

In 2018, Hollywood insider Barry Katz interviewed me on his highly regarded podcast, *Industry Standard*. He spent twenty minutes just talking about those famous Rolodex cards and my process. I lugged one of them in to show him too. Barry was so taken with the thing he asked to take a picture with it. Amazing how such a simple idea can impress so many. Thank you, Dad!

Armed with my credentials, my character, and of course the Rolodex edge, I packed up my car in the summer of 1993 and began life's next stage. After seven months on the road finding myself while discovering America, I arrived in LA, finally ready to apply my strengths to a legitimate career. It was then that I learned none of it meant shit.

Everyone in LA who was looking for a mailroom job at a top agency was just like me. Most were far better, at least on paper. I remember one particular interview I landed by leveraging my limited Rolodex — the legendary former ICM (International Creative Management) literary agent, Tom Strickler, who has now dedicated his life to improving Los Angeles area schools. He started the interview by saying, "I only hire Harvard graduates, but Chris Moore [Producer — *American Pie, Good Will Hunting*] raved about you, so I felt obligated to meet you. That said, you will not get the job." I thought he was kidding. Turns out, he wasn't. I continued to hit the pavement and lined up several other job interviews only to get rejected over and over again. I was running out of money fast.

Thankfully I had a backup plan, or at least, I thought I did. When I cut out on my own in Hollywood I knew if things got tough, I could always wait tables or bartend. I was friendly, had a bartending certification, worked in bars and restaurants in both high school and college, and could certainly serve food and drink with the best of them. Plus, some of the higher-end restaurants in Beverly Hills and Santa Monica were industry hangouts like The Ivy or Chasen's or Morton's. I could get noticed at those spots, perhaps leading to an interview for a mailroom gig. Serve a Hollywood power broker charred beet salad and calamari with the right dazzle, and you never know where it could lead.

It seemed like a sound idea, but I soon realized I was pretty naive. Due to Hollywood's influence, nowhere else in the world is there a higher concentration of beautiful, charismatic people, grossly overqualified to carry your food or serve your drinks. LA is like the Olympics of waiting tables and bartending. At each restaurant I applied, I found myself outclassed and extremely low on the seniority pecking order. Some of those jobs had a sort of hierarchy not unlike the training processes implemented at studios and agencies in town. First, you start as a dishwasher and barback, then busboy, then waiter-bartender apprentice, and then, finally, a glorified server capable of making a six-figure income. That said, the road to such was long and arduous, and it wasn't a career path I was interested in.

So, I took the best job I could find with the quickest route to making a few bucks: The Olive Garden in Westwood, right down the street from UCLA and the studio apartment I shared with a friend from college, John Strauss. Ironically, the Olive Garden provided the first — and possibly only — time in LA when I was able to put my formal engineering education to work.

On my first day, they sent me to school — "Hospitaliano School" — a corporate term used by the restaurant's corporate owner at the time, General Mills. The week-long program trained aspiring servers how to properly wait on tables, but more importantly, how to make money for the corporate parent. "Hello. Welcome to Olive Garden," isn't just about being pleasant. It's about starting the art of an upsell to every customer a waiter serves. The highest profit margin items were appetizers, fancy non-alcoholic drinks, alcoholic beverages, and desserts. If you sold only entrees and soft drinks, you were fired. If you sold entrees with multiple "up-sale" items, you were praised, and maybe, just maybe, if your dollar average was high enough, you'd get a bonus and your photo in a frame behind the hostess station with the words: *Employee of the Month.*

"I'm Chris, I'll be your server today." Smile. Smile. Smile. "Here are some fresh garlic sticks to enjoy on the house." Bait. Bait. Bait. "Can I get you all started with some appetizers and wine while you look at your menus? We have a great special on Chianti today as well as our famous calamari dish."

To me, the upsell felt fake. Almost like a con. Your customers had no idea what you were doing, yet they fell for it every time. Heck, I even fell for the con when I was a customer at the Olive Garden. I just didn't know it at the time, but Hospitaliano School woke me up to it.

These upsells are so important that the Olive Garden had an algorithm built into their computerized point of sale system that tracked the amount of upsells a server made for each customer served. A customer was only calculated when an entrée was ordered. The assumption was that almost everyone who dines in the restaurant will buy an entrée. Therefore, a table of four will buy four entrees. For an add-on or upsell average, the entrée count is divided into the total non-entrée/soft drink bill to come up with the average per-customer add-on/upsell done by a server on a given shift. The higher the average, the better the server. The lower the number, the worse the server, and if it was too low, you either went back to Hospitaliano School or got fired. And here is where my formal education and engineering degree came into play.

Numbers! One thing about an engineering degree is that it forces you to think about numbers. It also makes you think about how numbers apply to everyday aspects of life in both theoretical and practical ways. So, of course, when I understood the importance of average add-ons/upsells per customer, I immediately started thinking of how I could make my per-customer average as high as possible. However, rather than do it for my own gain, I wanted to do it as a modern-day, waiter version of Robin Hood. Why? Because I felt bad for the customers. We were tricking them into buying items they never intended to purchase. And let me tell you, the customers at this particular Olive Garden weren't particularly well off. They couldn't afford add-ons. They were students or people from the burbs coming into town to celebrate a special occasion. Conning them out of money was not cool at all. But if I solely focused on the customers' well-being, they would win, and I'd feel good. But I'd also lose my job in the process. No add-ons, no job. Therefore, I needed to figure out a strategy that kept me employed and also kept customers from being conned.

I concluded an attack from both the sales side and a simple math strategy would work best. With sales, I'd simply sell: "Hello. I'm

Chris, I'll be your server today. Here are some fresh garlic sticks to enjoy on the house. While you look at the menus, I'd like to make some recommendations. Our selection of appetizers is incredible. I recommend parties like yours order appetizers and share them, family style. While you think about it, how about I get you started with some calamari and a bottle of wine?" Smile. Engage. Entertain. Compliment. Listen. Sell. And, sell again.

With respect to the math strategy, that was obvious to me. Lower my customer count to the smallest possible number. How? By convincing customers not to buy an entrée, I was saving them money. If I could do that, then technically that customer never existed because no entrée equals no customer, so any appetizers, desserts, fancy drinks, and such I sold were complete gravy and calculated against a super-low customer base overall for my per-customer average. Get it? If I did it perfectly, meaning zero entrees and only add-ons, my per-customer average would be infinity. But of course, there were always customers who wanted entrees, and an infinity average would probably cause alarms with corporate anyway.

Bottom line, my system broke records. I had the highest average per customer ever. And, even better, my customers got great value every time. Not conning them meant they enjoyed great, reasonably priced meals. And quite frankly for the restaurant, the better margins on appetizers, desserts, and drinks were much more profitable anyway. Both sides won. Not only that, but I was also Employee of the Month twice in a row. I was an Olive Garden God, and a top-secret Robin Hood for all my customers. My numbers and customer feedback were so good, I was worried the restaurant was going to promote me to a job at the corporate level. And knowing that I was pretty broke at the time, it may have been a job I'd have to take. Such a financially forced career choice would've killed any chances of working in Hollywood.

Speaking of being pretty broke, I did need to supplement my income with one other job at the time. The job that I chased allowed me, once again, to utilize some of my college education too. I took the

SAT exam for a company called Ivy West for a side job tutoring kids on how to master the SAT. I remember driving down to their head-quarters in Marina Del Rey to both apply and take the exam. It was in an apartment overlooking the marina—the same marina Gilligan and crew left for a "three-hour tour." Ivy West's founder was an Ivy Leaguer himself, roughly a decade older. He liked me and thought I'd be perfect to teach rich kids in Malibu, especially since I had just moved there—20440 Pacific Coast Highway, a 1400-square-foot, three-bed-room I shared with three other friends: my fraternity brother and beverage director at the swanky Regent Beverly Wilshire Hotel (the one where Richard Gere took Julia Roberts in *Pretty Woman*), John Strauss, his best friend from high school and aspiring filmmaker, Jeremy Haft, and a friend we recently met, banker Dave Brooks. The home stood on a cliff, hanging over the beach, and it was awesome. We each paid only $500 per month for the place. A small price for such a prime home. The highly discounted rent was a result of the massive fires that had swept through the iconic beach town a few months earlier, burning down most of southern Malibu. No one wanted to live there at that time. It was a ghost town on the beach. Even the famous Moonshadows bar, directly next door to our home, lacked patrons. A typical night there was the four of us nursing a single cheap beer at the bar, with Vince Neil from Mötley Crüe, who lived down the street, sitting next to us, and regulars Alec Baldwin and Kim Basinger dining at a corner table. Yeah, it was that kind of hangout, but it was hardly populated.

I took both the English and math portions of the SAT for Ivy West, hoping to qualify as a tutor for both. Yes, I was an engineer, and I never was all that good in English courses growing up. But I did take an introductory writing class during a summer session once. Maybe my English skills had improved since high school?

"Chris, we're hiring you. Malibu will be your location. We have lots of rich kids up there who need help now. You start tomorrow," the company's owner said after grading my exam.

"Both English and math?" I asked.

"Fuck no. Only math. You scored an eight hundred, which is perfect, as you know. To get the job you can only miss one question, so you easily qualified."

"Why not English?"

"Seriously?" He thought I was kidding.

"I didn't score well?" I asked.

"Let's just say I can see why you were an engineering major."

So, at least I was making some side loot tutoring math SAT skills to privileged kids in Malibu. And between the two jobs, it did leave me some flexibility to get to interviews for a *real* Hollywood job.

For instance, one of the first *real* Hollywood jobs I interviewed for was with Emilio Estevez of *Breakfast Club* fame and his producing partner, Jonathan Brandstein. I remember driving on the Disney lot for that pivotal Hollywood-virginity-breaking moment as if it happened yesterday. I was so excited. I had never been on a movie studio lot before.

Emilio Estevez could not have been any hotter in Hollywood at the time. I was super nervous. The job was an assistant position at his company, Avatar Productions. Emilio was in the thick of *The Mighty Ducks* movies and on a roll with hit movie after hit movie. As a result, his company had one of the biggest deals in town, and Brandstein, Emilio's partner at only twenty-four years old, was one of Hollywood's top up-and-coming executives. The meeting had come through my fledgling Rolodex. I had reached out to an older Cornell alumnus one day when I arrived in LA. I had never met him before, but he was a fraternity brother and connected to others I sort of knew. We met on a whim. He liked me and made a call to Tom Selleck—yes, the actor and his good friend. Tom said his buddy Emilio was looking for another assistant at Avatar Productions, so Tom made a call to Emilio, and the stage was set, as they say.

I mainly met with Jonathan, though Emilio did walk in for a few minutes. Jonathan had to keep taking phone calls throughout the interview because a hot movie script was on the market, and both he and

Emilio wanted to buy it as producers so they could make it into a movie at Disney. The script was called *Mango*. It was essentially an action-comedy about a chimpanzee and a cop who fight crime together. Or at least that's how I remember it.

"Isn't that the same idea as the movie *Every Which Way but Loose*?" I asked.

"Hmmm. I guess so, but who would remember that? This script is hot! Everyone wants it!" Jonathan responded.

His office was phat! Big, modern, richly appointed, and organized. A super cool Eames lounge chair and matching couch faced an expensive-looking coffee table covered with a plethora of massive hardcover photography books—too big to place on standard bookshelves. Bang & Olufsen speakers hung on the walls. I always dreamed of owning a pair of those someday. I grew up thinking B&O speakers were the kind of thing someone bought when they had truly made it.

"We offered half a million dollars for it," he added.

Holy shit. Half a million dollars! For a movie script?

The meeting lasted about ninety minutes, but the interaction between him and me was probably only thirty minutes of that. The rest of the time he was on the phone fighting for the *Mango* script, telling the agents selling the script that he and Emilio were the only ones that could make a hit movie from it.

"We are the producers of *The Mighty Ducks*. Emilio is the hottest star in Hollywood. We are the ones for *Mango*," Jonathan barked into the phone. It was intense to watch. Almost surreal. But I loved it. It was so Hollywood!

Ultimately *Mango* went to other producers at another studio for more than what Jonathan and Emilio were able to offer. I can't remember the exact price, but it was close to a million dollars. Yes, one million dollars!

"You are a super good guy and very impressive. That said, we really need an experienced assistant," Jonathan ended the meeting saying. "Let's stay in touch, though."

Which we did. Jonathan remains my friend today, and he has a very detailed card in my Rolodex.

I tracked *Mango* over the next couple of years out of curiosity too. Eventually, the studio that bought the script realized a similar movie had been made back in 1978 starring Clint Eastwood. It was called *Every Which Way but Loose*. *Mango* was never made into a movie as a result.

While basking in Olive Garden glory, one of the managers called me into his office after a shift. It sounded like he had big news. Oh boy, here it was. The big talk where they'd offer me the assistant manager job and the career path of a lifetime. *This is the opportunity you've dreamed of.* Ugh!

I walked into the manager's small office behind the kitchen. He was sitting behind the desk looking super serious.

"Busy night tonight." I grabbed a seat on a stool in the corner. All those employee rights posters and five-step CPR and "How to Help Someone Who's Choking" instructional diagrams surrounded me.

"Chris, this is a tough meeting for me," he said.

Weird. I straightened up in my chair. It wasn't exactly how I thought he'd begin the meeting.

He pushed a tape into a TV/VCR combo bracketed above us and pressed play. It was a CCTV camera shot pointed toward the dessert trays inside one of the kitchen's walk-in refrigerators. It was a spot I knew pretty well. Anxiety suddenly filled my veins.

A date popped up, subtitled at the bottom of the screen: January 30, 1994. In the bottom corner there I am. You see me go into the walk-in, fork in hand. I head straight to the tiramisu trays. I grab one. Eat it. I grab another. Eat it. I grab one more. Eat it. I grab the three plates and hold them in my left hand. I use my right hand and spread the remaining full plates around, so it looks like no tiramisus are missing. I walk out.

"That ring a bell?" he asked. "I'll put it on fast-forward so you can see some more."

Oh shit!

One of those fuzzy lines cuts through the screen as a result of the 5X fast-forward effect, but it was still easy to see what was happening. Dates would pop up. I'd enter the walk-in fridge. I'd attack the tiramisu trays. Then I'd leave. New date. New entry. New crime. New date. New entry. New crime. Over and over.

"Okay. I get it." I was super nervous now.

"Two hundred seventy-three. We counted two hundred seventy-three tiramisus you've eaten since you started here."

"I'm sorry." I felt bad. We did get some free food each shift, but the privilege was never meant for multiple tiramisus.

"I'm sure you are."

"I'm addicted to tiramisu. It's the one thing I can't *not* eat. If I take a bite, I can't stop. I can't be around the stuff." I attempted the victim card.

"That seems obvious." He sped up the fast-forward so I could witness all the crimes.

"Well, I have been breaking records around here. Perhaps we just add my tiramisu count to that and call it a day?" I joked uncomfortably, not knowing how to react. "I mean, how much does each of those cost anyway? I've more than made up for it all with my add-on-per-customer average. You've mentioned many times how profitable my tables are."

"That's not the point. You could've come to me with this addiction. We could've worked out a discount or shift allotment or something," he explained. I could see he was torn on what he had to do about this. "Instead, corporate feels like you stole the desserts and tried to cover it up. Yes, they are fucking tiramisus and the whole thing is sort of stupid, but it does look pretty damning on camera."

"I get it," I said, feeling slightly scolded at this point. "I'm so sorry. Is there a way I can pay the restaurant back for it?"

"I'm now fast-forwarding. At ten times the normal speed the video of you is still playing! Look at all of those you ate!"

"You have to admit. It's pretty impressive," I said, attempting to make light of it.

"I have to fire you, Chris. I don't want to, but it's my only choice. I'm sorry."

"Seriously?"

"Yes."

"I understand," I said, getting up. "If it helps make up for my bad deed, I'm happy to share an item I've learned to make the restaurant more profitable."

"What is it?"

"Entrees. They cost the restaurant a lot. The smaller portions needed for appetizers cost you less, and their price points are more favorable to you. Appetizers can satisfy most customers, especially when a bunch are shared by the table family style, and they combo it all with a variety of desserts." He was listening intently. "Push waiters to sell appetizers over entrees and combine it with high-margin dessert selections. You'll make the restaurant more profitable."

"Interesting."

"Yeah, and the bill is roughly the same for the customer, yet they'll feel they got more for their money. Nothing better than happy customers and bigger profits."

"Everybody wins?"

"Yup. Everybody wins." And I walked out. Satisfied that I had kept the Robin Hood initiative alive, yet I also did a solid for my now-former employer.

6.

ONE DOOR CLOSES.
ANOTHER OPENS.

A FEW DAYS LATER, another opportunity opened. I was offered a temp job at William Morris. I accepted and started the next day. It was a two-week stint that never really ended. I made sure of that.

My job was to sit in a small room with a bunch of fax machines. I'd send out deal memos from the booking agents in William Morris's music department to promoters all around the world. That meant all day long I could read deals and learn how they worked. At the time, William Morris was representing bands like Nirvana, Pearl Jam, Red Hot Chili Peppers, the Allman Brothers, and Blues Traveler. Additionally, agent Peter Grosslight and manager Irving Azoff decided that they could get The Eagles back together again for a tour called "Hell Freezes Over" if they could guarantee the band one million dollars for each concert. That meant taking ticket prices from the normal $20 per ticket to a minimum of $70—a feat no one thought was possible. The result was sold-out shows throughout the world and a disruptive moment in the concert business. Quite frankly, it's why I now have to shell out $350 per ticket for very mediocre Hollywood Bowl seats to see The Cure.

At the same time, Pearl Jam and their Morris agent, Don Muller, who also represented Nirvana, were fighting Ticketmaster over ticket pricing. Pearl Jam wanted fans to get tickets to their shows for only $18. Ticketmaster, on the other hand, wanted to charge $21 for the privilege to hear music greatness. Pearl Jam ended up winning that battle, but Ticketmaster eventually won the war.

During my short music department tenure, I saw a lot of odd requests from rock stars. For instance, even though The Eagles received one million dollars minimum for each show, their rider, which is a special request list added to every deal memo, had a backstage catering budget of $60,000. That was more than most acts made for a concert. Another example was the heavy metal artist, Glenn Danzig. His rider requested three women, aged twenty to twenty-five, who could talk about sports, politics, and religion backstage after the show. Oh yeah, and they had to live within a $20 cab ride of the venue.

Between learning the structures of the deals, the fascinating tidbits in the riders, and from the conversations I heard around me each day, it was like going to law school without the professors, the college bars, or the prestigious degree. I gained a lot of knowledge that I would later use in negotiating historic, first-time music licensing agreements between the US and China.

Additionally, I learned another lesson: *identify those who hold the keys to power and court them.* At William Morris, there were many powerful people. At the time, Jerry Katzman, Norman Brokaw, and Walter Zifkin all ran the agency. There were also super agents like Brian Gersh, Mark Itkin, John Burnham, Mike Simpson, Arnold Rifkin, and Bob Crestani. Superstar clients like The Eagles, John Travolta, and Bruce Willis paid our bills, and there was the COO who was responsible for my micro-advancement within the agency. But no matter how hard I Rolodexed, I could never get to him. However, with a little aggressive ingenuity, I could get to his assistant.

William Morris's music department was in a separate building from the rest of the agency. However, since much written correspondence occurred between the music division and others, I recognized an opportunity to quickly identify key players, grab their interoffice mail, and personally deliver it to them. One of those people was Louise Wein, assistant to William Morris's COO, Steve Kram. Louise was in charge of interviewing potential agent trainees for the new slots in the mailroom. Therefore, any time a piece of mail destined for people in or around Louise's desk was dropped in the interoffice mailbox, I'd grab it and personally deliver it. And every time I did that, I'd find a way to swing by Louise's desk to say hello. Not only that, but Louise was also a super interesting person. Every time I saw her, I'd ask for new details about her story and what she was passionate about. Of course, each evening, I'd write all those tidbits down on the back of her card.

"You're too nice to be an agent," she once told me. It's a quote I put on her card too. She was the first to say that to me too, but I convinced her she was wrong.

"I can be an agent and still be nice."

"Okay then. Prove me wrong. And don't say I didn't warn you."

Louise coordinated interviews with six agents. Each had to give a thumbs-up for me to earn a coveted mailroom slot. She had never done that before with a temp. Especially one from the music department. Five months in, a two-week temporary job then became a permanent job at William Morris as an official agent trainee, making $300 per week. Yes, I kept that Ivy West job to make extra coin on weekends.

I started in the mailroom in September of 1994. Considering I had severely pissed off the entire William Morris Agency Alternative Music Department a few months prior, to the point where they never wanted to see me roam the halls again, it was quite a feat. And it's a story in itself.

LA's alternative radio station 106.7 KROQ was, and continues to be, one of the most influential entities in the rock and roll industry. If a song was played on KROQ, it made the song a hit, and it elevated the band to the next level. In the music fax room at William Morris, we always listened to KROQ. It kept us up to speed with breaking artists, allowed us to track when clients appeared on the station, and it kept us attuned to important music industry news. And on Friday, April 8, 1994, KROQ and its sister station KXRX out of Seattle broke the news that almost got me fired.

KROQ's morning show hosts, Kevin and Bean, took a call from an electrician through KXRX that morning. He happened to be working at a home in Seattle, Washington—Kurt Cobain's home. On the call, he informed Kevin and Bean that a body appeared to be lying on the floor of Kurt's guest house. The body was motionless and covered in blood. The electrician said it looked like Kurt Cobain, arguably the most influential musician at the time.

None of my fax room colleagues happened to be with me then. I was alone, and I had to decide what to do with such information. Since agenting was phone-call-intensive, it was rare that an agent had the radio on in their offices. Music agents obviously listened to music, particularly that of their clients or potential new clients. But the banter of newscasters or talkative DJs heard in an agent's office was rare. It was simply too disruptive.

Knowing full well that such terrible news was in the kill-the-messenger category, I thought a long moment about my next step. Do I brush it under the rug, or do I tell someone? I decided on the latter, so I ran to the office of Nirvana's lead agent, Don Muller. His assistant Jon Pleeter was there, and I told him what I had heard. Understandably, he started to panic. Considering the value that Kurt had to both his boss and the agency, the news couldn't have been worse. Was it true? Holy shit!

Other assistants overheard the conversation and gathered around. I started to repeat the conversation on their behalf as Jon planned his next move. Don Muller was in his office, meeting with a handful of colleagues, apparently unaware.

Suddenly, Jon's face turned white. He went completely silent, almost as if an evil ghost, standing behind me, was staring him straight in the eyes. I turned around to look at what he saw, and there was one of Don's colleagues, looking angry, red in the face, and as if he wanted to take a desk chair and bash it on my head.

"What the fuck are you saying?" he shouted. He got right in my grill. I could feel his steaming breath on my face.

"I'm not making it up. They are talking about it on KROQ. Listen for yourself," I responded, pointing to the fax room.

"Who the fuck do you think you are? Spreading rumors like this!"

"I was just telling Jon what I heard. That's all. I swear," I said, panicking.

The phone rang on Jon's desk. He picked it up.

"Nirvana's team at Sub Pop [Nirvana's record label] is on line one," Jon interrupted, yelling into Don's office. "Sounds urgent!"

"Get the fuck out of my face," the agent roared, staring me down for what seemed to be an eternity. He then stomped into Don's office, slamming the door behind him.

"What's going on?" I could hear him ask through the walls.

Someone, maybe Don, maybe someone else, quietly responded. I couldn't tell what was said, but an eerie moment passed.

"Holy shit!" the agent said. I could hear the tragic concern in his voice.

I turned back to Jon, and he just shook his head. Partially in disbelief. Partially in sadness. And partially, I couldn't help feeling, as if I caused the tragic news we had all just processed.

Kurt Cobain had indeed committed suicide. He had done so a few days earlier, only to be discovered that dreadful day. One of Don's, and the William Morris music division's, biggest clients no longer existed.

The rest of the day was a blur. Needless to say, I avoided Don Muller's end of the music department hallway the rest of that day. I avoided it for the rest of the month too. In fact, I avoided any potential interaction with Don and the rest of the Nirvana team until Louise finally rescued me from the music department later that summer. That particular dramatic episode taught me a very important lesson: *information rules, but always be careful how you share it*. To this day, I'm convinced Don and his colleagues think I killed Kurt Cobain myself.

After a short mailroom stint as an agent trainee, I spent the next sixteen months as Mark Itkin's assistant and was promoted thereafter as a television syndication and cable agent. At twenty-four, I was the youngest agent at William Morris worldwide. My career was on a continual upward path in what would become the most important and profitable business at William Morris: television.

And then I made my first lethal mistake: I chose to leave the security of the TV department. I moved to William Morris's film division. Movies were sexy and cool, and I yearned to be a part of making them. The film business seduced me. It was where everyone wanted to be back in the nineties.

Coincidentally, during my run as a movie agent, I did represent the great Stanley Lieber, a.k.a. Stan Lee, who was the inventor of most things Marvel, for a couple of years. I even sold one of his non-Marvel creations, *The Guardians*, to Disney, which became the eventual owner of Marvel. At the time, no one could have predicted how big Stan's creations would become, but many of the studios were starting to try them out by developing films from his creations such as *Spider-Man*, *X-Men*, and *Daredevil*.

One apparent flaw, other than being "too nice," at least with respect to succeeding as a motion picture agent—I'm a team player. I like working in groups and collaborating with others. That's fun for me. Being a lone wolf in the snake pit of the film department wasn't. I never enjoyed the solo artist's game.

But that was the world I joined. Sharing information wasn't the norm. Working with colleagues who often had ulterior motives. People were selfish and insecure. Schadenfreude was rampant. I was fresh meat, and though I could've been another shark in the waters, it wasn't something I wanted to do or even would've enjoyed doing. There were times I could have signed big clients, Chris Nolan, Ice Cube, Hayden Christensen, and Paul Walker to name a few, but doing so would have meant going behind a friend's back, excluding someone I worked with or throwing a hardworking person under the bus. I'm not built for that, and it cost me business.

Nevertheless, my salary grew, and I became a more expensive agent. As the industry shifted from original content to remakes, the film department got squeezed. And somewhere in the midst of all that, I became a marked man.

7

FIRED. AGAIN.

ON NOVEMBER 12. 2001, John Fogelman and Rob Carlson, co-heads of William Morris's Motion Picture Department, called me in for a meeting. I entered John's office where he sat behind his large desk. Rob sat in an Eames chair next to him. Seeing dead eyes and no smiles from people I considered both friends and colleagues, I suddenly felt very uncomfortable.

I grabbed a chair facing them both, and as I sat down, a song ended on John's office sound system. He always had music playing softly, and I don't remember the song that was playing. However, I do remember the one that came on next, U2's "Beautiful Day."

"Chris," John cleared his throat to begin the meeting, "we've decided to let you go…"

I looked at Rob. I could tell he didn't agree with what was happening, but it didn't matter. What was done was done. I don't remember a word that was spoken after that first sentence. I watched John's unemotional lips flap, but I couldn't hear what he was saying. All I could hear was Bono.

When the song ended, I was looking right at them, but I don't think I could see them.

They stared at me, waiting.

"Chris," Rob said as he leaned in.

Out of the two of them, I respected Rob more. The sound of his voice snapped me out of my daze.

"I know this is hard," he said, "but is there anything you'd like to say or ask?"

"Did you hear the song that was playing?" I asked calmly.

"I didn't." Rob looked at John, confused. "What was it?"

"'Beautiful Day,'" I flashed a lunatic's smile. "Ironic, right?"

"Chris, you know I think the world of you. I consider you a friend. We don't need to tell anyone about this. You have at least a year left on your contract. You can work from the office. Phase things out slowly," Rob explained.

John nodded.

"Not interested," I cut him off. "Everyone knows when someone is getting fired before the person who is actually fired. That's how it works in this town."

"Not in this case, Chris. We kept it quiet," John explained.

I knew he was lying. I could see it in his dead-eye gaze.

"Anything else you guys have to say?" I asked.

"Just that we'll help in any way. References—"

"I won't need a reference from people who fired me. Thank you both for your time today."

I got up and walked out. In the hallway, a few agents passed me, trying not to make eye contact. They all knew what had happened. I was sure of it.

That was my walk of shame. A slow, seemingly endless walk past the offices of a dozen or so colleagues. No one looked, yet everyone watched. There was Chris—dead man walking.

I finally got to my office. My assistant, Will Lowery, looked up from his computer. He stared at me for a beat, studying my face. Concern suddenly swept his expression.

"You okay?"

"Please let people know I'm unavailable." I grabbed my briefcase and took my suit jacket off the door hook. "I'm heading home for the day."

I never went back.

Louise was 100 percent correct. I was too damn nice to be an agent. And oh, how I wanted to prove her wrong on that. But instead, William Morris just chewed me up and spit me out. She knew what she was talking about. She warned me too. I was simply too stubborn to listen.

Make no mistake, my termination from William Morris was like a knife slammed into the heart of my being. It didn't just hurt. It attempted to destroy the very essence of who I was. As I've said before, once you become an agent, you are a "made" man. I was "made" at one of the top agencies in Hollywood. I was the kid people whispered about running the place at one point. I was in a state of shock.

Imagine if Tony Stark could no longer be Iron Man. Imagine if Clark Kent could no longer be Superman. Imagine if Peter Parker could no longer be Spider-Man. That was how I felt then. Being a motion picture agent at one of Hollywood's great agencies had become part of who I was. Losing that was losing a big part of myself. Or, at least that's how it felt at the time.

Two days after I got fired, I had lunch with a longtime friend, Konrad Leh. Still on the rollercoaster of emotion, I was on an extreme low that day: sulking, upset, lost, and completely dazed.

"Just bought my first house. I have a mortgage now. I have no idea what I'm going to do. I don't know if I'll ever work again. I'm so screwed," I said. "Jennifer's been amazing though. She's allowing me a pity party...for now."

"I love that you're still dating Jennifer," Konrad said. "She's great for you."

"That she is. I love her."

"Getting serious."

"It is."

"Chris, let me ask you something." Konrad leaned in and posed a delicate question, "I don't mean to pry. But did you save anything?"

"Save...? What do you mean?"

"Your mortgage and all your bills, food, insurance, future plans with Jennifer, whatever—how long can you last before you have to find another source of income?"

I took a long breath. "You have a pen?"

I ran the quick math on the napkin, and Konrad, watching intently, jerked the pen from my hand before I could finish. He'd seen what he needed to see.

He leaned back in the booth, squinting at me. The waiter brought over my blackened chicken with broccolini—my favorite lunch at The Farm, given I was on the Atkins diet at the time. Konrad waited for him to leave.

"Get the fuck over yourself, dude. You're fine! Take a vacation, enjoy life for once. When you come back, you can figure out what you want to do and then make it happen."

He could see that he had my ear.

"Getting fired will be the best thing that ever happened to you. I guarantee it. You never should've been a motion picture agent. Everyone said you were too good a guy to be one. What's done is done. You learned everything you could from that place. You filled three massive Rolodexes of networking. And you work your ass off. If that's not a recipe for success, I don't know what is!"

His words sunk in.

I flew to the Caribbean a few days later. I tried to follow Konrad's advice and taste the good life and recharge. From my balcony, I stared at the amazing crystalline-blue water, attempting to relax. I drank rum drinks, surfed, fished, listened to steel drum bands, and smiled at the guys with dreads. And then I got bored. And quickly. I was floating in the ocean, looking back at the hotel, and it hit me: *no one ever goes down in history for what they do on vacation.*

I had to get back in the game.

Anyone who has seen the movie *Jerry Maguire* will recall that as soon as Jerry walks out of the big sports agency, goldfish in hand, he immediately makes frantic calls to all his clients, trying to ensure the talented athletes he fought for successfully and loyally over the years stayed with him. But those clients, instead, fucked him. All but one— Rod Tidwell, a selfish prima donna at the end of his career. As Jerry passionately guides Rod through a miraculous comeback, it's Rod who radically changes Jerry's life for the better.

Something similar happened to me. Freshly back from LAX, I took the elevator up from the garage of our building and when the doors opened, Jennifer was waiting in the penthouse foyer. I put my bags down and hugged her, but she pulled back.

"Enough's enough, okay?" she said with a stern smile. "Get your shit together and make something happen. Get on the fucking phone." She handed me one of my largest Rolodexes, stressing her point. "You're too good. The pity party is now over."

A bit shocked at her tough love, I responded, "I know. I'm with you. Game on!"

8.

GETTING BACK ON THE HORSE

I DID SEVERAL ROUNDS of meetings at the top agencies looking for a job, while hammering the phones, calling all of my clients. I was in full Jerry Maguire mode. I pushed hard to keep them all, knowing if I could retain a few, I'd still make it work. Heck, if Jerry could do it with only one, I could too.

I put my big-ass Rolodexes on the kitchen table, working my way through each relevant card. I called everyone—clients, friends of clients, studio bosses of clients, and families of clients. An agent has two types of clients: the well-established ones who are in demand and consistently working, and those who have great potential and are even on the verge of becoming successful but have yet to make it big. The first type are the known, high-profile, and beloved actors, the writers behind television's biggest shows and the studios' largest film franchises, and the directors responsible for Hollywood's box-office hits. These clients are highly lucrative and often require less effort from the agent, posing little "time and resource risk." For obvious reasons, they are the best clients to have. The second type are the clients who make little or no money and often cost money to represent before they actually pay off. They require the most time to develop, soaking up valuable minutes and mental effort throughout the day. That said, like raising a child, these clients can also be the most rewarding. They are the uncut diamonds who an agent discovers, polishes, markets, and sells, who one day become the world's most valuable gems—if everything works out according to plan. If the plan doesn't work out, lots of time and effort is wasted. Overly-fickle Hollywood may never understand their true value. And, even if La La Land gives them a shot, there's no guarantee. A complicated global entertainment audience may choose to shun them instead.

One such client of mine was a Staten Island-born aspiring filmmaker named Dan Mintz. I initially signed him after seeing his first film, *Cookers*. It was a little independent film about meth cookers who start to use their own supply and end up killing each other in a house they mistakenly thought was haunted. I saw it as a mix between *Requiem for a Dream* and *The Blair Witch Project*. The film won a few film festivals, and I was impressed with the freshness of the directing. Dan was worth taking a chance on. He felt like a director who could be the next David Fincher or Michael Bay, especially given his background in commercial directing. More importantly, his style was unlike anything I had seen before. And it was only after we first met that I realized the source of his originality—where Dan lived and worked full-time: China.

Beyond his significant talent, I was intrigued by Dan. He was different than most artists I was accustomed to working with. An intense, abrupt, no-nonsense, tell-it-like-it-is, Staten Island-bred New Yorker, Dan also possessed an acute comprehension of people, particularly ones very few others understood: the Chinese. In a thick "Beijing street" accent, Dan could fully speak in Mandarin, and to watch him bark orders to his production team always caught me a bit off guard. When you saw him, you never expected Chinese to come out of his mouth. No one did. I think such shock value got him lots of sway with everyone around him too.

Though filmmaking was Dan's passion, at the time it was only his hobby. I came to learn shortly after meeting him that his main priority involved running the hottest commercial production house in China with two Chinese partners, Peter Xiao and Wu Bing. They started the company in the early 1990s before anyone even noticed China as a potential juggernaut of capitalism. Even better, that commercial production house had just signed its first full-service advertising agency client, Volkswagen. Yes, Volkswagen. One of the largest automobile manufacturers in the world was now a client of Dan's fledgling advertising agency. Even crazier, VW had been in the Chinese market since 1984, so by the time Dan and his partners signed them, VW was selling sixteen different models through four separate entities: three were Chinese joint ventures, and one was the imported German division.

I felt strongly I could help Dan in two ways. One, I could push him in town as the next great Hollywood filmmaker, and two, I could help his growing business in China increase internationally through my comprehensive Rolodex network. I got two swings at the plate with him and his company. After more diligence, I discovered something else; the depth of understanding he and his partners had of China, as well as their marketing creativity to engage China, was revolutionary. It sounds a little ethereal, but I can explain.

In order to sign Volkswagen as a client, Dan's company, DMG, had to beat all the big guns in the advertising world. To do that, they had to demonstrate DMG's understanding of the Chinese consumer went way deeper than their competitors, many of which were based out of Taiwan, Japan, or Hong Kong and not mainland China. Additionally, DMG had to show they could convert that knowledge into the appropriate creativity to attract Chinese consumers to buy VW automobiles.

Without getting too inside baseball, the winning pitch involved a traditional Chinese character that bridged relevancy for China with the global "for the love of automobiles" VW slogan. Such was the character for "love" 愛 which within it contained the character for "heart" 心. That "heart" character is the foundation for many other words, including "loyalty," "wisdom," and "ambition," essentially words defined by needing true "heart." Each heart-related word was then partnered with a specific model of VW, showcasing the underlying characteristic. A driver's model VW like a GTI would be paired with "ambition" whereas a versatile model like a Tiguan would be associated with "wisdom." The glue comprising the overall VW brand messaging in China combined the "love" and "heart" origin characters, resulting in a slogan "On China's road is VW's (and the people's) heart." That's the rough translation, but when Dan explained the case study to me, it was obvious they knew China really well. So well, in fact, I learned of American car companies applying similar relevancy strategies to attract more Chinese consumers and position their brands in smarter, higher-quality ways. And it worked for them too. To this day, I still marvel at how GM's Buick brand became such a stalwart luxury item in China. The Chinese aspire to own a Buick. As an American, I find pride in that.

At that point, my basic understanding of China was simply that the market would be huge someday, and lots of money could be made as a result. Dan's tutorial gave me an even greater *aha* moment. The result was putting a bet down on this potential client was well worth the risk of lost time and effort.

I drove to the Beverly Hills set of Dan's second movie, *American Crime*. Dusk had set over Opie's pond (yes, it was used in the opening of *The Andy Griffith Show*) in Franklin Canyon Park. Dan and his partner, Wu Bing, were shooting several exterior shots that evening. I met with them under a line of lighting balloons as the skeletal crew hustled to set up another shot.

"Didn't expect to see you up here tonight," he said as I approached.

"Just wanted to make sure my favorite clients were doing okay." I shook his hand and gave Bing a kiss on the cheek. "I also wanted to make sure you were committing to me."

"I haven't heard from anyone else at William Morris...so why not?" He looked briefly through his camera's viewfinder and tinkered with the locking ring. "Besides, I don't know anyone in the US anymore, so I need some eyes and ears here."

"Great. Count me in on that." I looked at Bing. "Whatever you both need, I'll get it done."

"Be careful what you wish for." He looked away from his camera, grinning at me. "It's China, so get ready to hang on!"

I had no idea what that truly meant, but I was happy. I had bagged my Rod Tidwell.

BE THE FIRST

"**Y**OU KNOW THAT VW pitch I walked you through?" Dan asked over the phone one night a few months later. He was back in China. He had finished the physical production of *American Crime* by then and was focused again on DMG's advertising business.

"Of course." I had taken the call while watching television with Jennifer. I sat up, focusing. It was getting pretty late in Los Angeles.

"I'm going to use a Hanson song for the television commercials. You know, those 'MMMBop' kids, but a different tune of theirs. I'm thinking we license it properly."

"Of course, you do," I said. "Why wouldn't you?"

"No one does in China, but let's be the first." He paused a beat. "Song is called 'I Will Come to You.' Jay will get you the specifics. Can you get this done?"

"For sure," I thought about which former William Morris music contacts I'd have to approach first. This request wasn't something I'd done before, and I knew my old music fax clerking days might come in handy. Rolodexes were ready to go. "Piece of cake."

"Love that. Talk later. Let's get it done." He hung up.

"You know how to do that?" Jennifer asked, having overheard the conversation.

"No. But I'll figure it out."

I sensed a new, yet challenging door had opened. I had my Rod Tidwell, and I believed in him. He believed in me too. That said, I needed to show him the money. If successful, the enormous sleeping giant on the other side of the door would reward me too.

"That didn't sound too confident." Jennifer cut me a knowing smile.

"Guess we'll see…" The stage was set. My long journey to China began that night.

Hollywood's relationship with China in 2003 was strained and filled with suspicion at best and filled with severe mistrust at worst. No one thought that China would play by the rules, especially when it came to valuable entertainment assets. Music publishing was one of those.

When I received that call from Dan wanting to use an American song for a new Chinese Volkswagen campaign, I got nervous. No one would believe China, or anyone in China, would do the right thing. The assumption immediately was that China steals everything—and music publishing was no exception. Fortunately, our CEO wanted to do it right. Even better, we wanted to showcase our ability to play by the rules. It would tee up new business down the road.

At the time, Hanson wasn't nearly the success it was back in the nineties. I remember thinking that getting the song would be pretty easy and relatively inexpensive. However, that wasn't the case. The song was owned by a few different entities—Universal Music, Sony ATV, and the band itself. Each was very excited when I called to say China wanted the rights. I could hear the chop-licking through the phone.

"China? You guys want to actually pay for a song to use in China? Wow! Didn't think I'd ever hear that during my career," an executive at Sony ATV said when I called.

"Yup! How much will it cost?" I asked. "It will run nationwide in a new brand campaign for VW. We need a buyout for all media—radio, TV, internet, et cetera. It will be for Greater China, meaning China, Hong Kong, and Taiwan. And it will be for VW's full brand, not individual models or products," I added. I wanted to get him thinking about how great this would be to build consumer awareness of Hanson, increasing the value of Sony ATV's publishing asset in China in the process.

"China's a big market, and you're using the song for a lot of advertising push. You're probably talking a million bucks or so," he answered. "I need to discuss with my colleagues first though, so that's just a ballpark."

"A million bucks? For a song from a band who peaked a decade ago? Most people don't even know this song. It's not 'MMMBop' or something," I argued.

I hung up shortly thereafter, very discouraged. Obviously, this executive saw the market as one to milk rather than one to massage and build a foundation upon. This kind of thinking would be a big problem for me. Everyone approached China as a transactional opportunity with a short-term focus only. Building opportunities over time was not a common thought. A longer-term strategy though was the key to any sort of success in China.

I needed to find an ally for this venture that would view things on the longer-term horizon. To me, Hanson was a band that could be reheated. There was an opportunity to do just that—in the world's largest market too. I decided to seek out the band's management. Managers in Hollywood tend to work with artists over decades, so they always think about longevity and building value over time.

In pulling out the Rolodex, I called old friends in the William Morris Agency music department. They connected me with Hanson's manager, Jordan Berliant. After all, the band owned one-third of their publishing, so they must have some say over things. Additionally, if

Jordan saw a longer-term opportunity, I was sure he could push things forward from a point of influence.

I was correct. After connecting with Jordan, I started to see some daylight. I had $150,000 to spend on the song. That was it. $50,000 for each entity. Maybe something significant for the band, but surely not something that meant all that much to the media conglomerates of Sony and Universal. That said, I did have leverage. China normally just runs with a song without paying for it. The big publishers were looking to change that dynamic. Closing the deal and publicizing it was key. Showcasing its template as a precedent could change China's ways.

"We like the song, and we will pay for it. Look at it as found money, and a case study you can use for China moving forward!" I told an executive at Universal music.

Jordan was sharp and forward-thinking. He knew the circumstance was a gift. He had the issue of a song that wasn't fully owned by his clients, but he was motivated to clear such a hurdle with the big publishers. He knew if he could get it done, it would open big potential for Hanson.

"Everyone with a TV, radio, or computer will know this song! That's a lot of people, Jordan. Hundreds of millions of Chinese will know your client and their music. Imagine the doors that will open," I said to him on one of our first calls.

"I get it. This is complicated and you have a tight budget, but I'll get it done," he responded confidently.

After some time, we did get it done. The VW campaign ran for two full years. By the end, many Chinese knew the song very well and they liked it. They liked it so much, many Chinese used the song during their wedding ceremonies. "I Will Come to You" became that kind of phenomenon, and Jordan took full advantage of it. He put a tour together for Hanson in China that following year. It was amazingly successful.

China became a great market for music after that deal. We closed other challenging music licensing deals using the Hanson success story as a case study in our pitches. One for VW used the song "How Do You Like Me Now" by The Heavy. Cost us roughly the same amount, even with all the greed on the publisher's side. And VW didn't stop there. They wanted the well-known song "ABC" by The Jackson 5 which required a larger deal. Though difficult to negotiate, we ultimately got it done.

Licensing music to China took off. Music publishers were suddenly in the incoming call business. The Great Wall of China had opened for another great American cultural export—rock and roll!

10.

MICHAEL JORDAN
PAVED THE WAY

"**M**ICHAEL JORDAN'S TRIP to Beijing this year was off the charts," Dan said over the phone one night in late 2004.

"What do you mean?" I asked.

"It was like the president showed up, but even bigger. They had to cancel some events because the crowds got too big. It was nuts."

"NBA is doing it right. So is Nike," I said, matter-of-factly.

"Yup, and we are tapped into both already, but we need to ride the cultural sports exchange wave somehow. It needs to be ours," he responded. "With Nike, we gotta play nice with Wieden+Kennedy [Nike's international advertising agency], and with the NBA, I gotta deal with the chaos of the CBA and the NBA guys here on the ground. Ain't easy."

"What do you want?"

"We need to bring a sport here. Another one. Another one that the Chinese can grasp easily. One that we are fully responsible for and make happen."

"Well, soccer is already happening, and I'm already talking to World Wrestling and Arena Football," I paused. "You thinking MLB or NFL or NHL or something?"

"No, definitely not. Chinese won't understand football or arena football. Heck, I don't even understand those. And, MLB makes no sense here. Too Japanese. NHL is a no-go. No ice unless you're in Harbin or Beijing. Too complicated too. And wrestling is simply too violent. If they want violence, they'll go the martial arts route." He gathered his thoughts. "I need something global too. Like we position Nike. They are a global company. Not American. The US-China relationship is always tenuous. Creates too much risk."

"Well, I got a buddy at IMG/TWI. Could dig into their stuff to find something," I responded, scratching my head a bit while glancing at my Rolodexes.

"What do they have?"

"Stuff like the World's Strongest Man, Wimbledon..."

"That's it!" he interrupted.

"What?"

"The World's Strongest Man! It's simple to understand and a total spectacle. Chinese will love that shit!"

"True. Big, muscular dudes carrying heavy things and heading to a finish line as quickly as possible," I agreed, seeing his point. "Plus, it's global."

"Exactly! Go *get* it." He hung up.

Our 2005 production of ESPN's World's Strongest Man competition was just as trailblazing as it was strange. Strange because no one understood why we wanted the competition in the first place. Trailblazing because we garnered forty million Chinese viewers for the finals of a sporting event never before seen in China.

"Insane. That's all I can say. You guys got us a bigger audience in one single night, in one single market, than we have gotten in total over twenty-five years of airing the show globally!" Geoff Cochrane,

Senior Production Executive at IMG/TWI, exclaimed when it was all said and done.

"That's one sure thing about China," I responded. "The country has people and lots of them! You make something culturally relevant; you break records."

Several months prior, I convinced Geoff, a friend from my days at Cornell and part of my Rolodex's earlier entries, and his team to shoot the competition for the first time ever in China. At first, the plan was to film it in Beijing, selling the idea of competitions on the Great Wall and in the Forbidden City. However, with the 2008 Summer Olympics approaching in a few years, Beijing didn't really need international exposure. As a result, the city's offer of incentives was lacking. Beijing showed little enthusiasm. The Olympics inspired their city. A Strongman Competition did not.

We expected other cities would react differently. Most would jump at the chance to host anything that offered international exposure. And they did. Ultimately, the best city for The World's Strongest Man was Chengdu. They offered the most. Though barely known by anyone outside of China, Chengdu did have a population of almost ten million. And more importantly, it was home to China's famous pandas, some of which I got to spend time with personally—pandas do love a nice belly rub!

Pandas also pioneered modern-day international diplomacy. They symbolized the ultimate in cultural exchange. Everyone truly loves pandas. And pandas loaned by China to various countries fostered amazing alliances over the years.

Chengdu's offer included hundreds of free hotel rooms, hundreds of police and military personnel, meals for the crew, VIP tours, special access, free production location access and facilities, free laborers, free equipment, and so on. The municipal authorities fought hard for the event. Their passion to showcase their city, which had just been completely modernized through government initiatives and private-sector partnerships with companies like Intel, was super convincing.

Chengdu's physical and tech infrastructure rivaled anything in the US too. We were sold.

The airport was a different story. When I arrived on a very weather-delayed flight, the whole facility was pitch black. The airport apparently closed at 10:00 p.m. Electricity shut off in that part of the city at that hour. We sat at the gate for an hour until officials switched emergency power on. After deplaning we walked through the dark airport with workers carrying flashlights to illuminate our path. Workers had to manually run baggage claim machinery until we all found our bags. The whole episode was pretty hard to believe for a city of ten million. I hoped we wouldn't regret our Chengdu decision.

Important to note, a few years later the whole airport was replaced by a spectacular new one. A few years after that, Chengdu was the hub for the largest high-speed rail network in the world. China knows how to build infrastructure — and quickly!

In Chengdu, even with its push into the modern world, being a white guy from the US made for an extremely unusual sight for the locals. I remember walking through a Trust-Mart, China's version of Walmart at the time, browsing for some souvenirs to bring home. They had a great Chinese wine selection, which, if you haven't had it, is pretty good if you pick the right ones. The bottles also make great gifts. You can't, to this day, get any of them here in the US. They typically come in individual ornate wooden crates, adding to their exclusive appeal.

As I was browsing, I started to sense my space being encroached upon. In fact, behind me, I could hear some whispering. I also could feel some breathing near me. I didn't want to turn around, hoping that whoever was too close would eventually walk by. However, after a few more uncomfortable minutes, I turned to accost the stranger and ask them politely to back off. When I did, I almost fell over from what I saw. It wasn't one person, but rather it was a hundred. They were following me around the store, taking pictures and simply blown away at the sight of a blond American in their city. Truly a once-in-a-life-time event for Chengdu locals, at least back then. Such was the case everywhere other than Shanghai and Beijing. Heck, even in Beijing, once you get outside the central business district, the locals still give you a curious stare.

Getting the Strongman Competition to attract forty million viewers was no easy feat. We had to make people want to watch it. And to do that, we needed people the Chinese could identify with. That surely wasn't a bunch of massive musclemen from Eastern Europe. Instead, we needed a Chinese strongman—one who could respectfully compete. He would be the key to local relevancy. If our Chinese contestant was eliminated early, our viewership numbers would plummet instantly. A Chinese competitor, who was able to compete at the level of the massive Eastern Europeans who typically dominated the show, was optimal. But that was a very tall task. Finding a Chinese guy as big as the European competitors was almost impossible. There are not that many six-foot-six, 380-pound muscular Chinese. And tracking down a local with the learned skills to tow an eighteen-wheeler a hundred yards was a challenge.

We did a "Search for the Chinese Strongman" competition several months in advance. It was quite a spectacle in itself, and through it, we found our guy—Gu Yanli. Immediately we started to transform him into a national hero, allowing the televised competition to ride on his shoulders. He wasn't the perfect candidate, but he had the potential to be our Rod Tidwell. Gu grew up in the rice fields of a sparsely populated area in Western China. Gu was strong, but more importantly, he was extremely charismatic. That alone made up for his relatively small size in comparison to the competition. He also didn't have the technique like the Eastern Europeans, so cracking a beaming smile and being quick with a joke came in very handy.

Our creative team came up with a solution to keep the charismatic Gu in the show, knowing his early elimination was inevitable. He'd play into a forced, made-for-television, mentor/protégé relationship—another culturally relevant touchpoint. Gu filled the role as protégé, and a fantastically charismatic American competitor, Jesse Marunde, acted as his mentor. We picked Jesse because he had a great chance of winning the event too, meaning he'd be competing for the run of the show. That way, when Gu was eliminated from the competition in the early rounds, we could still have him on screen, cheering his mentor on throughout the rest of the competition.

The plan worked. It made Gu famous. And more importantly, our consistently growing audience loved him.

Gu embraced his role. His involvement made the Strongman Competition relevant regardless of his placing in the event. Gu's lack of skills didn't matter. People cheered him on with more vigor than any other competitor. The show's spectacle, muscle-bound men carrying massive objects on challenging courses through unique settings, only amplified it. The Chinese audience loved him.

During the eighteen-wheeler-pulling race, Gu initially couldn't even budge the truck. I shook my head, fearing an embarrassing disaster. Others not only pulled the truck, but they moved the truck dozens of yards in a matter of seconds. Meanwhile, our guy couldn't even get it the least bit moving. That didn't discourage our live audience. Instead, they cheered on Gu with roars that deafened the people of downtown Chengdu. They encouraged him to not only try again but to try until he succeeded. Even better, the crowd's idea of success for Gu wasn't whether he won. Instead, they just wanted him to move the damn truck. One inch or one yard, it didn't matter. Just move it, Gu. Just move it! And they stuck with him, shouting support with thunderous applause for what seemed to be an hour.

Gu would pull with all his might, and nothing would happen. He'd take a quick breather, loosen his shoulders, crack his neck, and try again. This was repeated again and again. Instead of the crowd's energy deflating, they just simply got louder. I marveled at the sight. I couldn't help but smile, nodding my head when Geoff Cochrane and I caught eyes across the production. The crowd yearned for Gu to succeed. Geoff and I joined them in their supportive frenzy. So did the full crew and on-camera commentators. Even all the competitors. It seemed all of China wanted Gu to move that truck.

Finally, as the crescendo of the crowd's roar peaked, it happened. Gu grabbed the rope, took two big huffs, and started pulling again. Sure enough, the truck moved. It moved a good six inches too! The crowd went nuts! I'm talking earthquake kind of stuff. The windows of all the shops and buildings in downtown Chengdu rattled close to the point of shattering. It was mayhem!

When Gu finished his triumphant achievement, Jesse ran up to him. They hugged hard, smiling ear to ear. They ended their embrace and turned to the crowd. Jesse held up Gu's hand, signaling a new champion. Yes, Gu wasn't exactly a true champion, but for that very moment, it didn't matter. Our national hero moment was made! Relevancy to China achieved!

Sadly, Gu was eliminated later that day. It happened during the Ding-Carrying Competition, a Chinese-invented event that became part of the overall competition. Steeped in the history of China, a ding is a large, extremely heavy iron or bronze bowl that stands on only three legs. The three legs are positioned to create maximum stability and symbolize the coming together of three tribes of ancient China, joining forces under a central and all-powerful emperor. In short, the ding is an ancient symbol for unity.

Our creative team felt the symbolic and heavy ding would create much better relevancy for the Chinese audience. Typically, a full keg of beer was the object used for that event. Watching the strongmen come from all around the world to carry such an amazing and authentic piece of the country's lore was exciting, important, and relevant. Carrying a keg of beer was not. Audiences proved our theory too. Our Chinese broadcast partner CCTV5 posted record numbers each night during the show's airing, and the viewership grew steadily throughout the two-week competition.

Even with Gu eliminated, the significance of the show was continuously reinforced. The ding was just one example. Even better, Gu stayed on camera until the very end, cheering on his mentor at every moment. As a result, our overly enthusiastic crowds did the same. If Gu wanted his mentor to win, so did they!

The results were some of the highest holiday-period ratings ever for CCTV5, the Chinese equivalent of ESPN. Eighty-six hours of total television, over fifteen straight days, both on CCTV5 and Chengdu Provincial Television. It was the top national sports story over the run of the program and an amazing accomplishment considering the massive sports interest of China in general. Our Western partners ESPN, IMG, and TWI all called it, by far, the *greatest* World's Strongest Man competition ever. And, our Chinese broadcast partners still marvel at the fact that we could shoot a competition using two separate and distinct camera crews, one focused solely on English-language announcers with Western background sponsors, and the other focused solely on Chinese announcers with Chinese background sponsors, simultaneously.

On our final day in Chengdu, to celebrate our achievement, the municipal government along with a local Nike representative organized a basketball game. A team comprised of DMG and IMG/TWI executives played against the varsity team of one of Chengdu's high schools. With China embracing a new sport like the World's Strongest Man competition, Chengdu officials seemed to be excited to see how a bunch of Americans could do against their local youth in a sport they've known and loved for decades. We happily accepted the challenge as yet another form of cultural diplomacy. We played the game in the high school gymnasium in front of a standing-room-only crowd—not kidding. The bleachers were completely full! Most were wearing Michael Jordan t-shirts or some other NBA-related image.

After a competitive back and forth, led on our side by my colleagues Daniel Postaer and Geoff Cochrane, both great athletes, and a few impressive Chinese kids for the other, the score, which no one seemed to keep accurate track of, remained tied by the end of the game. When the final buzzer sounded, the crowd erupted. A tie!

And a tie between two very different teams from very different worlds. I couldn't help but think back to those American kids playing ping pong in China back in 1971. The surreal, yet feel-good moment each of those kids shared in such a competition back then must have been similar to what I felt thirty-five years later. I'm sure when Michael Jordan made his first China trip, one where a link was created between a country crazy for basketball and another where the greatest players in the world lived and played—he felt similarly too. There was a strange, positive magic to it. A constructive aura. Emotional too. I loved it. We all loved it.

Bottom line, history was made. China embraced the World's Strongest Man competition, an event and competition it had never seen before. It started with zero relevancy, and it ended as one of the most-discussed Chinese sports events of 2005 with a brand spanking new national hero right smack in the middle of it.

Create cultural relevance, and the Chinese will embrace it! Money will be made too—lots of it. The bilateral exchange of commerce and culture was alive and well.

11.

THIRD-PARTY VALIDATION

IN 2002, FREELANCE journalist Jamie Bryan, and I first met when he wrote a feature article for *Details* magazine about Hollywood executives who surf. Jamie reached out to me and some other friends, asking if we'd like to take part in the article. He wanted us photographed at our favorite local break, which at the time, was the El Porto section of Manhattan Beach. He met with each of us separately to talk about what we do specifically in the industry, and why surfing is still a part of our very busy lives. I agreed to do the article along with friends Jason Burns, an amazing surfer and partner at United Talent Agency, Rick Alvarez, a film and TV producer who was partnered with the Wayans brothers, and Matt Moore, who was a rising film executive at New Line Cinema. Dan Spink, the youngest brother of a very close friend of mine, J.C. Spink, joined us too. He had just graduated from college at the time.

The shoot and article came out so well, I was immediately won over by Jamie Bryan's journalistic abilities. Not only that, but the guy could surf, so we bonded over that too. He received a very special Rolodex card as a result.

A couple of years later, I reached out to Jamie again. I filled him in on my China exploits—particularly the impressive achievements of Dan and his partners at DMG. China was the Wild West and we were all making shit happen there. It felt like it was a story he'd dig.

And after we ended the call with some surf talk, I hung up thinking he was intrigued.

Hardly two days later, Jamie called and pitched a story about a foreigner taking a leap of faith, moving to China, and integrating himself into the nation's fabric to build a media business. That foreigner was Dan.

"What Dan and his partners are doing involves swaggering bravado. It's aggressive. It's fascinating and colorful. It begs to be a Robert Towne screenplay some day," he explained. "And what you do to create and facilitate business between the two countries, I'll want to address too. Not an easy task and a key ingredient in DMG's secret sauce."

"I'm psyched you see a story here!"

"Of course I do." He took a beat, gathering his thoughts. "The story's premise is a fish out of water living in a faraway land. That guy builds an empire with his partners. He has his trusty sidekick based in LA. He tells his sidekick what he can do in the world's most difficult, yet most promising market. His sidekick brings in international partners and businesses to fill that plan. You make people believe. You close deals. You massage the rough edges. Then Dan and his partners get it done on the China side. As a team, you all make history—again and again."

"Love that!"

"Then, of course, the nuance of how Dan actually gets stuff done in China creates the real entertainment value of the story. I need to see that firsthand."

"Great! Let's do it!"

Shortly thereafter, Jamie convinced *Details* magazine to fund it as a large feature article and hopped on a plane to meet me in China. He spent ten days following us through our endeavors in both Beijing and Shanghai. At the time we had large, permanent offices in Shanghai, but we were in the process of building new headquarters in Beijing, replacing our original Beijing offices.

That turned out to be a very pivotal moment in time for Beijing. The whole city was getting rejiggered. Our original offices had a makeshift wall all along the backside, as one day a bulldozer had shown up and abruptly cut our offices completely in half. It turned out, half of our building was in one development zone and the other half was in another. When the government decides to redevelop a city, it doesn't matter who's there. They move the tenants out and tear the building down. DMG was no different. We received a notice one day, and the next we only had half of our building left.

The good thing was that our new building was almost completed. Jamie and I both got to put on a hardhat to tour it. Even though it was a gleaming thirty-story building, it seemed to be in a rather rough-around-the-edges neighborhood. Dan explained we were standing in the soon-to-be heart of the central business district. It was hard to believe at the time, but today it's easy to realize how right he was. When Beijing wants something done, they do it. Those in the know can take advantage of that.

Shortly after the trip, Jamie finished the article and handed the materials over to *Details*. They passed on the story even after funding the entire trip. *Details* simply felt it was too business-focused—not hip and cool enough for its audience. That didn't deter Jamie though. He stood firm. He loved his angle, and he knew there were other outlets for it.

Jamie sent the article to Will Bourne, who was then the editor-in-chief of *Fast Company*. Moments after reading, Will committed to publishing it. He even asked for Jamie to add length and additional details. Will also inserted more photos to the final version.

The issue hit newsstands shortly thereafter, and the rest was history. That one article put us on the map. It provided an amazing third-party validation of what was going on in China, and how we were making the impossible happen. Jamie was able to touch and feel our business, capabilities, resources, ingenuity, aggressiveness, and infrastructure, and he put it on the page for the world to read. It allayed suspicions of China and unkept promises—at least for us. That article became one of the strongest arrows in my quiver of sales ammunition. With that article, I could convince people that DMG was legit. To persuade anyone to take a chance on China—legitimacy is *everything*!

12.

CHINA'S LOVE FOR BASKETBALL

WITH THE 2008 Olympics quickly approaching, our company was rapidly becoming a go-to entity in China for anything related to the culture around sports, particularly for international clients looking to reach targeted consumers and market to them in the most relevant way possible. Nike was one of those clients, and the culture they wanted to continue to tap into, and subsequently grow, was that of basketball. With the NBA already a well-known commodity in China, and with Michael Jordan already selling his branded Nike products faster than they could be supplied to Chinese stores, Nike looked beyond both for growth. Additionally, the sting of misplaying LeBron James's marketing back in 2004 (remember the dragon slaughter?) was still fresh in everyone's minds. Setting a new tone moving forward to distance the company from that crucial misstep was key.

That's where The Battle of the Nine Gates came into play. DMG worked closely with both Nike and their international agency, Wieden+Kennedy, to create the ultimate high-profile and record-setting three-on-three basketball tournament made for the hubris-filled Beijing city street basketball player. There were no NBA or CBA pros in this tournament, just regular street ballers and lots of them. Even better, it took power forwards and centers out of the equation. The reason? Because the average Chinese player isn't physically built for those positions. This tournament was made strictly for guards, point guards, and a handful of small forwards.

The Nine Gates tournament combined the Western roots of true New York City streetball into the swagger of Beijing's inner-city, modern-day youth culture. The competitions were laced with bilateral mixes of hip-hop music, outrageously designed uniforms, and graffiti-inspired decor. Beijing's best artists joined forces with the top icons of New York's street culture underbelly. And, of course, all of this set the stage for some really solid pick-up hoops!

The finals were held smack in the middle of the Forbidden City, which was normally an off-limits location. The Chinese government never allowed access for any sort of commercial endeavor there, especially one associated with a Western company. DMG's *guanxi* (high-level relationships, particularly with key government officials), however, helped nullify that restriction. We also continued to press a *global* positioning for Nike's brand in the market. And that narrative aided DMG in gaining key government approvals. Nike wasn't *American*. And it wasn't even *Western*. Nike was *global*, just like basketball itself, allowing the brand to survive any geopolitical flare-ups between China and the Western part of the world.

Over the course of the event, 5,300 teenagers competed for 1,340 teams. It was China's largest outdoor basketball tournament ever. And for cultural relevancy, each of those 1,340 teams represented one of the city's nine ancient gates and the specific neighborhood surrounding each. It's a tribute to the city's rich history. Beijing was originally walled. Supplies and personnel had to move in and out freely to keep the city humming. Therefore, each gate was used for different reasons and had a vital purpose. One gate was used for food. Another for water. Another for prisoners. Another for trade. Another for fuel, and on and on.

"It's pop-culture-meets-ancient-turf-wars as the kids of Beijing stand behind their gate, one of the original nine gates along modern-day Beijing's second ring road," Dan said in a May 16, 2007, *Ad Age* article. "The tournament gives the Chinese something to stand for, it represents actual turf, their own part of town and a chance to be the local gate master. So, it's kind of a West Side Story idea, but one that's all about Beijing."

"Please bring back those badass posters from the tournament," I said to my colleague, Daniel Postaer, after the event. "We'll hang them up in the LA office."

"I would, but kids ripped them down from the walls and kept them. Collector items apparently. Kids were pushing and shoving to get their hands on them. We had to constantly replace them. It was crazy."

"We did Nike good with that event."

"Heck yeah, we did. Nike loves us. We brought the right kind of relevancy. Goodbye 'Chamber of Fear' [a reference to the titles of those troubling advertising spots in 2004]. We did good for basketball too. NBA loved it," Postaer explained. "And now that we represent Kobe, he's going to want the same treatment!"

"We'll get it done. He'll be selling more than Jordan in no time."

"Yup, but it's never easy. We need to get working ASAP."

"Understood. Let's get a meeting on the books with Rob [Kobe's agent, Rob Pelinka] ASAP when you're back," I responded. "What's the big play with him first?"

"We need to help launch the Nike Hyperdunk shoe, and we need to do it when Kobe is here in Beijing for the Olympics!"

"Hmmm. Crazy timing. We'll need to organize the chaos," I assumed. "What's the concept?"

"'Rise Up and Man Up'! Or as the Chinese refer to it, '*Zhan Qi Lai.*'"

"Okay. And the forum?"

"We'll take what we executed with Nine Gates but apply it to a five-on-five tournament. And this time we'll have it judged by LeBron, Carmelo, Chris Paul, and Kobe—who, by the way, has the number one selling basketball jersey in China—more than Jordan and more than Yao if you can believe that!" Daniel was excited about the event. It was obvious. And his relationship with Kobe and his agent was blossoming into something he was passionate about too. "And, instead of six thousand players like Nine Gates, we'll have at least fifteen thousand this time."

"Damn! What kind of guanxi shit do we need to pull off for this one?"

"Nothing crazy," Daniel said, sarcastically. "Just a bunch of guerilla marketing everywhere that isn't allowed. And a televised finale at Shanghai's 1933 building [an art deco monument known throughout the nation as the core of all things hip and cool, and the center of China's reinvention from ancient relic to modern awesomeness]. And a lot of people to control because the crowds will be intense."

"Okay then. We better get started," I said, cranking up the hip-hop song created for the Nine Gates event. The song oozed of Beijing's newly discovered confidence and urban-American attitude. Roughly translated, it said:

> Give me a basketball.
> I will bring you to a new era.
> I just want to compete with you.
> Attack you above your head.
> and force you to the corner.
> No matter what you want to do.
> I will play you one-on-one.
> Even if you are number one.

The Battle of the Nine Gates was the largest event Nike had done to date in China, a market worth $750 million in annual sales even back then. It obviously led the way to bigger and more eye-popping endeavors in China for Nike involving basketball, China's proudly adopted major sport from the West. But the future wasn't just bright for Nike. It was beaming for the NBA too. One-third of the traffic on NBA.com was generated from China, and the NBA had merchandise already in more than fifty thousand outlets nationwide. On top of that, more than 300 million Chinese played the sport recreationally, and more than 350 million people watched various NBA broadcasts, airing live as early as seven in the morning. The beginning of the biggest growth spurt the NBA and Nike would ever experience had only just started. After all, this was China, and breaking records was a daily routine for the market.

And, as far as the "Zhan Qi Lai" event, it went off better than anyone anticipated, further thrusting Nike, the NBA, Kobe, LeBron, Carmelo, and Chris Paul into the stratosphere of Q-score altitudes. When Kobe grabbed the microphone surprisingly during the peak of the event and yelled "*Rise Up!*" in Chinese, the crowd erupted to levels akin to our Strongman Gu pulling that eighteen-wheeler. It created an aftershock reading at the local university's seismic center and a rumble that shuddered the nerves of every Nike competitor.

"Basketball is China's biggest sport," Dan said to *AdAge China*'s reporter, Normandy Madden. "Having four of the world's biggest basketball stars at the culmination of this campaign is an incredible coup. It's a sign of solidarity and will galvanize a generation around their favorite sport."

Kobe and his NBA friends not only came to China. They wanted to be there. And Kobe proved that by saying something in Mandarin, proclaiming that it was China's turn to stand up on the world stage. Yes, Kobe and his friends expected to win the gold at that Olympics. But he knew he was doing it on China's home turf. He proved himself to be a true cultural diplomat, but he also played the game right in order to tap the riches of the market for himself, his peers, Nike, and the NBA.

Cementing a cultural bridge to make billions was the name of the game for Kobe that day. He had two of the five forces of diplomacy working harmoniously. There was no cold war on his horizon!

13.

CHINA'S LOVE FOR MOVIES

LIKE ME, THOMAS Augsberger is a bridge builder too. In particular, he has decades of experience forging a tight relationship between Germany and the US in the film business. Germany was Thomas's Rod Tidwell. The back of his Rolodex card had some color to it as well. A family man, Thomas finds time to ride fast motorcycles and share stories of his early days as an opera singer. Yes, an opera singer!

I knew Thomas because he was instrumental in getting me my first producing credit. He put the financing together for a small movie called *Waiting*.... I'm tremendously proud of that cult classic and its writer/director Rob McKittrick, not to mention producer Chris Moore, who was responsible for me getting into the movie business, and Chris' former assistant, Jeff Balis, who initially shared the script with me during my days as a literary agent at William Morris. I highly recommend the film. The cast includes Ryan Reynolds, Anna Faris, Justin Long, Dane Cook, and John Francis Daley. It's a fun flick. We made the film for only three million bucks, and it grossed seven times that.

After the Beijing Olympics ended, I desperately needed movie studios to believe that DMG could distribute their films in China. Yeah, we could produce commercials. Yeah, we could make great television. Yeah, we were a top-notch advertising agency. Yeah, we knew our way around the business of sports and creating and executing massive culturally relevant events for the likes of the NBA, Nike, Kobe, LeBron, and the CBA. And yeah, we had proven ourselves as pivotal when moving all kinds of mountains behind China's Great Wall with our guanxi. We closed the Bund in Shanghai for VW, orchestrated an event in the heart of the Forbidden City for Nike, shot commercials on the off-limits Great Wall itself, and we were known to pull off VIPs from their commercial flights that landed on Beijing airport's tarmac and usher them through a special customs area hidden from the masses. Yeah, we did all that and much more.

By then we had even brushed elbows with Hollywood's movie business a few times. Though uneventful production-service and consultancy kind of work, it still counted. The first was helping Quentin Tarantino's team garner access to government-owned soundstages for his film, *Kill Bill*. The second involved facilitating on-the-ground production logistics for Miramax's (yes, Harvey Weinstein's studio) epic war drama, *The Great Raid*. The third, Fox's *Flight of the Phoenix*, required DMG's guanxi with the Chinese military to approve landing rights for the production's private jets.

Additionally, with each production, DMG worked closely with Chinese customs officials to clear the import and export of specialized production equipment—a simple task in most countries but not in China. In fact, to this day, Steven Spielberg's Panavision cameras from his 1987 production of *Empire of the Sun* still remain in the back of a moldy Chinese customs storage facility inside Shanghai's airport.

Such a frustrating customs episode was so common, even my alma mater William Morris fell into that ditch. And when they did, I got the call.

"Our office equipment for our new Shanghai office is stuck at customs—apparently permanently too. Can you guys please help?" a former William Morris colleague asked.

"Ironic, don't you think?" I asked, fully aware he knew I had been fired from his employer.

"Yeah, it's an awkward call to make. I admit that," he responded. "But you guys are the only ones who can help."

"I'm just busting your balls," I said. I could feel his relief through the phone. "I hold no grudge. We'll get it done."

And we did.

But given those past few brushes with Hollywood's business in China, we still didn't know shit about distributing movies. Or, at least in the traditional sense. That said, we did have a bunch of the dots around the skill connected already. And, in China, sometimes just connecting dots around a specific objective is just as good as connecting them directly.

The way China's film distribution system operated, at the time, played right into our area of expertise. China Film Group, a.k.a. CFG, coincidentally used the media buying power of many of DMG's brand clients, so we were an important partner to CFG. DMG was in charge of where that media spend was put, and our clients loved to activate media spend around the distribution and marketing of movies. Heck, they even liked to have their brands integrated into Chinese movies themselves.

That was one way CFG would finance films, and that was key to our new endeavor. CFG was one of the largest players in the production of Chinese films. And they were the only way to get a film distributed in China—a monopoly. If someone was close to them and had something of value to them, CFG was able to return the favor as any good partner would. DMG had that "in" with CFG. Or, as others would call it, DMG had guanxi with China Film Group and its leader, Han Sanping. That meant DMG had a true, solid, battle-tested relationship with CFG. People in China knew that, so now we needed people in Hollywood to recognize that too.

Thomas Augsberger knew everyone in town, and even better, he knew the C-Suite executives at Summit Entertainment. In 2008, Summit had some of the biggest non-major-studio movies in Hollywood. And since we were still unproven in this space, the major studios weren't interested in working with us yet. We needed to earn our stripes. So, we needed a company like Summit to give us a shot. And a $75 million-budgeted, Alex Proyas-directed, and Nic Cage-starring film called *Knowing* was exactly that.

I asked Thomas if he could introduce me to Bob Hayward, Summit's COO and co-founder. Thomas obliged. We went to see Bob together, and in that meeting, I was able to convince Bob that we could take one of his biggest films and release it on theatrical screens in China.

"No non-studio title has ever gotten a theatrical release of any real scale before," Bob stated confidently. "And, for sure, no non-studio movie has ever gotten a quota slot."

Bob's reference to a "quota slot" was the twenty films China let in annually from international studios. Those select films were given wide theatrical releases through China Film Group and a whopping (just kidding) 13.7 percent share of their gross box office. At that time, only the major studios were able to secure such a coveted designation.

"Well, we will make *Knowing* the first," I responded.

"Can he?" Bob asked Thomas.

"I don't know for sure, Bob, since China is pretty darn mysterious to me and almost everybody," Thomas responded. "That said, Chris is a man of his word, and he has always come through on his promises."

The rest was history. Thomas vouched for me, and I vouched for DMG. That was all Bob needed. He hadn't made any money in China up until that point, so if suddenly there was an American in his office saying he could make millions there, and his good friend Thomas Augsberger vouched for it, well then, that worked for Bob.

"Give me a few bucks up front," he said. "I always get a little something. You put a few bucks up front, I'll tell my team to stop looking for anyone else."

"How much?" I asked. I knew he'd want something.

"A few hundred," he responded.

"No way." I shook my head. "Heck no. I know the players you may get some hundred-thousand-dollar offers from, and even if they pay you, and that's a big *if*, you won't see a dime after. With us, we'll pay you a little something, and then, when it works and we get you that quota slot, we will all make some dough. Real dough. And you'll get a check on the backend."

"I don't believe that."

"Look, with China, talk is talk. Right now, all I'm doing is talking. We'll give you $75,000 and a cut of the backend," I said, getting up. "We'll then walk the walk next year. You'll see. We'll make some money together, and you'll get more on the backside. *Knowing* will be the first non-major-studio film ever to get a quota slot," I walked towards him, extending my hand. "Bragging rights for Summit too!"

"Deal," he took my hand, grinning. "Thomas, you had better be right about this guy. I may have given up a couple hundred grand here."

"You haven't given up anything," I stated, opening the door to his office. "What you did do though, is found a great partner who is going to open China for you and your studio!"

I left with a deal closed and a big grin on my face.

14.

PUNCHED IN THE GUT

MONDAY, SEPTEMBER 15, 2008, was probably more influential in shaping my view of China and the US-China dynamic than anything else in my life. It was the day Lehman Brothers declared bankruptcy.

One of my closest friends at the time was an executive board member at the firm. He was also one of its biggest moneymakers. In the months preceding the financial crisis, a group of us would talk about how Lehman's share price continued to drop precipitously. Lehman wasn't a statistic to our group of friends. It was humanized because we knew someone who was living through it. There wasn't a guarantee Lehman would go bust, but many of us suspected it. And we all marveled at how such a stalwart institution of finance could fall apart so easily during that summer of 2008.

Therefore, when Lehman died, it didn't surprise any of us. What did, however, was how dramatically it affected my family's finances.

The weekend before Lehman's demise, my wife's close friend stayed with us in our 1929 Tudor-style Hancock Park home. It was a beautiful place we financially stretched for in order to have the perfect home to raise our young children. My wife's friend was married to a guy who also worked at Lehman, so most of that Sunday involved panicked calls relaying the latest rumors of how things seemed to be playing out for his company and, more importantly, his career. When

Monday morning arrived, and the bankruptcy rumors became reality, an eerie silence overtook our home.

She then got the call from her husband. He was ordered to get his belongings and leave Lehman's offices immediately. Watching her face as she heard the news brought the direness of the situation into an even more human and emotional form. It was never just a news item on CNBC because of my close friend, but seeing someone else in my home so directly affected by the collapse made it even worse.

After my wife and I helped nurse her wounds that morning, I had to leave for an early lunch. It was at the Daily Grill in Studio City, a restaurant I hated, since the last time I was there I got a call from a hot actor client, Lucas Black, saying that he was firing me. I remember the episode well. I got on the escalator from the parking lot and my phone rang. Lucas was on the line. He said it was a tough decision, but he felt a sense of loyalty to another representative, so he was firing me. I got to the next floor. I walked into the Daily Grill and sat down for my lunch meeting. I can't remember who it was with, and I stared blankly into their eyes. I did not hear a single thing communicated that hour. The firing was brutal because Lucas was a big part of my business at the time. He had just starred in a new installment of *The Fast and the Furious* and had just received a multi-million-dollar offer to star in another Universal movie called *Wanted*.

On September 15, 2008, I reluctantly hopped on to that same escalator heading to the Daily Grill again. Midway up, my phone rang. It was one of my private wealth managers at UBS. I'll refer to him simply as Mark.

"Hey. I'm walking into a lunch. Can I call you back?" I asked.

"Ummm. Yeah, that works. I just wanted to make sure you heard about Lehman." He sounded worried.

"Yup. Of course. I think I told you about my buddy who works there. Been watching the train wreck all summer. I'm well aware and not surprised."

"Yeah, but do you know how the bankruptcy affected your port-folio?" He was nervous.

"I'm sure it's crushing the overall market today, and my structured notes are riding the various indexes. I'm not too worried. Those instruments have been great to me over the years. I'll ride it out," I said rather confidently, hopping off the escalator.

"It's not that minor of a thing, Chris," he said. The seriousness of his tone jacked my blood pressure. "Your portfolio has gone to zero."

My heart sank.

"What?"

"Your structured notes. The instruments that rode the indexes over the years and multiplied three times to the upside? Those were tied to Lehman bonds."

"What the fuck are you talking about, Mark?" I yelled, standing outside the door of the Daily Grill. "If I knew that, I would've gotten out of them long ago. I knew Lehman was in trouble. I've been following it closely."

"I'm sorry. I don't know what to say. Those prospectuses sent out by UBS detailed how those instruments worked."

"What are you saying, Mark? Those three-hundred-page booklets with microscopic writing in them would've walked me through how the structured notes that you pitched me more than a decade ago were tied to Lehman bonds, which, in the event of bankruptcy, would go to zero, taking my whole portfolio to zero also?" I was both livid and scared. People walking into the restaurant were scurrying around me. I must have had crazy eyes and sounded like a madman. "As I recall, this was not something I was ever told about by you."

"You should've read the prospectus. It was all there."

"Did you know how these structured notes worked? Did you know how they were tied to Lehman?" I asked, blood boiling. "Tell me the truth. Did UBS ever tell you how they worked? Did you even care? Are you saying you just simply sold me a product with no idea how it worked? What the fuck, Mark?!"

"You should've read the prospectus, Chris. I'm sorry."

I hung up shaking. Every dollar Jennifer and I had saved was in those structured notes.

On Monday, September 15, 2008, Jennifer and I were officially broke.

Like my previous lunch disaster at Daily Grill, I don't remember whom I was meeting with, and I honestly can't remember anything that occurred after. The next memory I had was September 16, 2008, driving to Brentwood Country Club to play golf with Daniel Postaer and his father Larry. During that rush hour drive, I listened to CNBC. There was talk of a TARP bailout package. Congress was being pressured to pass it to keep the rest of the banking system afloat. Congress was reluctant though. Why bail out the bad seeds who caused the financial crash? No kidding! I was with them on that. Such a bailout would cost taxpayers almost a trillion dollars and go straight to the banks who, at the time, were absolutely hated—and for me at that point, *hate* was a very tame word.

That morning, I also continued to hear how many of the speculating idiots inside the banking system who created financial weapons of mass destruction couldn't be fired, fined, or thrown in jail. Why? Because they were the only ones who understood how to possibly unwind the very apocalyptic instruments that they created. The ones responsible for the whole mess.

My mind was a blur during that entire round of golf. I felt bad, because playing golf with Daniel's father, who is one of the great iconic advertising business maestros, was always a special treat. I do, however, remember one moment. I was on the tee box of the par 3 hole alongside San Vicente Boulevard. My phone rang. It was Mark again.

"Your colleague, Bruce, still hasn't called me back. That coward refuses to take my call. He knows he screwed me and my family," I said.

"Forget Bruce. He was a pawn. Didn't know shit about what he was pitching you."

"What the heck are you guys going to do about this? My savings are gone! Completely gone! I have a wife, two young kids and an expensive house in Hancock Park that apparently I bought at the peak of the market," I huffed.

Larry and Daniel gave me a slashing-throat signal. Cell phones were not allowed on the course and I was making a scene. The commotion was annoying to a handful of golfers around us, causing concern in my group.

"You going to listen or yell?" Mark asked, matter-of-factly.

"Talk. I'm listening."

"Bottom line is UBS didn't instruct any of us on what these structured notes were. We had no idea. We were just told to sell them. You need to write a letter. A strong letter. Saying that UBS intentionally kept your wealth managers in the dark. It was all about selling product. Get what I'm saying?" he asked. "You and I never had this conversation either."

"I get it."

I hung up. I took a swing, hitting my ball a good twenty yards farther than I had ever hit a seven iron before. I was jacked with adrenaline and super pissed off.

As the months and years passed since Lehman's bankruptcy, I saw many issues in my beloved United States of America that shed light on flaws I was unaware of. No one seemed to understand the complexities of what was really going on day-to-day on Wall Street, and even worse were the regulatory bodies who were unable to properly patrol it. Additionally, none of the rich and powerful people went to jail for ripping off poor and powerless people. Just look at Angelo Mozilo, Jon Corzine, Dick Fuld, Kenneth Lewis, Ralph Cioffi, Matt Tannin, Steve Cohen, and others. What happened to the S&L crisis days when all corrupt C-level execs went to jail? What happened to the days since Enron and WorldCom, when wrongdoers were thrown in prison? Now many of the people that caused the collapse got off by saying the institutions they ran were too big to govern. Therefore, they weren't responsible for the evil deeds done by those below them. But then again, we designated several entities as "Too Big to Fail." And

"Too Big to Fail" means true capitalism simply doesn't exist in the United States of America anymore. And don't get me started on how corporations get fined for criminal activity, but no individuals go to jail for that criminal behavior. A corporation doesn't make a decision. Humans inside of them do. If something was done that broke laws, actual people made those decisions and directed that course—not the corporation itself. It's so messed up.

I learned our form of "capitalism" allows people to make big money on apparent risks where they have no skin in the game. Consider underwriters of loans, the very people in charge of determining whether a borrower was creditworthy or not. They would vet a borrower and then hand off the loan to another party to take the risk.

And then, of course, there were the rich and powerful guys who ripped off other rich and powerful guys. What happened to them? Jail. The Big House! Why? Because if you are going to commit a crime in America, make sure the victim is poor and powerless. Jon Corzine was smart enough to do that. His victims were poor farmers. Bernie Madoff, on the other hand, wasn't as smart. He ripped off other rich and powerful people, so he went straight to the slammer. If he targeted Corzine's victims instead, Madoff would be alive and well on both Wall Street and Worth Avenue—making trades, watching polo, and sipping a Bellini.

But why do I mention this all? Because the 2008 financial crisis, and in particular the Lehman Brothers bankruptcy, opened my eyes to flaws in the American system of capitalism, justice, regulation, and governance that I had never noticed before. Understanding those flaws, while also studying the aspects of the US that are truly our strengths, gave me great insight and perspective on what I would continue to learn about China and how I could apply it to my efforts in maximizing the monetization of cultural exchange between the two countries.

15.

AIM HIGH

"THERE ARE A lot of people who talk a lot about how to do business in China, but I actually got *Knowing* in," Mintz told Jonathan Landreth of the *Hollywood Reporter* in an August 19, 2009 article.

He was accurate. Our promise to Bob Hayward became a reality, and both DMG and Summit reaped the rewards. As a result, Bob's studio continued to give us films to release in China. Others did too. *Twilight, Resident Evil, Kick-Ass, The Eagle, Priest, Red,* and *Killers* were some of them. DMG garnered highly coveted theatrical releases for each in China, both surprising and impressing everyone in Hollywood. For a market that only took the biggest and best from major studios, we were getting it done with that next tier of Hollywood films.

DMG also found success in producing our own Mandarin films for the local market. The blockbuster and Communist Party-pleaser, *The Founding of a Republic,* was one of those. Showcasing such a pro-China story on the big screen gained DMG even more fans with the Chinese government—a very smart move that paid off in spades, providing greater guanxi for the company. A lot of that goodwill allowed smaller DMG productions like *No Man's Land* and *Go Lala Go!* to find big success in the market too. The government bodies overseeing China's film industry really put the wind to our backs.

"We have found success in marketing and distributing Hollywood's movies. We have found success in making our own Mandarin language movies. Now we need to combine the two," Dan said one evening in 2010.

"What do you suggest?" I asked.

"We need to make our own Hollywood movies."

It was August of 2011. We just finished production on a film called *Looper*. Bruce Willis, Joseph Gordon-Levitt, and Emily Blunt starred in the movie for director Rian Johnson, a highly prized independent film director whose debut film, *Brick*, was the toast of Sundance a few years prior.

Looper was a badass project with some serious street cred in Hollywood. I was super proud to be involved with it. Every film, no matter the size or scope, takes a village to accomplish. *Looper*'s village included an independent financier/production company, Endgame, along with Rian's producing partner, Ram Bergman, and studios Sony/TriStar Pictures and FilmDistrict. Fantastically talented people surrounded this project, putting the film's pedigree in rarified air, especially one that started independently rather than at one of the major studios.

Looper was an amazing story for Hollywood, as it marked the first true collaboration between US filmmakers and their counterparts on the China side. It wasn't just some *Crouching Tiger, Hidden Dragon*-type of obvious fit either. The project had a big Western star, along with other Western actors who were all favorites of the top critics. *Looper*'s budget was sizable at roughly $35 million too, so it had real risk.

Rian Johnson was "hot," as they say in Hollywood, and very much in demand. Years later he became one of the choice directors Disney tasked with shepherding the *Star Wars* franchise. Rian also wrote and directed 2019's critical darling and box-office hit, *Knives Out*. Add to that, Johnson's script had all the markings of a potential commercial hit with buzz-worthy stars, an "it" director, a much-talked-about script, and a good-sized budget. Genre-wise, it was a sci-fi thriller, set both in the not-so-distant future and also forty years after that, as time travel was a key element in the plot. And most striking was that the original script had no China relevancy whatsoever in the film. Absolutely none. No Chinese characters, no Chinese locations, no Chinese references, no Chinese anything. Other than the United States, the only other country mentioned and used in the original script was France.

With great persistence, we eventually convinced the filmmakers to change every one of *Looper*'s plot points involving France to China—the actors, the locations, the references, everything. Every mention of something French transformed into something Chinese. And in the process, we also brought China into the financing, development, production, marketing, and distribution of the film. It was no easy task to get the filmmakers to agree to any of this, but we got it done. Money talks, and when filmmakers see a way to increase the budget to get more shooting days and increased production resources, they'll listen. Even better is when you can showcase how China can enhance the story. They just needed to believe the money was real and that the changes in the script would make the film better. Convincing everyone took some time and effort, but we eventually made the entire *Looper* village believers.

That across-the-board incorporation of China into a high-profile Hollywood commercial film began to change the bilateral cultural relationship between the US and China in a positive manner. Two of the five forces of diplomacy were alive, well, and blossoming. For the movie-making business, it opened the door to a larger-scale monetization of what would soon become the largest film market in the world. In other words, *Looper* shifted the bilateral dynamics, bringing competitive superpowers closer together through artistic collaboration, but that was an unplanned, beneficial side effect.

Watching movies shares the cultural magic of basketball. *Making* movies creates the same positive collaborative side effects experienced by the NBA, Kobe, Jordan, and Nike too. We witnessed equivalent diplomatic rewards on our own projects like The World's Strongest Man and The Battle of the Nine Gates. However, like the sports industry, both Hollywood and DMG focused on the business of it all too. Making money in one of the largest film markets was the initial and most prioritized goal. That was all anyone cared about. No one in *Looper*'s village really gave a shit about China. And for sure, deep down, China couldn't really give a shit about us. Diplomatic altruism was simply a beneficial shrapnel of capitalism.

In a January 18, 2011, *Hollywood Reporter* article, Jonathan Landreth continued to cover DMG's exploits, but this time the focus was *Looper*. He cited a few key elements that made the film so groundbreaking for the two countries. According to Landreth, by casting Chinese actress Xu Qing as Bruce Willis's wife, it *"could help the movie skirt Beijing's annual twenty-title cap on imported films,"* a reference to the protectionist China import quota, placing a limit on foreign films entering the market each year, thusly enabling China's local film industry time to develop without an overabundance of Hollywood competition. Additionally, strengthening *Looper*'s relevance in the market through the strategic implementation of Chinese elements allowed the film to circumvent that limit, positioning the film for a substantial piece of the then-$1.5 billion box-office pie—a sum that had increased 64 percent from the previous year in a market that would hit $10 billion annually by 2019. And Landreth also highlighted that *"DMG's design department is mocking up a futuristic Chinese note that will be used as money throughout the movie,"* referring to several props and computer-generated buildings for Shanghai's skyline created to showcase China's prowess in the future.

Call it supercharged brand integration, but the brand in this case wasn't a consumer product, but rather a country itself: China. And our successful implementation of the brand resulted in a reward from China's government: a bigger cut of the film's box office. By August of 2011, the physical production of *Looper*, both the US-located and China-located portions, had completed. Only the post-production portion was left, and the date for the film's global release was set for September 28, 2012.

Though China's regulators hadn't approved that date for us yet, the buzz on the film was already strong, and Hollywood was paying very close attention given *Looper*'s aggressive and trailblazing China-market monetization ambitions. DMG's China operation had successfully accomplished the China-located portion of the production and was focused on qualifying the film as a US-China co-production, a status never given to a major Hollywood film before. Such a designation granted lots of benefits, particularly the ability to release the film in concert with the US release, to market and promote the film early, and to garner a 43 percent share of the film's box-office gross rather than the standard 13 to 17 percent at the time.

Hollywood still couldn't believe that such an esteemed filmmaker like Rian Johnson would take a gamble on China and the chaos associated with the country at the time. *"Why the heck would Rian alter his script and production to involve China? That's completely fucking nuts!"* executives would tell me. *"And, besides, even if Rian gets the job done, China will find a way to screw him and the financiers for sure."*

Using history as an indicator, such an assessment rang true. However, they didn't account for DMG's track record for making the impossible possible.

That said, the whole damn thing was really a high-profile test case that everyone in Hollywood secretly wanted to fail. It was vintage Hollywood schadenfreude on one hand, and a true skepticism that China would deliver the promised rewards, if the risk actually paid off, on the other.

It was obvious the next thirteen months would be nerve-wracking as we awaited *Looper*'s ultimate fate with China. Lots of potential business was on the line, and Hollywood analyzed the risk/reward profile of duplicating our innovative initiative. If we failed, Hollywood would continue its begging and pleading to Chinese authorities to let their films in the market. If we succeeded, all Hollywood players would attempt to replicate our every move, hoping to repeat the same accomplishment.

And it wasn't just Hollywood looking at this case study either. American and international businesses in other industries hoping to break into China were also watching extremely closely. Trillions of dollars were on the line. Yes, trillions!

And so were leaders of various countries, including, most importantly, that of both the United States and China. A new template for diplomacy was surely at stake.

And journalists—Chinese, American, and international—were all covering it. They gladly supplied the dry kindling for all that scrutiny by all the different parties from all over the world. The result? Often overly critical reporting creating explosive reactions.

Let's face it, films are already so high-profile on an international scale, and the potential success of this bilateral film collaboration could present a template for other forms of constructive diplomacy and commerce. *Looper* was a case study loudly showcased on the international stage. Global capitalism—trillions of dollars' worth—cast one watchful eye, and international diplomacy—one that could prevent another cold war—cast the other.

Simply making *Looper* gave credence to a new form of "Ping Pong Diplomacy," especially since the actual production of the film was successful and covered by journalists in a very favorable light already. However, the jury was still out as to whether the endeavor would have a successful conclusion. If the film succeeded financially, it would definitely soothe a very tense Sino-US relationship, providing a proven and practical example on how to maximize profits through bilateral cooperation. However, if it failed, it could be embarrassing on a global scale—not just in terms of P&Ls, but also as a weak template for diplomacy.

Such a high-stakes, slow-moving train wreck *or* historic, game-changing success had another thirteen months of intrigue to play out. So, for me as the company's Motion Picture Group President and North

American GM, I couldn't just wait to see what happened. Our business needed to continue driving forward, and I had to find the next project. But this time we wanted a film from a major studio, and the bigger the better.

So, I went big...*really* big!

I reached out to Nate Moore, a good friend with a rather detailed Rolodex card. He was an aggressive and innovative production executive at Marvel. I wanted the next great US-China collaboration to be a mega-budgeted Marvel film. I knew he could help.

I wanted *Iron Man*.

16.

THE SECOND ACT: CHASING MARVEL

NATE CAME THROUGH. On August 17, 2011, Daniel Postaer and I drove on to the Manhattan Beach Studios campus to meet with Marvel COO Tim Connors and Marvel Business Development executive Benjamin Hung with the purpose of landing *Iron Man 3*. If victorious, we would change how Hollywood's major studios approached China.

The last time I visited this particular studio lot was a decade earlier as a William Morris agent. I went to see my client, Dwight Yoakam, on the set of Sony's *Panic Room*. The sprawling soundstage had a real-life $6 million New York City brownstone built inside it. Elaborate plumbing in the stage's ceiling simulated a raging storm. An almost-endless craft service table extended the length of the set, piled with fruit, PowerBars, fancy snacks, and any kind of non-alcoholic beverage and barista-fresh coffee drink imaginable. Completely expected from a major studio movie—excess ran rampant. Even the shooting schedule, detailed on walls around the set, went almost to infinity. Acclaimed filmmaker David Fincher required ample time to get every shot perfect. His demand for excellence demonstrated in the finished product—meticulously created works of precision art for the big screen. *Panic Room*'s cast included Jared Leto and Jodie Foster, two of hottest stars at the time and also perfectionists themselves. Money was no object. Hollywood at its most gluttonous.

That decade-old memory spoiled me. I expected to see something similar visiting Marvel. After all, this was the studio largely built from the storytelling genius of Stan Lee. It created the rebirth and box-office sensation of *Iron Man* in 2008. And Disney recently made a $4 billion calculated gamble on the iconic comic book company and its treasure trove of five thousand characters. Marvel should've been living large in my opinion.

The security guard pointed in the direction of Marvel's offices and suggested where to park. There wasn't a reserved spot for us, apparently. I found that unusual. Reserved parking spots for guests were typically a given for studios.

We walked into Marvel's lobby. "Unassuming and a bit disheveled" described the scene best. Daniel and I announced ourselves to the receptionist who looked like a stereotypical fanboy rather than the typical corporate greeter. The reception area had no seats, so we were led to an adjacent conference room with a large table and a dozen chairs. None of them matched. I grabbed a seat near the door and leaned back. It then abruptly broke.

"What the *heck*?" I shouted, barely catching myself. I stepped away. It continued to fall off the hinges while I watched from a safe distance.

"Looks like Marvel puts all their money into their films," Daniel laughed.

The receptionist walked in.

"Shit, I forgot to warn you about the chairs," he said, seeing the broken chair. "Tim and Ben will be joining you in a minute."

He left. Daniel simply shook his head.

The guys then entered the room. They grabbed chairs, knowing which were in working condition.

"Hope we didn't make you wait too long," Tim started, carrying a friendly grin. "Good to finally meet you, Chris. Nate says some great things about you."

Small talk ended quickly. Tim and I led the core conversation from there. Daniel was ready when needed. He was the perfect addition to any meeting given his vast experience of working on the ground in China. Daniel also carried his father's tremendous wit and charisma, making him the ultimate wingman. He is an extremely hard worker who exuded competence and simply made people feel comfortable that we could deliver. When pitching executional capabilities in China, that was all anyone cared about. *Can you deliver?* Why? Because so many people had been burned in China, no one believed shit anymore.

"Did you see the article in *The Wrap* the other day?" I asked. "Good description of our film agenda."

The Wrap, one of the key industry-focused trades in Hollywood, broke a story I gave them exclusively. The power of third-party validation. That *Fast Company* article was a big one for us obviously, but I had to continuously keep our accomplishments out there publicly. Hollywood forgets things quickly. It doesn't care what you did years back, the town wants to know what you did yesterday, and was it successful? My good friend, J.C. Spink, taught me the art of such a craft. He mastered it in many ways. There was no one better at keeping his name out there than J.C.

"Need to stay top of everyone's mind or you go extinct." he'd say.

To do such, J.C. kept his relationships with journalists balanced. He had information he could share with them. A reporter did him right, he would whisper back, exclusively, a piece of breaking news. He stressed the importance of such trading, and I learned from that. Each journalist who helped him would receive an equal favor in return, allowing more goodwill down the road. And, since J.C. was known to have his ear to the ground better than anyone, journalists knew he'd be good for a tip. And that tip would lead to a printable story.

A steadfast believer in "any press is good press," J.C. used such a mantra to create the flame that attracted moths — and lots of them. For more than a decade he was arguably the greatest salesman of cinematic projects in the business. If he had a project going to market, you could guarantee a reporter would write about it. The article would create heat, and that heat would create a sale.

J.C. mastered the sizzle. And the sizzle sold. But it did come at a price.

J.C. possessed larger-than-life flaws, and he held no shame about them. Such an openness carried a bravado, leading at times to a lack of discipline in the public eye. An example was his openly candid and public battle with producer Roy Lee. The *New Yorker* ran a piece about it, bringing to life publicly J.C.'s fondness for high-end escorts. When asked to confirm the allegation, instead of denying, J.C. instead corrected the reporter, calling them "strippers." He then proceeded to provide more color for his rated-R exploits.

The article came out on June 3, 2003. Being the *New Yorker*, the story exposed J.C.'s entertaining character flaws well beyond the Hollywood audience. The publication reached a large national audience. That meant J.C.'s parents in Philadelphia might come across it, greatly worrying Spink. He didn't care about anyone knowing everything about him unless it was his parents. They had to be shielded, and continuing that censorship was a must.

On the day of the article's publication, J.C. frantically made calls to childhood friends back east. He asked them to buy up any and all *New Yorker* hardcopies in the Philadelphia-metro area, a desperate and expensive, yet also successful plan to keep his parents from coming across the controversial exposé.

Another issue J.C.'s overt openness and favor-swapping created was a "cry wolf" syndrome. Leaking artificial heat on one too many mediocre projects caught up to him at times. Hollywood insiders got weary of any news related to a project of his.

"You're really telling me you got five hundred thousand dollars for that piece of crap?" I'd ask. "I heard everyone passed, and the blogs are trashing it."

"Yup!" he would respond. "It's true!"

"I'm calling bullshit."

"Technically, it's a mid-six-figure offer," he'd say, offering a hint of spin. "I'm not lying."

"How?"

"The studio offered five thousand."

"Dude, you can't count the zeroes after the decimal point!"

"Is that in some rulebook I'm not aware of?"

"You're nuts!" I'd relent.

I'd have that exact same conversation with him several times. Pushing well past the gray, it did eventually catch up to him. Skepticism built, becoming too big a challenge to overcome for his lesser projects. He could always sell his best projects no matter the town's suspicions, but it was his B-level projects that became harder for him to sell. People learned to smell the hype. And still, despite it, J.C. did sell more mediocre projects than anyone. Even crazier, some of those mediocre projects went on to become successful films.

"Hollywood works from a position of fear," J.C. would say. A very important point I learned from him.

"Everyone is scared. They'll believe in something, but they'll be too scared to fight for it. My job is to give them cover. I'm giving them a story. They can then walk into their boss's office and say 'This is a hot project. Everyone wants it. Even the press is talking about it. We should buy it.'"

And that's the truth. People are scared, but with the right story, they will fight. And for J.C., that resulted in movies including *A History of Violence*, *The Hangover*, *The Ring*, and *The Butterfly Effect*. Fear would've killed those films. They never would've existed. Instead, buzz brought them to life, and J.C. and his producing partner, Chris Bender (who later produced Disney's big-budget remake of China's beloved *Mulan*), benefited. Hollywood did too.

And so was my reason for mentioning *The Wrap* article right off the bat. Whatever we pitched from that point on had to be relayed to a boss and the boss's boss for approval. With a smartly timed article in a Hollywood trade, both Tim and Ben had cover. It mitigated fear.

"Yes, that article was impressive. It made the rounds internally," Tim responded.

I smiled.

"Great! It summarizes how a partnership between DMG and Marvel could work. Collaborating, we can help Marvel unlock the potential of the China market."

"We need better box office results and to build brand awareness there," Tim responded. "That is for sure."

"That's the goal. The twenty million *Iron Man 2* grossed there is not enough. The Chinese should crave all things Marvel, and that can happen. Marvel just needs the right partner with the correct strategy," I explained. "That's where we can help."

"We will build your brand, and we'll position it as one that is global," Daniel chimed in. "Consumer products to theme park attractions to other Marvel-branded content. Going way beyond just box office."

"The *global* narrative is key," I added. "As a global brand, Marvel avoids the negative blowback of potential conflicts between the US and China down the road. And you know those flare-ups will occur. You can count on that. Being global immunizes Marvel. Being global will be Marvel's trump card through almost any geopolitical conflict."

"Ike would love to hear that," Ben said, referring to Ike Perlmutter, Marvel's CEO and Disney's biggest shareholder.

"We're all on the same page, obviously, so what do you suggest?" Tim asked.

"Well, there's a bit of a secret sauce we tapped into that plays into the agenda of the Chinese government. Think of it in the most macro sense to understand it best. The Tiananmen Square uprising in 1989 is a nightmare scenario that China's Communist Party never wants to face again. To combat that, they are trying to pull people out of poverty on a massive scale that the world has never witnessed before — to the tune of four hundred million and counting. That is how many Chinese have risen from poverty to a middle class — so far. That's insane!"

"Agree. Incredibly impressive," Tim agreed.

"That social elevation requires lots of resources and long-term initiatives. You can't just create skilled, middle-class jobs out of thin air to replace farming, mining, and dangerous low-skilled factory work. It takes time and money and strategy."

"And those have limits, I'd imagine," Tim butted in.

"Exactly. Keeping 1.4 billion people just happy enough so that they don't revolt is no easy task," I responded. "Especially when there are limits on resources and time. It's frankly why the government can't make them all happy. 'Just happy enough' is the best-case scenario, and even that's a stretch."

"I never thought about it that way," Ben interjected. "So how many more can get to the middle class?"

"Not clear yet, but they're going to push the limits." I had their attention. "That's where we come in."

"How?" Tim asked.

"Let's apply that thirty-thousand-foot view to the micro-level. What Marvel and DMG do well is making movies and building brands." I took a beat to look both in the eyes. "Leading into 2008, the only thing that mattered to the Chinese government was hosting the greatest Olympics in history. That was China's coming-out party. And that Olympics was nothing less than spectacular. Size, scope, expense, grandeur, logistics...you had it all."

"True," Ben agreed. "On top of that, they had Michael Phelps too!"

"No kidding. Phelps was an animal!" Tim exclaimed.

"We took full advantage of that — *big* time!"

"How?" Ben asked. "Give the CliffsNotes version."

"Well, after that crazy run, he made only a handful of carefully selected endorsement deals. One of them was with DMG and our client, Mazda. Boom!" I explained. "China market only. Seven figures annually. A huge win for all parties. Everyone wanted that guy to endorse their brands."

"Definitely a super-hot commodity," Ben agreed. "Nice work!"

"China *loved* him!" I exclaimed. "At least at first."

"Huh?"

"Well, I was on a family ski trip shortly after we closed the deal. A text came early one morning from a colleague in China."

"This is a crazy story," Daniel hinted.

"No kidding," I agreed. "On the text was a grainy photo from a random website. Michael Phelps was smoking a bong. Almost a fake-looking photo. Below the photo, my colleague texted, 'do you think we'll have an issue with this?'

"I responded, 'I hope not.'

"He responded, 'I hope not too!'

"I started getting my gear on. And I helped my wife suit up our kids. Totally occupied, I heard a text chime. Then another. Then my phone rang. Then it rang again. Then it rang again! Then it rang *again*! I glanced at my phone. Colleagues were texting the same photo from various websites. It went completely viral.

"'Oh shit!' I said to myself. And then I get a call from Daniel!"

"Ha! I remember that call," Daniel joined in. "I called you to read an email from one of our PR executives and a crazy text from our Mazda account manager."

"What did it say?" Tim asked.

"It was crazy," Daniel responded. "Our head of PR shot out an email saying, 'A photo just surfaced of Phelps taking hits off a bong. *Today Show* is putting together a last-minute piece on it and Matt Lauer is doing a story in the morning for *Weekend Today*. Someone needs to go on the record about this.'"

"Holy shit!" Tim practically shouts. "Heart attack kind of stuff, right?"

"No kidding!" I said, taking a breath. "I got a call from our CEO. He was pissed and said that Mazda's China executives were in full meltdown mode. I told him I'd get on the phone with Phelps's agent at Octagon, Peter Carlisle. We needed a plan immediately. Needless to say, I didn't ski that day."

"So, how did it play out?" Ben asked.

"Long story short, we made lemons into lemonade."

"How?"

"We came up with a smart 'Own It and Apologize' strategy for Michael Phelps. No ducking. No excuses. Come clean," I explained. "We got his agent behind it, and then Michael agreed. We scripted the apology, and he read it on camera for all of China. Really owned it and spoke from the heart!"

"What exactly did he say?"

"The gist was more than an 'I did a bad thing, so please forgive me' type of apology. It was deeper than that. And he spoke directly to the Chinese people. Like he was there with them, one-on-one." I pulled my computer out. "I'll read the speech."

> To all my Chinese friends,
>
> As many of you know, I've made a mistake that makes me feel very regretful. Recently, many Chinese friends who support me have written comforting and encouraging words online to me. I truly appreciate your sincerity and your caring.
>
> When I fell into this current trouble, your warmth and caring lifted me up. Due to your strong support and kind encouragement, *I have strength*. I promise I will change myself from this point on to the future, continue to train hard, *and I will make you proud again*.
>
> China is a great country; your culture is deep and powerful. I feel *China's tolerance, forgiveness and warmth* from the bottom of my heart. To the youth who are the same age as me: *please learn a lesson from this*. Be positive in life and do the right things. Thanks again for your support and encouragement. I look forward to returning to China again soon....

"Did it work?" Ben asked.

"Yeah, it did! And then for the ads, we brought him right back to the Water Cube where he won all his golds in 2008. The commercials resonated, and Mazda sold a boatload of cars! Absolutely killed it!"

"How?"

"The whole episode and the way Phelps handled it played out super well! He garnered respect and sympathy. The mistake and his humbling apology brought a human quality to him. He became much more relatable," I responded. "Think about it for a second, the guy broke practically every Olympic record in 2008. He's physically a freak of nature. Heck, he's almost superhuman! Anyone, let alone any Chinese person, would be an idiot to sit on their couch and say, 'If only I trained more, I could've done what Phelps did.' That would be preposterous. Yet, after the famous bong incident, the Chinese felt like, 'That guy makes mistakes just like everyone else, and he owned it! He apologized. I feel for him. I like him because of his flaws. He's more like me than I thought.'"

"The Chinese rallied around him. He's now forever tied to China's history. And smartly, we were one of a few agencies influencing our brand client to stick with him through that terrible time. That was risky, but we had a clever plan, and it worked," Daniel added.

"Lemons into lemonade!" Tim said, grinning.

"Yeah. Phelps activated cultural diplomacy through sports. His ability to be human, approachable, flawed, and emotional, added a personal aspect to it. He sincerely touched the hearts of the Chinese. He will make even more millions as a result."

"I get it," Ben said. "One heck of a story."

"So back to what I was saying, Phelps's Olympic achievements notwithstanding, think about the Chinese resources and logistics and execution put into that summer. Insane, right?" I asked rhetorically. "So, when the festivities ended, the Chinese government took a sigh of relief and then started planning their next agenda item."

"Which was?"

"Prioritize industries to build into the best-in-world status and use those industries to broaden the middle class. The film industry was one of those, and someday China wants to be number one at making movies. *And* they wanted to become the largest film market in the world!" I explained. "Both goals, if successful, would create skilled jobs and foster entertainment content for the masses. Think about that: a larger middle class and great entertainment. I'd say that helps keep people just happy enough that they don't revolt. Say *so long* to another Tiananmen Square incident! Mission accomplished!"

"So that macro is really all you need to know. Deliver on that, and you put the wind-to-the-back of Marvel in China," Daniel explained.

"Let's break it down. Hollywood studios are Western propaganda machines. Marvel is one of those. So, things are already working against you in a soft-power sense." I took a swig of water. "Then, even worse, the making of a typical Hollywood film uses nothing China-related, meaning no Chinese artists, no Chinese crew, no Chinese locations, no Chinese plot points, no Chinese investment, no Chinese anything. So, what does that do for the Chinese government agenda of building a robust middle class? Absolutely nothing! It has nothing to do with helping to create middle-class jobs in China, period. That's a big problem!

"Compounding that are Hollywood films because they harm job growth in China's film industry. Why? Because the actual Chinese local-language films that are using Chinese people to make them get crushed by Hollywood films. Chinese consumers like Hollywood movies way more than their own, so they aren't buying tickets for their own homemade product. That means lower revenues for local-language films, which means smaller budgets and shorter productions and less personnel. Or, in other words, fewer Chinese workers are used to make films.

"In the government's eyes, all Hollywood films do is spread Western culture, eat away at local-language product, suck revenue away from Chinese consumers which is then exported to the US, and contribute nothing to the government build-a-middle-class mandate," Daniel stressed.

"So why even let Hollywood films in?" Ben asked.

"Because, remember, the Chinese government needs to make people just happy enough so they don't revolt. If letting their people see films from Hollywood helps to satisfy that objective, they'll let a few trickle in theatrically. Others, they'll let flow into the black market for DVDs," I responded. "In the first scenario, Hollywood monetizes. In the second, Hollywood doesn't."

"Never really thought about it that way," Tim said. "So, what do you suggest?"

"Let's make China a financial and creative partner with Marvel. Let's start with *Iron Man 3*."

"How?"

"Let us first co-finance, co-develop, and co-produce the film. And then let us market and distribute in China."

"Marvel needs to sell to two customers. First is the government. If you get past them, then you can sell to the second: the consumer," Daniel added.

"Got it," Tim said. "No one has done this before with a major motion picture, though. If we're going to be the guinea pig, we'll need big upfront financial comfort."

"And getting Kevin [Feige, Marvel's President of Production] on board creatively won't be easy," Ben added bluntly.

"Fair. We'll put on our thinking caps and get back to you." I got up from my seat.

"Fantastic," Tim responded, shaking my hand. "I think there is something here."

"There definitely is. Guaranteed!"

Daniel and I walked out of the Marvel conference room, through the reception area, and across the parking lot to my car.

When the doors shut, I fist-pumped him. I grinned ear to ear.

"Score!"

"Boom!" Excitement spread across his face. Then some concern. "Ike sounds tough though. Everything goes through him, and it sounds like he'll want some big money to do this."

"He's an interesting character for sure. In fact, a friend warned me that he could be ruthless."

"How so?"

"Apparently, after the Disney deal closed, Ike called most Disney executives directly, demanding to speak to each immediately. When one didn't respond, he called again, leaving a message to call back ASAP. When a very short amount of time passed without a response, he called again, telling the assistant to get her boss immediately. In one situation, the assistant panicked, reaching out to colleagues to find her boss. Ike held the whole time until the executive was found."

"What happened when he was found?" Daniel asked.

"I heard the conversation went as follows:

"'Hello, Ike. Nice to meet you over the phone. Sorry about the wait.'

"'Do you know how many strikes a batter gets in baseball?' Ike asked the nervous exec.

"'A what?' The guy was confused. Totally caught off guard.

"'How many strikes do you get? You know the game, right?'

"'Yes, of course. I'm sorry.' The exec was left scratching his head. No idea where Ike was going. 'Three strikes.'

"'Correct. And you already have two with me.' Then Ike abruptly hung up.

"That executive was stunned. Couldn't stop shaking the rest of the day, so he just left. Took sick days the rest of the week too, apparently. Took a while to recover."

"Yikes," Daniel responded.

"We just need to get a deal to work financially and creatively. Ike will want to make money, so we need to show a path. If he signs on, then we need to get Kevin excited creatively. Two masters to please here. Let's get on the horn with China tonight."

"Roger that."

Daniel fiddled with the stereo.

"Living on a Prayer! Turn it up!"

"That's what I'm talking about!"

We both started singing along with Jon Bon Jovi. We were pump-ed up!

"Postaer, we pull this off, DMG could go public! The founders will love us! Marvel will love us. Disney will love us. And China will love us!"

"Game changer for the US and China on a cultural and business level for sure. This is big time."

"Living on a prayer, baby!" I said, driving out the studio gate.

"No kidding."

17.

THINK OUT OF THE BOX

THE DEBATE INTERNALLY at DMG over *Iron Man 3*'s potential box office in China was heated. Ultimately, the distribution team estimated a low-end of $35 million and a high-end of $50 million, which, even in 2011, was too conservative. Those numbers wouldn't sway Marvel, and more importantly, Ike. Even worse, Disney would battle any co-financing arrangement even with Ike's support.

Disney was already the most established American media company in China, so what did they need us for? Yes, I knew the answer, but did they? And even if I made all the right arguments, would Disney even care? They already were building a theme park in Shanghai, which was a project in the works for more than a decade. Disney possessed great confidence in their China-market acumen as a result. Disney firmly believed they needed no outside help. That was not good for us.

"Those estimates are too low," I argued with a colleague. "Hundred-million-dollar grosses from co-productions and imports will start to be commonplace. Heck, *Kung Fu Panda 2* and *Transformers 3* did that already. If we start promoting *Iron Man 3* from the launch event through the release, that's an insane amount of consumer awareness! I think that should justify an eighty-million-dollar gross. Versus *Iron Man 2*'s twenty million, that's four times. Then roughly double the amount of revenue we all keep because of co-production status, that's like nine times. That's real dough. That's game-changing. That gets a deal done!"

"I don't want to sound too pessimistic, but *KP2* had major Chinese relevancy and a fucking panda! And *Transformers* had toys and a TV series in China before the movies ever came out. Costumed super-heroes such as Spider-man or X-Men, while popular stateside, are very new and unfamiliar to the Chinese. An eighty-million gross for *IM3* might be a very best-case scenario—not one we should promise or, heaven forbid, guarantee," my Beijing-based colleague, Andy Anderson, responded.

"There will be twelve thousand movie screens in China by then! We need to be in the Marvel business. We need to think big picture. I need a big number to offer. Otherwise, we've got nothing," I countered. "Let's keep thinking about this over the next couple of days."

Here's the crazy thing, even when we came up with the number, that was only half the battle. The Chinese government would demand certain creative, production particulars, approvals, and partnership requirements to get their full support and obtain a co-production status.

I outlined those in a draft of our offer:

A) *Five to fifteen production days on the ground in China,*

B) *at least one supporting Chinese actor,*

C) *the ability to read the script for censorship issues and to suggest creative "China relevancy" via plot changes, Chinese locations, Chinese roles, and so on,*

D) *good faith cooperation by the Marvel team,*

E) *consultation on potential global release dates, especially since we needed to avoid China's foreign-film blackout periods,*

F) *credits for our Chinese executives and the company, showcasing China's involvement, and*

G) *marketing, branding, and promotional control in China.*

I read through them out loud and winced. Even for me, it was tough to digest. For Marvel, I couldn't imagine.

We had a young, bilingual attorney in our Beijing office named Tim Shih. He helped me formulate our offer from a legal perspective.

"The China portion of the production shall be run through the Chinese side, in this case DMG. Yes, it will be in partnership with Marvel's production and creative team, but the government will also mandate such an arrangement. It must appear as if a Chinese studio is actively involved in the making of this film. Cooperation will aid in garnering final co-production approval by CFG," he explained.

I winced again. Even mentioning stuff like that will make Marvel believe I'm a spy for China. Or at least a Communist Party sympathizer.

"The goal is to make the best film possible. It should be for all parties. Any China priorities that compromise that goal can't be forced," I explained.

"If we can't get all we need, we could lose status with the government. That will cost us money through lost revenues," Shih insisted.

"I get it, but Marvel can't feel like they are forced to make a Chinese infomercial," I countered. "They'll pass on this deal for sure. They can't sense any of that."

"Okay, I'll consider the exact wording legally."

"Just try to make it strong enough in legalese, so we know Marvel will at least *try* to cooperate during production."

"Got it."

"Tim, the bottom line is Marvel will want *full control* creatively in making this film. They will never give us anything but that. All we can do is outline what we really need from them and hope they give us something close to that. That's the best we can do. If they screw us, they will screw themselves since the movie and the brand won't resonate as well as it could."

"Okay. But it does concern me from a legal perspective."

"I understand, but if you give me eighteen months in the trenches with them, they'll appreciate the importance of our asks. I can get them to play ball over time, but it will be a process. All we can do now is put on paper how we hope this deal will work. Cool?"

"Yeah, cool. I'll get you the draft by end of the day China time," he said. "Get some sleep."

We made the offer the next day.

"The offer is missing a 'wow factor,'" Tim Connors responded over the phone, barely a moment after I emailed it. "I don't see it, so I won't take it to Disney or Ike."

I called Tim Shih, waking him.

"We need to pony up more! Sleep on that please, and let's talk when you wake up."

We connected again during his morning.

"There was some good news from Connors," I started. "Assuming we pony up more money, they did offer us the opportunity to create a teaser at the end of *Avengers* for the China market. That would give us a chance to tease a potential character, either The Mandarin or Shang-Chi. It's our decision as to which."

The development team in Beijing felt Shang-Chi was the safer role to promote since he was a "good guy" and a hero, while The Mandarin was clearly a nemesis to Iron Man. Strictly thinking about how the "Ministry of Propaganda," which reports directly to the Politburo, would view it, you always wanted the Chinese character to be a good guy or a hero, not a villain. Remember to them, China is good, and the West is bad. The Politburo wanted white-knight messaging. The country was spreading its wings globally, and it wanted to be viewed as a friend to the world, not an agitator or adversary encroaching on long-established borders through an Imperialistic strategy.

But American hubris, and often ignorance, commonly led to studios putting the Chinese in an antagonist role. Additionally, Hollywood didn't want to waste the part of a hero on a Chinese actor. But a villain role? No big deal. And simply putting Chinese people in a film was mistakenly thought of as the guaranteed price for admission to China's lucrative market. So, studios did it. That was a bad move.

That was exactly the mistake both Sony and MGM did in the reboot of the film *Red Dawn*. In the remake, the story took the Wolverines, the brave young American heroes of the film, and pitted them against an invading Chinese army instead of the old Soviet Union-backed, nondescript Latino force that was in the original film. Though the reboot was entertaining and decently well-crafted, the strategic move to portray China as the film's hated antagonist was a huge mistake by both studios.

Not only did China forbid Sony and MGM from ever releasing *Red Dawn* in the country, but because the movie was made with such ignorance to the Chinese point of view, they also punished both studios beyond *Red Dawn*. China issued very poor release dates to Sony and MGM for other movies. And in some cases, China flat-out rejected normally approved films from those studios. Such severe corporate punishment resulted in the studios reshooting, editing, and using VFX work to alter all images of a "Chinese Army" to one that was North Korean instead.

For this reason, a Marvel antagonist like The Mandarin was risky. It posed a high-stakes gamble, not just for us, but also for Disney and Marvel. If it backfired, it could prohibit a release of the film in China. Even worse, it could prevent both studios from gaining any traction in China for other films coming later. Worst case, a temporary blackballing, similar to what Sony and MGM received from China, was even a possibility.

And that would just be the sentence for the US studios involved. For us, the wrong use of a character like The Mandarin could shut DMG down forever.

"From a strictly 'which character is more interesting' standpoint, The Mandarin is more riveting because he is super intelligent, he is a skilled martial artist and he possesses the ten rings from an alien spaceship which allows him to teleport, among other special powers," Alan Chu, our Beijing-based development VP, explained, sharing a dissenting point of view. "He grew up with a major chip on his shoulder and is able to harness all that into who he is today. There are more layers and depth with this character."

Such an assessment would foreshadow problems ahead, unbeknownst to us. Marvel not only had final cut and approvals, but they were also looking to make the most globally entertaining and profitable film possible. Thinking first about China was not their priority. A super-complex, yet flawed character full of surprises? Now that was a different story.

"That makes a lot of sense, but it also scares me," I responded.

"Scares SARFT also," Alan mentioned, referring to the State Administration of Radio, Film, and Television, the bureaucratic layer that took orders from the Ministry of Propaganda. Below SARFT was China Film Group. They oversaw, regulated, and controlled all the distribution of films in China, once SARFT approved it. "Their reaction to The Mandarin is very negative."

"By the way, let's pass on *The Avengers* teaser opportunity. Agree?"

"Yes, Dan said that also. Too expensive and not enough time."

"Okay. I'll let Marvel know."

"The Mandarin scares the shit out of us."

"Why?" Tim Connors asked.

"He is way too controversial for Chinese censors."

"Why is that?"

"Because The Mandarin looks and acts like the stereotypically derogatory Chinese man. Not only does he have a long spiny beard that he's constantly straightening with his fingers, but he also regularly speaks in uber-'Chinglish,' constantly saying Chinese-cliché types of proverbs," I explained.

"Come on. Seriously?"

"Yeah. I'm serious. Additionally, his character's main motivation is to kill Iron Man!"

"You don't know that for sure."

"That's what scares me more," I responded. "So that leads me to ask...if you wanted us to tease The Mandarin in the end crawl of *The Avengers*, does that mean Marvel is definitely using him in *Iron Man 3?*"

"I don't know."

"Ask yourself this, then. If Marvel does use him, could he be a *Red Dawn* kind of antagonist that gets us all banned from China?"

"Don't be so dramatic," Tim responded. "Besides, creative won't tell me anything, and the script hasn't been completed yet anyway."

"I wish I wasn't being dramatic."

"Don't freak out yet. Let's see." There was a tell in his voice. I heard it.

The Mandarin was going to be in *Iron Man 3*.

18.

TAKING A CALCULATED RISK

THE MANDARIN WAS at best a neutral wildcard. But, more realistically, he was a Dragon-slaying, LeBron James-Nike-brand-and-business-damaging mishap of a character. And at worst, The Mandarin was a *Red Dawn*, company-destroying, banished-from-China nightmare. Even more frustrating, I wouldn't know for sure if the character was being featured until I was able to read the script. And it was entirely possible that the creatives may still be undecided on exactly how to use The Mandarin in the plot. The mystery was massively stressful because the stakes were extremely high.

On September 8, 2011, I did get some rough details of what was being bantered about creatively regarding The Mandarin. Marvel had also given me some hints on what China-specific production opportunities were coming to life.

"There is an action sequence that takes place in Mongolia. It could shoot in China. Iron Man and Iron Patriot will be in the scene—in costume. Therefore, no Robert Downey and no Don Cheadle. Body double/stuntmen will be doing the on-location work. Is this a problem for the Chinese government granting co-production approval?" I asked Dan over the phone.

"Yes."

"A villain dressed as The Mandarin may be in the film. He's a bad guy. The audience assumes the character is Chinese. *However*, a reveal at the end of the movie is that this character is actually a Caucasian impersonating a Chinese character. Is the initial perception of the villain being Chinese a problem for a co-pro?"

"A complicated, but pretty firm *yes*."

"The initial production schedule for this sequence was probably for five days on the ground. Is that enough for a co-pro?"

"No," Dan responded. "Please get us some creative freedom that works for us. This is ridiculous. China will crush us and the movie if this is the best we can do."

"I'm trying," I said, knowing exactly how he'd answer those questions beforehand. "And you can tell Connors yourself too. He's coming to Beijing. Wants to see DMG headquarters and meet the team."

"Great," he responded. "We'll show him a great time and do our thing, but get me some good news about all this stuff beforehand."

He hung up.

For Tim's pending visit, we planned to pull out all the stops. Even though he wasn't Ike or Kevin, we knew he'd go back and report to them on everything he saw, touched, and felt. We wanted to blow him away. We wanted him to rave about China.

First, a warm welcome at the Beijing airport by the PLA directly at the jetway. Then, a VIP whisk through customs. Professional Formula One racers staffed our multiple stretch Mercedes-Maybachs, extended SUVs, and Bentleys, so Connors would witness our prowess with Beijing's nightmare traffic. The number of vehicles in Beijing was definitely no match for DMG drivers—ever. These guys sped through downtown's congestion faster than any police could. They also had police lights and sirens built into each car's front grill, tricking innocent drivers to pull over as they raced by. And if traffic wasn't moving, our guys would simply drive on the sidewalks.

DMG's treatment of VIPs was by far, the best in its class. In the previously mentioned *Fast Company* article I mentioned earlier, Jamie Bryan described it as:

> Like many people, Dan Mintz takes the time to meet his business associates at the airport; unlike most, he does it in a chauffeured Mercedes S600, escorted by a Shanghai police car. The Benz pulls right to the belly of the 747 inching its way to the gate, and the Staten Islander emerges into the brisk evening air—a bundle of affable, regular-guy energy in black pants, a sweater, and sneakers—and bounds up a stairway specially positioned so that he can intercept his colleague, Chris Fenton, before he gets siphoned off down the jetway and into an interminable customs line. As the pair emerges, joking, from the plane, nine Chinese military police officers stand at solemn attention along the path to the waiting car. Fenton sinks gratefully into the backseat while Mintz, the founder and head of Dynamic Marketing Group, one of China's fastest-rising advertising agencies, dispatches an employee with Fenton's passport to claim his luggage and handle customs. "We don't wait on lines here," Mintz explains with a smile.

Tim's treatment would be similar. Before his visit I outlined his tastes, utilizing a very in-depth Rolodex card I had meticulously created since our first encounter, and a potential itinerary. We wanted to nail it. *Iron Man 3* was on the line.

"Tim is pretty health-conscious. Not a 'club guy' or an all-night partier. Someone who enjoys a good dinner and an experience. Family man. Married with two kids, a boy and a girl, ages four and six. He likes to work out. Age is between forty to forty-five. Not a suit-and-tie guy. More casual. Slacks and button-down. His assistant was the only one who mentioned he may not eat much beef or pork, but she wasn't sure. He tends to go with the flow," I relayed to our team directly from his card.

"Flying in on Air China 1342 on September twenty-second. Let's try to get someone interesting sitting next to him. Please see who else is on the plane. Similar to my Beijing flight with Universal execs this summer, we should shuffle seats.

"Do our traditional Forbidden City treatment—DMG Style!" I added.

The Air China/Universal note referenced a trip when we hosted two of the studio's key international executives in Beijing, Jack Ledwith and Abhijay Prakash. I was flying over with them both, so I called colleagues with close ties at Air China to secretly switch my seat so that I could sit next to Abhijay. I already knew Jack pretty well, but Abhijay was a new acquaintance I wanted to get to know better.

In filling out Abhijay's potential Rolodex card, I stumbled across a published paper he wrote while attending Wharton called "Comprehending the Narrative Power of the Curse of the Bambino." I, being a Yankees fan, found that interesting. Definite common ground, even though we'd be on opposing sides. Abhijay was obviously a diehard Red Sox fan.

Having leverage with airlines to pull off a forced change of seats was nothing China-specific. William Morris had that kind of leverage back in the day too, and its former CEO, Norman Brokaw, would apply it regularly on trips to New York. He'd have his assistant find out who else was in first class and then switch him into a spot next to the person with the most potential for business. Concerning Air China, DMG could accomplish the same thing.

I remember grabbing my seat next to Abhijay prior to Jack boarding. Abhijay probably assumed I was residing there temporarily to share some chit-chat. Then Jack came up the stairs to the second deck. He saw me sitting there, a bit surprised.

"Hey, Chris. How are you? Mind if I sit?"

"Not a problem. Where's your seat, though?"

"You're sitting in it."

"I don't think so. Here's my ticket stub."

He glanced at it, shocked. Before he could presumably ask if I'd be willing to change seats, I jumped in.

"I think I just got a little lucky." I smiled, looking back at Abhijay. "Now I get to talk to Abhijay about his published paper on the Curse of the Bambino!"

"How'd you come across that?" Abhijay asked, completely surprised. "Did you read it?"

"Of course I did."

Jack, sensing he'd lost the potential battle over switching seats, walked off.

"You want to switch?" I offered politely. If he did want his rightful seat back, I surely would've changed. Jack was a good guy.

"No, that's OK. I'll be sleeping most of the trip anyway," he responded, putting his carry-on in the overhead compartment.

"I can't believe you read my paper. Wow!"

Bottom line, it was a very constructive flight.

The private tour of the Forbidden City, another arrow in our quiver, landed the whale every time. I never knew exactly how my Chinese bosses got it done, but they did. Jamie Bryan again described it best:

> After the general's dinner, Fenton and Mintz are standing just outside the Forbidden City when a police car pulls up and drives them into the massive inner courtyard framing the fabled Jin Shui Qiao, or Golden River Bridges. This is a special accommodation Mintz has arranged only once before, and as the cops patiently stand by, the pair steps out for a brief walking tour, with Mintz explaining the significance of various ornate monuments looming against the clear night sky. The buildings' scale alone is breathtaking, and Mintz reveals himself as a reverent if self-taught

student of the history around him. "This," he whispers, "is as close as anyone can get to feeling what it was like to be the emperor."

With Tim, we'd take full advantage of the good weather given the time of year, showing him the Forbidden City during magic hour. As Jamie mentioned, Tim would also experience the palace the same way any emperor would during their respective reign, in complete silence. Only the echoes of his dress shoes hitting the ancient stone of the ground beneath him would be heard. He would walk the countless courtyards and corridors this way. The whole experience symbolized power and ability—the power of shutting off the center of Beijing's energy and buzz entirely and the ability to replace it with comforting, yet deafening silence. An emperor would want it no other way. Our guests deserved the same.

We would make sure there was no way Tim left Beijing not wanting us involved with *Iron Man 3*. We would make sure his experience was one for his memoirs. And we would want him to tell his colleagues how he was now a believer in us.

We could deliver on Marvel's China goals. We were the ones.

"Tim is definitely impressed by the DMG show. He's super interested in what we can do and offer. Dan is having dinner with him right now," a Beijing-based VP, Billy Neo, alerted me on the night of the twenty-third. "I am picking Tim up at 6:00 a.m. at his hotel to take him to the airport. All good."

Dan followed up later that evening with "Seal the deal when Tim is back! We did our job! Now you do yours!"

19.

DURAN DURAN AND J.C. SPINK

SEPTEMBER 27, 2011

"**WHAT ARE YOU** doing right now?" a voice asked over the phone. It was J.C. Spink.

"I just put the kids to bed. Jennifer and I are about to start watching *Real Housewives of Beverly Hills*," I responded, grabbing a spot on the couch next to my wife. "Why do you ask?"

"Who's that?" Jennifer whispered.

"J.C.," I responded, covering the phone.

Jennifer smiled. As crazy, inconsistent, and larger-than-life as J.C. was, Jennifer always had a soft spot for him. She also knew how much his friendship meant to me.

"Come outside," J.C. said, matter-of-factly.

"Outside where? My house?" I asked. I got up to look out the window.

"Yeah!" he responded. "I'm outside your gates."

Yes, he was. I saw his well-worn black Jeep Wrangler sitting curbside in front of my home. His horn blared. I could hear it both through our double-paned windows as well as through the phone.

"Okay. One second. Let me grab some shoes," I said, slightly annoyed. I scurried around looking for something to put on my feet. "And stop with the horn! The kids are sleeping!"

"Where are you going?" Jennifer asked, walking towards me. We were both looking forward to a little reality television to cap off a busy day.

"I just need one second. J.C.'s outside. Wants to chat about something," I responded, sliding on the only footwear I could find by our front door. It was a pair of hotel slippers. I used them to get my newspapers in the morning. Given I was in pajama bottoms and a t-shirt, I figured that would do the job. "I'll be right back."

I opened the front door and propped it open gently behind me. I didn't want to awaken our kids. I walked through the driveway and buzzed myself out of our pedestrian gate. J.C.'s Jeep was there, just down the stairs leading to the street. He had Duran Duran's "Hungry Like the Wolf" blasting on the stereo. The passenger door was open, making it even louder.

"Dude, you're going to awake the neighbors," I yelled, reaching over the passenger seat to turn down the volume.

"Come on! This is a great tune!" he said, returning the volume to its original state. "I need to show you something. Get in the car."

"What is it?" I asked, sitting down. "Everything okay?"

"Dude, look at your life," he said, grinning. "Look at that fucking house. Every time I see it, I'm like, what the fuck! How awesome is my buddy, Fentoni!"

I turned back to look. I did like my home.

"What about it?" I asked.

"It's fucking beautiful. You live in Hancock Park. A classically beautiful house. You got yourself an English Tudor. A gated motor court. Not a big one, but one, nonetheless. A guest house too! An insanely awesome and gorgeous wife. Super cool kids. A perfect boy-and-girl pair too," he explained enthusiastically. "You almost got it all!"

I laughed, not sure where he was going. But he was J.C., so that was always par for the course. He definitely had something on his mind, but I wasn't sure what.

"Close the door!" he demanded. He had a bit of a shit-eating grin on his face, but I trusted him. "You got to hear this song. It's my new favorite."

That made my mind a bit more at ease. J.C. loved music, so it wasn't surprising that he may have had some epiphany about what was now his new favorite song from the eighties. Such sudden self-realization occurred almost weekly with him.

"Okay, but I got to go back in afterwards," I said, closing the door reluctantly. "Jennifer and I have appointment television with the Bravo Network. Can't leave her waiting long!"

Considering it was a soft-top Jeep, I wasn't super convinced the acoustics were all that improved by a closed door. J.C. was oblivious to that kind of stuff, but whatever. I played along.

"See, that's what you're missing! Spontaneity," he shouted over Duran Duran. He started searching for the song he wanted on his stereo. "When was the last time you just went out and had fun on a Tuesday night?"

"On a Tuesday, it's usually just for a business dinner or something," I responded. "Come Undone" by Duran Duran started to play.

"Yes, here it is! Great tune. Was one of their later tunes. Simon wrote it after his depression years," J.C. exclaimed, shifting his Jeep into drive. He slammed down the gas pedal, and we peeled out. I was flung backwards by the sudden acceleration.

"What the fuck, J.C.!" I yelled, re-adjusting. "Turn back! This isn't funny!"

"You're going out tonight!" he demanded. "Time to do something random on a Tuesday night!"

"J.C., that ain't happening tonight! Turn the car around!" I yelled, staring him down.

"Nope. You're going out with me!" he stated, not even looking back at me. We squealed around the corner, jumped the curb and took off down Melrose Avenue. "We're going to the Duran Duran concert!"

"Duran Duran? I can't go to a Duran Duran concert. I'm wearing pajamas, J.C." I shouted, pinching my pajama pants and holding them up for him to see.

He looked down at my legs and started laughing.

"So am I!!" he yelled back, pinching the clothing on his legs for me to see. "Look!"

I looked down, and sure enough, he was wearing pajamas also. Even worse, he was wearing what looked to be a pajama top too! The only slightly non-sleepwear he wore was a pair of Nike slides. I was envious, a much better option than my hotel slippers.

"You're nuts, J.C.! Seriously!" I yelled.

He drowned out any of my objections with the stereo. It was cranking.

"Maybe I am nuts, but who cares! We're going to see *Duran-fuck-ing-Duran*!" he screamed out the window. "Enjoy the ride, Fentoni!"

"Seriously? We're doing this?" I asked helplessly. It fell on deaf ears.

"Consider yourself kidnapped!" he screamed, staring at me with a shit-eating grin that reeked of amusement and positive energy. The look on his face made his excitement level contagious, though. I was won over. I was suddenly excited to join this latest J.C. adventure.

And thank goodness, since at that point, I was stuck anyway. I have to also admit that the idea of seeing Duran Duran in the intimate setting of the Nokia Theater was pretty damn cool too. Even better, because the kidnapping was executed by J.C., Jennifer was okay with it. Any extra time I could spend with J.C. was well spent in her mind. She knew he was a wandering soul and someone who needed a close friend. Jennifer also knew that J.C. was full of crazy, yet sometimes wonderful ideas that many times inspired me. It was a win-win in her mind. It was thoughtfulness like that which always made me realize how special Jennifer was and still very much remains. I love that woman!

After numerous near-death lane changes and missed turns, we finally made it to the parking garage of the Nokia Theatre. J.C. pulled into a fire lane and parked the car. He never feared the nuisance of being towed or getting a parking ticket. He mostly believed any hassle or expense incurred from that kind of disregard for authority was simply the cost of convenience. After countless times arguing with J.C. for having such an impractical belief, I eventually learned to live with it. J.C. wasn't going to change, and surrendering to his conviction only meant a few extra taxi rides when a towing took place anyway. To J.C., the upfront convenience and the thrill of the risk were all too worth the potential downside. And besides, he never had to really deal with the ramifications anyway. That was what his assistants and business manager were for in his mind.

"I still can't believe we are in pajamas," I said to him as we walked up from the garage to the venue. "This is so crazy!"

"Yup!" He just smiled.

"Let's just stay incognito, cool?" I suggested, hoping we'd avoid seeing anyone we know. "These seats aren't industry comps, are they?"

He was silent. A grin on his face formed again.

"Wait," I grabbed him as we walked towards the security line. "Where are the tickets? Are they 'House Seats'? We aren't dressed for that. You realize that, right?"

"Relax!" he said, continuing to walk to the metal detectors. He handed security our tickets. "They aren't 'House Seats.'"

"Thank God!" I responded, relieved.

"Enjoy the show. Great seats!" the security guard said. He then pointed across the room. "Head to the usher over there."

"Thank you," J.C. said. His grin was even bigger now.

"Follow me," the usher directed. The theater was dark. We arrived just before Duran Duran came on stage.

"Good seats?" I asked, realizing we were walking towards the front row.

"You could say that," J.C. responded, adjusting his pajama bottoms.

"Here's your row," the usher said, shining his light on the first seat. "Front row. Doesn't get better than that."

"No, it doesn't," J.C. agreed, respectfully forcing his three-hundred-pound, pajama-clad body through a few people in our row to get to our seats. They were smack in the middle of the first row.

"Good, I'm glad no one will see us in these ridiculous outfits," I said sarcastically.

"Don't worry, if they can't see us from a distance, they'll be able to see us on the monitors!" J.C. joked. "Look, I know you'd rather have on your leather pants and polyester shirt, but we are in the fucking front row of a Duran Duran concert!"

"I know. It's pretty epic. I'm with you!" I responded. I was excited, though I did wish I had underwear on and perhaps some sort of pajama bottoms with a stronger waistband to prevent an accident if you catch my drift.

"I've reached the age where I need to put glasses on to see the set list!" a voice said into the microphone. I could see his silhouette. He was hardly a couple of yards from me. It was the great Simon Le Bon!

And boom, the James Bond theme song, "A View to a Kill," kicked in at a thousand decibels. With it, every spotlight shone like the sun upon Simon. Even better too, those lights brought to life on the monitors everyone standing in the crowd within six feet of Simon!

"Look! There we are!" J.C. shouted, looking at the massive monitors set up on both sides of the stage. "Dude, dance! Everyone is watching!"

I looked up at the monitors and there we were, pajamas and all, right by Simon Le Bon. I then glanced at Simon who had just started singing. We caught eyes—awkward! He gave a quick look at both J.C. and me, then did a double-take. Clearly, we were the first pajama-wearing front-row fans he had seen on tour. Considering his front row had had lingerie-clad models back in the eighties, and now it was

Spink and I sporting loose pajamas, I'd imagine he found some irony in it all. Simon cracked a quick grin and kept going.

I shook my head. I couldn't believe it, but that was such a vintage J.C. Spink moment. He couldn't give a shit that he was on camera constantly during the show wearing the most ridiculous outfit. Bottom line for J.C., this was what Hollywood was all about. Work hard and play hard using the favors you built up over the course of your work to get front-row tickets to Duran Duran. Then kidnap one of your best friends to remind him to soak up every day by living life to its fullest. Under-dressed or not, it didn't matter. What mattered was living it up, having the experience, and sharing the experience.

My phone vibrated with a text message. I looked down.

"Are you at the Duran Duran concert? With J.C. Spink? Wearing pajamas? In the front row?" a friend in the theater asked.

"I am," I texted back. I looked up at the camera behind Simon, smiling.

"Epic!" my buddy responded. "Simon keeps doing a double-take. Not sure he knows what to make of you guys. It's hilarious!"

I looked at J.C. He was having the time of his life. Part Hollywood mogul and part big sweaty middle-aged guy living it up at a Duran Duran concert. He caught my gaze, giving me a grin with a cool head nod.

"Thank you!" I mouthed, knowing he gave me quite a story that night.

"No," he responded, leaning himself towards my ear. "Thank you, Fentoni. Seriously. You are the one of the few I can truly count on."

20.

MOMENTUM

SHORTLY AFTER TIM Connors got back to LA from his Beijing trip, Marvel executives began to cooperate. Nothing was mentioned, but everything was good. He had the experience in Beijing we wanted him to have. That was obvious. It felt like we'd get a deal finally closed. Both sides understood what each other wanted. We knew how, in theory, we could work together to achieve a Chinese co-production.

Some of the requirements on our side would bite the dust. Some on theirs too. But there was a path to a deal. And both sides understood that we could work together on necessary contractual changes down the road if needed. A bond was formed, and trust had been earned at a basic level, at least enough to commence the collaboration. Marvel even asked for creative ideas on how to insert China relevancy into *Iron Man 3*. That kind of request almost felt surreal. This thing was finally feeling real.

A smart, young creative executive under Kevin Feige named Stephen Broussard became our point person. Through the production process, he became a close confidant to me. He also became a shoulder to cry on when Marvel couldn't deliver on some items, or when things went awry.

"Okay. So, Stephen will chat with our creative team. They'll sketch out rough ideas for Chinese locations. Then we'll all brainstorm on how those sequences can be Marvel-quality, yet also practical," I said to Tim Connors, recapping action items we discussed in a September 2011 meeting. "Then a meeting will be set with you, Stephen, Kevin, and Ike while Mintz is in LA. The agenda to discuss DMG creative thoughts on *IM3* co-pro sequences."

"That's the plan. Agreed."

We shook hands. Parts of the deal were finally getting closed. Each layer comprised a battle victory in the greater war.

Shortly after that, Disney gave its first projection for *Iron Man 3*'s box office in China—$44 million. Now if Disney went without our services, their share of that $44 million would be somewhere between 13.7 and 17 percent of the gross. Let's call it 15 percent, so they'd net a whopping $6.6 million as a "lone wolf," a terrible return for such a large media company. Although, as bad as that projection was, the modest sum at least doubled Marvel's next-highest-grossing movie in China.

With that line in the sand, we knew we had to better it—and by a lot. A "Show me the money" kind of thing. Disney expected to gross that amount simply by submitting the film to China Film Group. That was simple and painless. It also wasn't risky. Our way, on the other hand, required Marvel to jump through hoops, lots of them, some challenging and some just a pain in the ass. And in some cases, they may make Marvel look like panderers to the Communist Party. The latter posed a potential public relations nightmare or even a potential fanboy revolt, and neither was appetizing. But the upside was 43 percent of the box office and the ability to raise the projected $44 million much higher.

"Disney's distribution team is only going to care about making more money and not risking anything to get it. Their projection is important, and we need to beat it. We need to beat it big. And we need to instill confidence that we won't screw things up. The hoops we make Marvel jump through can't jeopardize anything they are building in China, particularly the Disney brand and its theme park," I instructed our Beijing team over a conference call. "It's vital to understand their point of view when making our financial proposal. We need to back it with intelligent reasons for each of our creative requests. We must convince them it won't damage anything. It can only help, not hurt. And of course, it will make a better film."

There continued to be friction between our Beijing team and Disney's Beijing team at that point too. We had to remain cognizant of that. As in any industry, people are territorial and protective of their jobs. If our plan worked, wouldn't Disney's Burbank headquarters want us doing all of their films in China? And, if so, what happens to their film people in Beijing? Are they needed anymore? They could all lose their jobs.

That wasn't the reality, but it was how we sensed Disney's China office viewed the situation. As a result, we needed to handle them with kid gloves. Maybe they didn't have greenlight ability, but they had the ability to poison things. We did our best to assuage their fears with our consistent messaging that we would make them all look good. Essentially, they back us, and we will back them. We will be fantastic partners that are transparent and collaborative. It was an all-win situation for them. We told them that if the film succeeded, they could own it internally. They could boast of supporting DMG and Marvel all along. However, if it didn't work, they could escape blame by simply saying they supported Marvel. It wasn't their idea. They were always wary of the call at the time. They simply agreed, being good team players.

Disney China had nothing to lose. They had everything to gain. We reiterated that over and over until they started to believe it.

21.

THE MIDPOINT: GAME TIME

SKIPPING FORWARD A bit to January 2012, the contracts between DMG, Marvel, and Disney were almost closed. Marvel's creative team was open to our input on the script, or at least going through the motions of such. After all, they were Marvel. We were not. Even though we continued to bond nicely with the Marvel team, they still viewed us as a nuisance. Less of a nuisance at that point, but a nuisance nonetheless.

Tim Shih and I continued negotiations with a large team of attorneys from both Disney and Marvel. We even had Paramount chiming in from time to time. They still had a legacy participation in the film, a lasting, lucrative remnant from their sale of Marvel to Disney. Skype calls with me in Los Angeles, Tim in Beijing, Marvel's legal team in LA and New York, and Disney's attorneys in Burbank, Hong Kong, and Beijing occupied many of my evenings. On some calls, their side outnumbered Tim and me as much as ten to one. That made it a rush for me. Getting the *Iron Man 3* deal done seemed like David versus Goliath in many ways. Our slingshot was completely outmatched, but we remained undeterred.

With Marvel's business and legal teams almost fully on board, we still had creative to win over. After all, Kevin Feige and his team had almost full autonomy, even back in early 2012. Success after success gave Marvel's creative team more and more control. To retreat from such independence was both counterintuitive and, for some inside Marvel, borderline repulsive. It wasn't like we were coming at it from an A-list filmmaker's creative perspective either. Instead, we were viewed as "The Chinese." As such, we garnered little respect creatively. Marvel did not view us as independent-thinking, filmmaker-friendly, fanboy-appreciative, mythology-obsessed cinematic-universe-savants. If anything, Marvel saw us as shills for the Chinese government or even worse, we were creatively ignorant enemies.

In late February of 2012, Dan and I were invited to read most of the *Iron Man 3* script. We were given roughly ninety minutes to do so in a small room at Marvel's offices.

"Do you have a bunch of blank pages in the middle of the script?" I asked Dan, pausing from reading. He was across a small table from me.

"Yes," he responded. "What the fuck?"

"Hang on. Let me ask the assistant outside," I suggested, getting up to open the door. "It's locked."

I knocked a few times. An assistant unlocked it from the other side.

"Are you already finished?"

"No, but we were wondering if there's an issue with your copy machine?" I asked, flipping through the blank pages for him to view. "These are all blank here."

"Oh. Sorry. I forgot to tell you," he responded nervously, like his omittance of such a fact would get him fired. "There is a scene in the script that is highly confidential. Only Kevin and a few others are aware of what is in that scene."

"Yeah, but we need to read it," I responded. I was slightly aggressive. After all, my CEO was in the room with me. He was used to getting what he wanted, and DMG was putting a lot of money on the line—to the tune that was deep into eight figures!

"You can't. Top secret," he said, emotionless. "I'm sorry."

He left the room, closing the door behind him.

"Did he lock it again?"

I checked, turning the knob.

"Yes." I shook my head. "Weird."

We went back to reading. It was a bit stressful. The script was pretty long, and they'd only given us ninety minutes. Not only did we need to read the script, but we also had to think of ways to implement China relevancy. That was no easy task under such a limited period.

When the time elapsed, the assistant entered. He gathered our scripts, glancing around each of us for written notes or other ways we might have broken rules. We had not.

He then led us to another room. In it were Marvel executives Broussard, Ryan Potter from Marvel's business affairs team, Charles Newirth from Marvel's physical production team, and Tom Glinkowski, who worked closely with Broussard. Tim Connors didn't attend.

As is pretty normal in Hollywood, executives tend to bounce around a lot. Tim wasn't any different. Though he was the biggest advocate of DMG's involvement in *Iron Man 3*, he abruptly left Marvel just as we were approaching the finish line on the deal. He took the COO role at Legendary Pictures, another self-contained studio that was hot off of Chris Nolan's reboot of the *Batman* franchise and *Inception*. A few years later, Legendary was bought by the massive Chinese company, Wanda, led by a somewhat controversial CEO named Wang Jianlin. A Hollywood studio being bought by the Chinese? That was a reality few would've believed possible when we all gathered at Marvel that day.

The meeting was brief, involving the creative and production requirements needed in *Iron Man 3* to aid our collective co-production goals. That said, no one in the room was a decision-maker. Their priority was to give us color and advice for a much larger and more specific meeting scheduled for the following Monday, March 5. Kevin and all the top Marvel executives would be in attendance. This pre-meeting allowed us to ask some questions and formulate some ideas on how to make March 5 as constructive as possible. They also were looking for tidbits from us to give Kevin a hint of what we were thinking.

"What did you think of the script?" one of them asked.

"Solid. Fun," I responded.

"At least what we could read of it," Dan chimed in, slightly irritated. He was obviously referring to the missing pages.

"Yeah, what was in those missing pages?"

"Don't know exactly. Only Kevin does. He'll fill you in if he thinks it's necessary on Monday," Broussard responded.

"Got it. We'll work on some ideas to pitch in the meantime," I said, leaning back in my chair.

"Try to keep them brief. We don't have much wiggle room," Potter stated. "Production timetable will be super tight. We have to make the release date next spring. We won't have much time to waste, and we surely can't do all that much in alterations or extra shooting."

"We get the drill," Dan said, continuing to show some irritation.

"What's the latest with *Looper* right now? Disney wants some info, and we're all curious too," Charles inquired. "We're hearing it hasn't gotten its co-production status yet."

"It hasn't yet, and it won't until we get closer to the late September release date," Dan responded, shuffling a bit. He'd get irritated when people expected China to act like a normal market. It simply wasn't, and China didn't want to be, either.

"It's not all that important or even expected right now," I interrupted, sensing Dan's frustration. "We have the wind to our backs with *Looper* in the market. We've been marketing and promoting it since day one. We had a launch event. We have constant press attention. We've had Joseph Gordon-Levitt over there for the launch and the shooting. The coverage of him being there was amazing. We took over his Weibo account as a result too. We are constantly building his followers and those of the film. We are doing exactly what satisfies the government mandate of incorporating China into every facet of the filmmaking and film promotion process. We—"

Broussard interrupted me, "What's Weibo?"

"Think of it as China's Twitter," Dan responded. "You have actors over there with twenty million followers. It's powerful, and we are in the millions with Joseph already."

"Bottom line is the consumer is aware that this movie is coming," I added. "No other US film would ever have that kind of awareness this far from release. It has never happened before." I paused, looking each executive in the eyes. "If we can do this for *Looper*, imagine the attention we'll create for a massive Marvel movie."

"Yeah, but will *Looper* even get a release? Time travel is banned there. Then you've got criminal stuff in the plot. It happens right in Shanghai! Drug use too!" Potter stated. "Censors are going to hate it, won't they?"

"It doesn't matter," I responded. "We checked all the boxes on this film. We satisfied the government agenda. This film is a collaboration with China's film industry. China was, or is, involved in the development, financing, production, production locations, plot points, cast, marketing, promotion, and distribution. We hit all those key elements."

"Yeah, but is that enough?" Charles pressed. "Isn't that all stuff that works for a co-production anyway? I mean, if it can't get through censorship, how will you even make money based on an increased rental? Forty-something percent of zero is the same as thirteen-something percent of zero."

"Want me to answer?" I asked, looking at Dan.

"Go for it," he responded. I could tell he was thinking of the script we just read and Monday's meeting. As a CEO, he wanted to meet with other CEOs. The chain-of-command system in China reigned large, differentiating it from the West. Things trickled down in China to subordinates. The highest level only dealt with their own.

"Think about the plot for a second. A majority of the plot takes place in the future," I began. "Last January, *Hollywood Reporter* described the vital role of our design team, but they didn't elaborate much. Well, let me tell you, they were on the front lines. Their hard work massaged the government, and it wasn't by verbal lobbying. Instead, they used creativity and relevancy to lobby. They showcased a future China powerfully in the film. It was music to the ears of the Politburo and a delight to the Communist Party municipal officials in Shanghai. Our team illustrated how beautiful and sophisticated Shanghai can and will be. China was powerful and the center of the world in *Looper*. Yes, it had the balance of thugs and drugs and other negative attributes, but the film tilted the weight of the world towards China, and our team designed the majesty of that in the city's futuristic skyline. We made Shanghai the most modern, technology-advanced city in the world."

"Do they even know what they want Shanghai to look like that far in the future?" Charles asked.

"Well, if any country does, it's China. They are the home to the twenty-five, fifty, and hundred-year plans!" I responded. "But, in reality, no. Not really. But they are okay looking at potential examples of designs and ideas and choosing from those. And that's what we did. We showed city officials potential building shapes and skyline outlines. Then we guided them to the ones we thought worked best for the film. We presented impressive high-resolution graphics that blew the government away. Our modeling team even brought those designs to life with scaled models that officials could touch and feel. Pre-visuals and storyboards depicted exactly what the scene would look like, including our actors among the models."

We showed the designs on my computer. An image of Joseph Gordon-Levitt was superimposed in each slide. I left copies of the images behind so they could use them to impress Kevin and other senior colleagues. I also gave them actual stills from the on-location production of *Looper*. The stills next to the design images illustrated what the finished version would look like. They were impressed. Asking them to pass along the materials internally made total sense. Pictures speak a thousand words.

"So, let's discuss censorship in more detail," Dan interrupted, looking at me.

"I know that's on your mind, and your colleagues will want to know how it works," I added.

"Indeed," Broussard said.

"The road will be long and bumpy, and we are not even there yet on *Looper*. We've had to reiterate that to everyone on that film. We need to pre-sell *Looper* to many officials while making changes to the subtitles along the way. This needs to happen before we can officially submit the 'final' film to China Film Group, the State Administration of Radio Film and Television, et cetera. As we are bending the rules to the breaking point, getting *Looper* through censorship will not be easy nor quick, but it is trailblazing and needs everyone's support. It could take three to four months. Such will be the process with *Iron Man 3* too," I explained.

"And just like with *Looper*, we will need a copy of *Iron Man 3* as soon as it is completed," Dan stressed.

"Can you promise protection of the asset in China?" Potter asked.

"You better believe it. We got big dough in *Looper*. If it gets pirated…well," Dan started saying.

"We get screwed," I finished for him.

"Exactly." Dan paused.

"Having promoted many films in China for both major studios and our own, *Looper* is our most exciting yet, but *Iron Man 3* takes it to the next level. We've made that clear to Ram, Rian, and everyone on that film. DMG will be promoting *Looper* as a 'large and much-anticipated Hollywood-China co-production.' Film District will start to push the movie a few months out. We will start earlier. We need to build awareness in a market that is getting more and more cluttered," I further explained.

"I told Ram that our media campaign will be three hundred sixty degrees, including TV, print, outdoor, promotional, and digital. But we need materials, including key art, trailers, behind-the-scenes footage, everything. We need everything yesterday," Dan added.

"Bottom line, our *Looper* process will be a great training ground and template for *Iron Man 3*. And we can keep you apprised along the way, prepping you accordingly," I added.

"There's a boatload of moving parts," Potter said. "More than just making a movie."

"Yup. And some involve items that Hollywood is not comfortable with yet," I agreed. "Let's face it. No one wants to give high-resolution trailers or cuts of films early to China, especially given security and piracy issues of the past. But, if you can trust your partner to protect those assets, then real money is to be made. More time to promote and market. More time to prepare censors. More time to lobby China Film Group for a day-and-date release."

"That all adds up to more box office revenue," Dan stressed.

"Some of DMG's clients, like Mazda, will be involved with *Looper* too. We pitched them an idea they loved with Joseph Gordon-Levitt and Michael Phelps. An established artist and a world-class athlete go on a cultural tour to promote the film," I explained. "There is nothing better than mixing the universality of sports and culture! It's like 'Ping Pong Diplomacy' on steroids!"

"That's a cool idea," Charles said. "It's a feel-good play. It's super emotional. It excites the human instincts. It's aspirational."

"Yup! First, two days in Beijing. They attend Mazda's new model launch at the Beijing Auto Show. Then two days in London. Joe watches Phelps compete. Then three days in Shanghai so Phelps can watch Joe at the Chinese *Looper* premiere," I added.

"That's brilliant," Broussard said.

"We'll apply the same kind of ingenuity and innovative ways to promote *Iron Man 3*," Dan said. "But we'll be even more battle-tested with *Looper* under our belts."

The meeting ended shortly thereafter. Excitement filled the room. They bought into the plan. All we had to do was deliver the goods the following Monday in front of all the big dogs of Marvel!

Agenda: IM3 *Chinese Co-Production — Creative Specifics*
Date: Monday, March 5, 2012
Time: 1:00 p.m.
Location: Lantana — Conference Room (Avengers *Production*)
Attendees: Kevin Feige — Marvel, Dan Mintz — DMG, Louis
    D'Esposito — Marvel, Chris Fenton — DMG, Stephen
    Broussard — Marvel, Mitch Bell — Marvel, Charles
    Newirth — Marvel, Victoria Alonso — Marvel, Mike Ross —
    Marvel, Ryan Potter — Marvel, Kwan-Ting Ho — Marvel,
    David Galluzzi — Marvel, Rob Steffens — Marvel, Ben
    Hung — Marvel

Game time!

With *Avengers* only two months from its massive global release, the Marvel filmmaking team was in mad-dash mode. They were way behind with post-production on the $200 million film. The clock ticked so rapidly that it was an all-hands-on-deck situation consisting of "drop everything and finish the damn film!" Disney had set the film's release for May 4, 2012, long ago. Delivering the massively complicated film on time was priority number one.

Marvel viewed this meeting as a major pain in the ass. The integration of China into *Iron Man 3* was the last thing on anyone's mind at Marvel. The meeting didn't take place at Marvel, either. Instead, it occurred at Marvel's temporary post-production facility in Santa Monica. Every key Marvel executive relocated there. It was home until the delivery of *Avengers*.

A hustled anxiety filled the air. You could feel it throughout the building. Timing clearly wasn't perfect for our meeting. Nor was the location. But we had to make do.

I arrived with Dan. The receptionist led us to a lobby where we waited. And waited. We weren't the first concern of the day, not by a stretch. But Dan had flown to Beijing after our last Marvel meeting and then flown right back for this sit-down. Crossing the Pacific was practically like commuter flying for both of us by then. Marvel didn't know that, though, and because of that, they felt compelled to keep the meeting on the books.

I went through my notes ranging across all facets of the script. The Mandarin was a top item. We worked up fear tactics of how such a character could negatively impact all of Disney's business in China, including that of Marvel, in the event SARFT deemed the character completely inappropriate. My notes covered Chinese roles, location specifics, themes, villain characteristics, line changes, controversial lines, additional scenes, plot ideas…pretty much anything and every-thing I could think of. What we could actually accomplish in that meeting was a wildcard. What Marvel would listen to was even more of a mystery.

Our team flagged some particular character lines from the script. Would Marvel give us time to discuss them? Would they even change them? We weren't sure, but flagged lines I needed to address included "watching bamboo grow," "destroys my faith in science," "cash for the technology," "gas-and-oil president," "own your actions," "Chinese delivery box," and "embrace change." DMG's lobbying team cited each as a potential problem. I could've speculated what the reasoning was with each, but I was never told for sure. Colleagues felt strongly that censors in China would find each insulting. That was the gist and knowing I had to make a case for eliminating each made my stomach turn. I couldn't help but feel like a sympathizer for the communist agenda with those requests.

On the positive side, I did have one big idea for a Chinese character. I was super excited about it, and Dan liked it too. I did a lot of research to create the role so I could provide enough evidence to possibly win Marvel over. I did something similar with *Looper*, winning Rian

Johnson's approval for certain creative changes over time with strong arguments that worked with his vision. And by bombarding Johnson and his producing partner, Ram Bergman, with front-page articles about China every day, I was successful.

Another example of a similar creative sell that was gaining ground, not at Marvel, but rather at Paramount Studios, occurred when I pushed a big, China-relevant idea with the filmmakers for the tent-pole *World War Z*. I got a call from Paramount's President, whom I'll refer to as "Tall Exec" (he was extremely tall in a business where most are short!), about the big-budget zombie film starring Brad Pitt. The movie was in post-production, and the filmmakers realized the third act didn't work. They had discussed two different fixes. One involved reshooting the third act in a very contained and economical way. The other involved China tossing in big money to fix the third act in an even more spectacular and expensive way. In exchange for outside investment, Paramount would give the Chinese investors the China-market rights to exploit. The only problem was zombies are censored in China. Anything in the world of the undead is off-limits. Monetizing the film in China was therefore close to impossible.

But I also knew if Paramount could make the movie relevant to China, then such a strict censorship law could be overruled. Achieving this goal required some innovative and creative solutions, though. It's not that simple to take a finished film, dispose of the original third act, and then create an entirely new third act, all while making it China-friendly. And one more challenge, it has to be seamless with the movie's first two acts.

Assuming we could accomplish those goals, the film still needed to be good. And good for audiences worldwide, not just China. A tall task to say the least.

For me, I knew that if I read the *World War Z* script a few times and did some out-of-box thinking, I might be able to come up with a clever solution that would work. The film's concept was simple: "Zs," or zombies, were the film's antagonists, and they were taking over the world via a virus that was spreading without containment. Our hero, played by Brad Pitt, was a scientist attempting to find a cure against a rapidly ticking clock, and if he couldn't find one quickly enough, humanity as we know it would cease to exist.

One Achilles' heel Brad's character stumbled upon was that Zs could be defeated if they were in cold weather because the freezing temperatures slowed them down. And when the Zs lost speed, their ability to kill was mitigated so humans could successfully fight them.

During act one, a character asks if anyone knows what happened to the Chinese after the virus broke out. Another character responds "China went dark," meaning no one knew what the fuck happened to the 1.4 billion Chinese. Throughout the rest of the film, China was never mentioned again. Of course, when I read that single reference to the Chinese in the script, I knew that the simple line, "China went dark," would be offensive to both the Chinese people and government. Not only does a line like that keep censors from letting the film into China, but dialogue like that could potentially cause retaliation against Paramount overall. Combine that with zombies, which were already taboo, and the whole film was a big fat zero when it came to anything positive for China relations or monetization.

There was a great opportunity with that line, though. And I saw another lemon-into-lemonade situation. With the Chinese completely missing in action, it was easy to imagine Brad Pitt's character wanting to find out what happened. Perhaps he felt that China fell prey to the virus, wiping out the entire population. Or, perhaps the Chinese had figured out how to battle the Zs. And even better, perhaps the Chinese were working on a cure to the virus.

Imagine how amazingly fruitful such a creative change in the plot would be for Chinese support of the film? It would influence censors to let the film in for sure. Additionally, it would allow Chinese audiences to root for their own, as they were heroes in the movie now. And if done correctly, the film could be much better.

I remembered a random fact from a science class—temperatures decrease three degrees with every thousand feet of increased elevation or every hundred miles traveled away from the equator. In the script, Russia had some success defeating the Zs primarily because of their northern geography and cold weather. Brad's character headed to Russia as a result. He wanted to find out what the Russians were learning about the Zs, and in the process, he stopped through Israel, where he learned a valuable lesson from the Mossad. The Mossad makes decisions using eleven members. If ten members decide on a certain course of action, the eleventh dissenting member is the one they follow. The Mossad decides to go against common opinion to keep enemies off balance.

My idea was to have Brad's character in a Russian village just north of China. While he's there he asks, "Where are the Chinese? Shouldn't they have migrated north to battle the Zs with you?"

The Russians respond, "We think the Chinese are all dead. If any of them were alive, they would've headed north. If they headed north, they'd be in Russia, but there have been no Chinese coming across the border. They went dark, and they have stayed dark."

Brad's character then responds, "I refuse to believe 1.4 billion people are all gone, especially ones as resilient and inventive as the Chinese."

We cut to Brad's character sitting next to pilots in the cockpit of a Russian An-124 cargo plane equipped with a small version of Brad's laboratory.

One of the pilots asks, "Why are we flying over China airspace? There is nothing here. No one survived."

Brad responds, "My hunch is they did survive. Keep following that railway below."

Brad points to the high-speed rail that creates a long line straight into the distance. Surrounded on both sides by tall mountain peaks, the railway climbs the great Tibetan plateau.

There are portions of the railway which reach almost seventeen thousand feet in elevation. It includes the highest rail tunnel in the world, the highest train station in the world, and 675 bridges. Bottom line, the railway is a technological feat and one China would love to showcase to the world. What better way to do that than in a major motion picture from Hollywood?

The co-pilot then says, "That's strange. I don't think I see that lake on any navigation map."

He points ahead, shuffling through navigation documents. In the distance, a large, dark-colored mass extends from one mountain base to the other, rising up the plateau. It does look like a lake, but there's a uniqueness to it.

"That isn't a lake. That's why we came," Brad's character says.

And as the plane continues to head towards the "lake," we start to see what it really is. It's a mass of humanity extending into infinity up the entire plateau following the railway. It's most of the missing 1.4 billion people from China. They fled for high elevation rather than towards the northern border where they'd be forced to relocate to Russia.

Along the lower elevations, the Chinese are locked in a battle of battles, China's PLA is using every weapon and soldier available to fight the Zs. The Zs have slowed significantly due to the elevation and cold, but they are still a tremendous force. Scars on the tundra remain from earlier portions of the battle. The fight's location alternates higher and lower as the temperature and weather changes.

We also notice the railway has a purpose.

"We need to figure out a place to drop me and my equipment," Brad's character says. "It needs to be near that train. That is their lab. They are keeping it near the battle zone so it can study the fresh kills. It's on the train because it can slide up and down the plateau as the battlefield moves."

"That's brilliant," the pilot says.

"Yeah, I had a feeling the Chinese wouldn't go down without a fight. They are hardy souls and can push the envelope on innovation when backed into a corner. My bet is they solve this problem before any of us," Brad's character adds. "I need to drop in now."

That was the gist of the idea. Paramount loved it, as did Skydance, Paramount's co-financing partner. Creatively, it made for a better movie. It also made the third act eventful in scope, size, and satisfaction.

And for financing purposes, Chinese investors would love it too. Why? Because it delivered on China relevancy and China prominence. It showcased the most technologically impressive rail line in the world, the backdrop of one of the world's greatest plateaus and mountain ranges, China's PLA, and the scientific, innovative, and medical prowess of China. That meant the government would love the film and support it. The messaging was so pro-China that any normally censored items in the film would be ignored. That meant big box office in China, even with a movie chock-full of China-censored zombies. In theory, it was a guaranteed win-win for every party involved.

I was hoping to deliver a similar, creatively innovative idea to Marvel that day. I was also hoping, if not praying, to win similar enthusiasm from Marvel for it. Anxiety coursed through my body. There was a lot on the line.

"They're ready for you," a production assistant said to us.

I broke out of my daze. I put my game face on.

"Follow me, please."

"I'm letting you do the talking," Dan whispered to me, getting up. "This thing should be a fait accompli by now. Not sure why we even need to do this."

"Roger that. But if it goes south, don't get angry. Please keep it cool."

He nodded, slightly scowling.

I was nervous. My gut had me prepared for the worst. I rehearsed arguments in my head just in case I had to get things back on track.

"Just get it done," he said.

The conference room door opened. We walked in.

There they were. All the people on that list and more. A long conference room table filled with some twenty executives. Others sat along the walls. Dan and I grabbed the seats left nearest the door. At the far end sat Kevin Feige, wearing a Marvel baseball cap, and his co-president, Louis D'Esposito. Kevin handled all the creative. Louis handled all the barking and business-oriented hatchet-man kind of stuff. Both exuded lots of confidence, though Kevin carried a much softer demeanor, being an artist/filmmaker. He wasn't the least bit scary. Louis, on the other hand, very much was. I think he embraced it too.

"Appreciate you guys coming down here to see us. We obviously are in a jam to finish *Avengers*, so meeting here was the only option given the crunch," Kevin announced, starting the meeting.

"Thanks for making the time," Dan said, grabbing a seat.

"Not a problem. So, let's get down to business," Louis said, looking towards Kevin, who nodded. "We don't have much time."

I pulled out my notes.

"I believe you wanted to talk about our creative ideas for implementing China relevancy."

"Yeah, well," Louis jumped in. "The thing is, we talked about everything internally. There was lots of discussion about bringing you guys on board, doing some China stuff creatively, shooting some things on the ground there, all of that."

Oh shit. Here it comes.

"Bottom line, we don't think it's going to work." Dan shifted uneasily in his chair. I could tell he was ready to do his resting-angry face any minute. He sensed what I was sensing. This deal was going south in a big way.

"I'm sorry?" I asked. "What do you mean?"

"We aren't going to do this. We can't. It's too complicated, and quite frankly, Disney just doesn't support it."

"Yeah, but Ike does. We're in the middle of closing a deal. We've agreed on almost everything," I said, slightly panicking. "Heck, Tim Connors came back raving after his time in Beijing with us!"

"Tim doesn't work here anymore."

"But he told you, what he saw in Beijing. We can move mountains. We are the perfect partner!"

"Yeah, well, it just got too complicated. Ike doesn't think it's worth a battle with Disney," Louis explained. "Quite frankly, Kevin and I don't see it being worth the aggravation either. Additionally, there are lots of risks according to Disney's China office in doing something your way. Lots to lose."

Other executives started to fidget a bit in their chairs.

Dan was pissed. I could feel his vibe raging next to me.

"We have smart, creative thoughts. We know how to do this. We can make Marvel millions more on *Iron Man 3* and billions more with your brand. We deserve some time on the floor to make our case."

Louis and Kevin looked at each other, nodding reluctantly.

"Sure," Kevin said. "Go ahead."

"Thank you." I looked down at my notes. "The way I see it, Marvel is to the Hollywood movie business what Michael Jordan and Nike are to the NBA and basketball. Marvel is an emotional entertainment *global* brand. Hollywood movies are a form of culture. The same for Michael and Nike—emotional *global* basketball brands—with the NBA's version of basketball being the ultimate form of sports culture. If done right, the brands become ingrained into the culture of China. Like Jordan and Nike have done, while continuing to build on that foundation. Marvel can do the same. Hollywood movies are becoming culturally important to China just like NBA basketball. Marvel can become the iconic, emotional, and premium global brand riding that wave if you play it right. Or, it can be simply seen as an import from the West, or, even worse, *America*, which is what you are right now." I took a breath. "That's not where you want to be. Your biggest hit there, *Iron Man 2*, made hardly twenty million in box office. Marvel deserves better."

"What are you saying exactly?" Louis asked, annoyed.

"I'm saying Marvel needs to show an interest in having China be a part of your success. When our client Kobe Bryant said, '*Rise Up!*'

in Mandarin during one of our Nike Olympic events, the Chinese adopted him, a global cultural star, as one of their own. He has made millions since." I looked around the room. "Mao had already designated basketball as something culturally significant for China, but that didn't guarantee the NBA, Nike, Jordan, and Kobe success in the market. They had to earn it. They had to want it. The same is true for Marvel. The Communist Party of China [CCP] has said they want China to be the largest movie market in the world, but that doesn't guarantee Marvel's success. You guys have to want it and put in the effort. We can be that guide. We will make Marvel successful in China, guaranteed!"

"It's risky, and we don't have time."

"We will create a practical and low-risk way to get it done," I responded. "Look, Yao Ming played in the NBA. Think about that. That took the NBA to the next level in the market. It's akin to us putting a Chinese actor into a Marvel movie. And, unlike Yao, that actor doesn't have to be an MVP. We're not talking about a lead role here."

"If it's easy, it's something to discuss. What do you have for us?"

I looked at Dan. He was frustrated. Though his face showed little hope, he nodded for me to continue.

"Hu Jintao is China's leader presently. However, he will most likely be replaced by another politician named Xi Jinping. What's interesting about Xi Jinping is that he, like most rising Chinese government officials, spent a lot of time in the United States, not just on vacations or short trips, but also on extended exchanges. He lived with a normal American family in Iowa for a period. It allowed him to understand America and the way Americans live and think," I explained, pausing a moment. "I think it's pretty amazing myself. US officials should probably do the same in China to understand them better."

"Where are you going with this?" Louis asked, looking at his watch.

"Well, you have a kid in *Iron Man 3*. He lives somewhere in rural America, possibly in Iowa."

"That's correct."

"Well, what happens if that kid is Chinese?"

The room was silent—crickets. No reaction whatsoever.

"What I mean is, what happens if we make that kid Chinese because his father, like Xi Jinping, is actually on an exchange in rural America and his son happens to be with him? Iron Man comes across the kid as he's struggling to find shelter. The Chinese kid takes him in and nurses him back to health. And then later, when Tony Stark is trying to save the day in the third act and he can't get his glove to complete the Iron Man transformation, this Chinese kid helps open the shed so that the glove can fly off to join Iron Man to save the world?"

"So you want us to put this guy Xi into our movie and have his kid be the kid who helps Iron Man?"

"Sort of, but it's not actually Xi, it just carries a storyline that is similar to his."

"That feels like an infomercial for China," Louis declared.

"It would if it made no sense, but it actually could be a viable, convincing subplot. A version of this happened in real life," I argued. "The economic benefit of something like this would be massive. Of course, around the world, we don't talk about what this subplot is, but in China, with the very officials who oversee co-production status, censorship, marketing and promotional activities, theater bookings, the number of screens, hold periods, ticket counts, and so on, this subplot would be explained and exploited! They will love it! This movie could be the ultimate cultural bridge between the world's only two super-powers. And the result will be millions and millions of more dollars for Marvel and Disney from this movie alone, and billions for Marvel in the future! It will birth the greatest cinematic brand from the West in China. Marvel will dominate as the biggest, most successful IP in China for decades."

The silence hadn't lifted in the room, but you could tell people had heard my pitch. No one was willing to show a reaction though, at least not until Kevin or Louis did.

"Look, I get this is a bit foreign to everyone here, so let me mention another reason to do this deal with us. It's something more than making money. It's diplomacy, and one created by culture. The NBA does it through sports. Marvel can do it through movies. Not to mention make a shit-ton of money in the process," I continued to explain.

"What does that even mean?" someone asked, almost sarcastically.

"It means that like a cell phone, there are five bars of service that keep countries working together versus going to war, or at least starting a cold war. The five forces of diplomacy. You need at least one force, or bar, working to keep the connection. Three of those five forces are politics, national security, and human rights. Three forces we don't agree with China on—at all. And frankly, we will never be able to change their minds, either. Best case, we agree to disagree with them on all three. So that leaves us with the other two forces: culture and commerce. And right now, those avenues are open for business between the two countries, though they could use some strengthening. By being a platform for culture, Marvel can bring the two countries closer together by collaborating with China through a Chinese studio, DMG, to make *Iron Man 3*. That cultural collaboration will create commerce, which will make the bilateral relationship stronger. It's a glue that binds the two superpowers, and Marvel can be at the epicenter while adding to that glue and manufacturing a much stronger bilateral bond. And that will make the world a much safer place for all of us."

Okay, that all sounded a bit peace-hippie-utopian when I said it out loud to a room full of Marvel executives that day, but I did believe it. I believe it even more today.

"Stephen, will you please escort Dan and Chris out of the room so we can discuss this," Kevin asked.

We walked out. The door shut behind us.

"What the fuck?" Dan asked. "They did not like that idea whatsoever. And that whole diplomacy thing sounds too rainbows and unicorns."

"I tried. It does feel a bit like I'm a communist sympathizer though, with all the stuff we're asking for. Like we're pandering. Almost begging. So, I figured I'd take the United Nations approach. I went full diplomacy mode. *Making a better world* kind of shit. I believe in it too. I truly do." I walked over to the water cooler.

I pulled out my phone to look at emails. I really couldn't concentrate on anything at the time. I just didn't want to talk about what we both had sensed was going on. Our biggest deal to date was about to explode in our faces.

"We need to go DEFCON 1," Dan said, approaching me. "I refuse to lose this deal!"

"Guys, we're ready for you," Stephen interrupted, standing by the door to the conference room. Saved by the bell.

"Friendly face, please," I said to Dan.

"I'm trying."

We walked in. The room looked exactly the same as the first time around. We took our seats.

"Okay. I will admit that we fully intended to kill this deal today, but we won't," Louis started.

Dan and I changed our posture for the better. Suddenly, a bit of positivity filled the room.

"That said, your Chinese-kid idea is not happening."

"Why?" I asked.

"Because we're not interested in having the sidekick from *Indiana Jones* in *Iron Man 3*."

Laughter filled the room. It was a moment of levity that was probably needed.

"It just feels 'too much' and heavy-handed, if you know what I mean," Kevin interjected. "We need to think about how that would look. And, in particular, we need to stay true to our IP, its mythology, and the hardcore fans that are so important to all things Marvel."

"OK. Makes sense."

"What do you have in mind?" Dan asked, seeing an opening.

"A doctor. A Chinese doctor. And this doctor would be responsible for successfully removing the RT [Chest Repulsor Transmitter] from Tony Stark's body, allowing him to live without fear that the shrapnel in his body will destroy his heart," Kevin explained. "And his name will be Doctor Wu."

"Doctor Wu? Interesting. What's the significance to the name?" I asked.

"Is it a character from the Marvel Universe?" Dan asked.

"No," Kevin responded. "Not Marvel-related. At least not yet."

"So why Doctor Wu?" I prodded.

"No real reason. It's just a great song by Steely Dan."

Everyone laughed again. And shortly thereafter, the meeting ended. No other items were addressed. No time to discuss lines that treaded on censorship issues. No time even for The Mandarin.

As we left the room, Dan and I looked at each other. Not wanting to speak until we got to the car, our expressions displayed both relief and confusion. Our collective feeling was probably best described as bittersweet. Most importantly, we kept the deal alive. However, understanding what Dr. Wu's role would be and how it would create the proper relevancy we desperately needed was completely unclear.

Adding to that opaqueness was the name, Dr. Wu. We weren't sure it was even Chinese!

22.

PLAY THE GAME BUT UNDERSTAND THE RULES

A **DEAL CLOSED. NOT** the perfect deal, but a deal nonetheless. Marvel's creative, business, and legal departments were all finally aligned. The combined Marvel force coerced Disney to play along. We were off and running, and that was all that mattered.

A month later, we held a deal-signing ceremony for *Iron Man 3* in Beijing. For the Chinese, such ceremonies were extremely important. Not only did they allow all the parties to get together for a symbolic signing of a contract, but they also allowed for important bonding over large banquets and late-night karaoke sessions—sessions I got extremely good at over time by learning to sing some very popular Chinese songs in Mandarin. Marvel sent over one of their top executives, Rob Steffens, to sign on their behalf along with several reluctant executives from Disney's Beijing office. Included in that group was Stanley Cheung, Disney's GM of China, who touted the deal as "a testimony to the importance of China to Disney and the local China film industry's [meaning DMG] capability to deliver a blockbuster title."

China Film Group chairman Han Sanping also attended. That was both significant and telling. He gave the Party line, touting this amazing co-production collaboration in the cultural area of film, in rough translation, as:

162

This international movie, created by US-China partnership, has a strong agenda of focusing on the full cooperation and support of the Chinese government.

That same day, CNBC whittled down the news as "Disney Making *Iron Man 3*' with Chinese Partner." The newsworthy headline was pasted on CNBC's side-screen throughout the day.

Solidifying my understanding of just how big this bilateral collaboration was, at least in the eyes of the Chinese government, I discovered my favorite section of Beijing's Silk Market no longer sold strange and unusual pirated Marvel merchandise anymore. The black-market Marvel store in Beijing's U-Town mall mysteriously vanished as well, and my favorite black-market DVD store in the Sanlitun alley, behind Beijing's Opposite House Hotel, had stopped selling Marvel titles too.

Bottom line, if the Chinese public thinks the government is excited about a collaboration with the West, you better believe you won't see anyone trying to monetize that illegal product or service moving forward. The newly supported business becomes "made," and only the parties directly involved in making it, both from the West and China itself, are then allowed to capitalize on it. No one else can from that point forward can utilize its name or likeness.

The symbolic flag had been planted in a way that China loves and supports. The biggest co-production/film collaboration ever between two nations had become official, and China was in full boasting mode. Our collaboration symbolized China's "coming out" in terms of their film industry's entry on the world's stage. For a country looking to create the largest film market in the world, the significance of this US-China partnership with *Iron Man 3* was massive. Now all we had to do was pull it off!

Conversations focused on the US-China *Iron Man 3* collaboration a few weeks later at the Beijing Film Festival, a nascent film festival that, similar to most other China government initiatives, intended to be the greatest film festival in the world someday very soon. *Avengers* was screening at the festival, so Marvel asked us to join them and one of the stars, Jeremy Renner, on the red carpet to continue touting to journalists our exciting new partnership. Such a public display would also have a nice spillover effect on the buzz generated for *Avengers*. Now that Marvel was "made," resulting goodwill would lead to greater returns for *Avengers*. That was assured.

DMG was definitely the toast of the festival, and we flew in influential Hollywood producers, such as Mark Vahradian, producer of the *Transformers* franchise, and Craig Flores, producer of big-budget tentpoles such as *300* and *Immortals*, to witness DMG in our glory. As major influencers in Hollywood, we wanted them to go back to Hollywood boasting about our prowess in what will soon be Hollywood's largest market.

"What did your boys think of the DMG event last night?" Dan asked me over bratwursts at his favorite German brewpub in Beijing. For a guy who lived in China, Dan rarely ate Chinese food.

"Mark and Craig loved it. They were super impressed. Amazed at the celebrity quotient we had in attendance and all the accolades we were getting for both *Looper* and *Iron Man 3*," I responded. "After that karaoke session though, we should've taken them to the Great Wall to see the sunrise. Next time, that needs to be on the agenda!"

"I think jet lag was catching up to them."

"Did you see the *New York Times* story today?" I asked.

"No. Which one?"

"'SEC Asks if Hollywood Paid Bribe in China.'"

"What the fuck?"

Dan was definitely caught off guard.

"Yup. And *Iron Man 3* is mentioned." I paused, handing him my phone. "The *Times* apparently reached out to Marvel. Of course, no comment was given."

He stopped eating his bratwurst to read the article. Concern took over his face.

"This is bad. Really bad. At least they don't mention Han Sanping," he said, taking a gulp of his Diet Coke.

"Yeah, well, the *Los Angeles Times* does, apparently. Let me see if I can pull it up."

He handed me my phone. I found the article and read it out loud: "'China Film Group's chairman, Han Sanping, recently visited Los Angeles and met with several prominent Hollywood executives, including top officials at Universal and Sony. Han was accompanied in some of the meetings by Dan Mintz, chief executive of Beijing-based DMG Entertainment, a Chinese-American media company involved in film co-productions and distribution in China.'"

"Holy shit! This article makes Han Sanping look corrupt!" I continued to scan the piece online. "'A spokeswoman for Disney did not respond to a request for comment. The Burbank entertainment giant recently signed a partnership with a Chinese firm to co-finance the superhero sequel *Iron Man 3* and film part of the movie in the communist country. Disney is building a $4.4-billion theme park in Shanghai and has a smaller one already open in Hong Kong.'"

"That is nuts! The US government is going to cause a massive loss of face for the Chinese with this. They are implicating government officials by name, and pretty much saying they are guilty of taking bribes!" Dan looked super nervous. "Could this cause Disney to freak out? Would they try to get out of our deal on *Iron Man 3*?"

"I have no idea, but it seems journalists are wondering the same thing."

"Why do you say that?"

"Because I just received emails from *Bloomberg, Reuters, Los Angeles Times, Wall Street Journal,* and the *New York Times* asking that very question!" I exclaimed.

"So, let me get this straight. Joe Biden just announced that he worked with the future leader of China, Xi Jinping, in order to negotiate a new film deal allowing more Hollywood films into the market. This would let Hollywood studios keep more of the box office they earn here in China. Yet another branch of the US government is saying that China is corrupt and doing things illegally, and Hollywood studios are fucking complicit in it?" Dan asked, both sarcastically and super annoyed.

"That seems to be accurate."

"And it's making news during the Beijing Film Festival? A source of great Chinese pride and an event symbolic of China's rise as a world-class movie industry and market?"

"Unfortunately, yes."

"And this is happening at the same time that the Chinese government is facing a change of leadership in the next year and is cracking down on the foes of the soon-to-be incoming leaders?"

"Like who?"

"Well, for one, I'm talking about Bo Xilai, who ran Dalian as Mayor and made Wanda's chairman Wang Jianlin ultra-wealthy during the process. Bo is now in jail, and Wang has recently disappeared," Dan explained. "And Wang is the one who is apparently buying AMC Theaters in the US."

Years later, as I mentioned previously, Wang and his company Wanda bought Legendary Studios. That purchase angered many in Congress and was a key catalyst that led to the restructuring of CFIUS, the Committee on Foreign Investment in the United States.

"All of those items are ironic and coincidental, right? Or are they neither?" I asked with a furrowed look on my face.

"Probably neither. Bo is in jail for corruption and for helping with the murder of that Brit, Neil Heywood. Wang is in trouble for being close to Bo, so he needs to do loud and exciting things on an international scale to spread the soft power of China. If he can do that, he keeps the government off his back. But truthfully, it sounds like he couldn't do it quickly enough, and now we don't know if he's disappeared forever or not. Can't imagine the US likes the idea of him buying a big theater chain either," Dan explained.

"Well, having the US government implicate the Chinese government for doing criminal things in the high-profile world of movie-making isn't going to make us friends here. That's for sure," I said.

"And that makes me nervous about *Iron Man 3*. In fact, this could cause issues with our release of *Looper*, too!" Dan said, dialing a number on his phone. "Let's get back to the office ASAP. We need to get some more information."

"Marvel is a *global* company. Iron Man 3 is an *international* film," I stressed out loud. "We need to push our troops to continue that messaging. Can't get stuck in the mire of another US-China conflict with so much money on the line."

"No shit! It's our money too." Dan had the phone pressed to his ear. "We need to stay above the fray of this geopolitical crap."

Deadline Hollywood, April 29, 2012:
Hollywood-China Gatekeeper

Now that the SEC has sent letters of inquiry to all the Hollywood majors regarding their China dealings, one name continues to come up: China Film Group chairman Han Sanping…. But gray areas may exist. In Hollywood, for example, a commonplace practice like awarding exec producer credit for a seemingly small contribution may be seen to run afoul of the federal rules which forbid bribery of foreign officials. Is hiring Han Sanping to produce or provide services illegal? Interesting that, for now, the Chinese exec has not been listed as a producer or exec producer on any upcoming projects that involve the U.S. For instance, Han is not a producer on Disney and Marvel and Beijing-based DMG Entertainment setting up Iron Man 3 to be co-produced in China.

And that seemed to be the gist of every article since the *New York Times* first broke the SEC investigation story. Yes, it was making my life challenging when it came to mitigating the fears of both Marvel and Disney. Anything having to do with China scared everyone in Hollywood now, especially those with high-profile and active projects there.

It also wreaked havoc on all things *Looper*. Both our release date and co-production status were in jeopardy, meaning we faced the prospect of being relegated to a much smaller cut of the box-office revenues. We also faced a potential worst-case scenario where China might forbid us from marketing and releasing the film—period. We did nothing wrong, but as retaliation against the United States for embarrassing the leader of China Film Group, which then embarrassed SARFT, the Propaganda Ministry, and ultimately the Communist Party, any sort of punishment was within reason.

"We have a lot of footage from the China portion of *Looper*'s production," I said to my Beijing-based colleague Billy Neo one evening. "I know they don't intend to put it in the film though. The cut is too long as it is."

"We need more in there. If the Chinese expected footage in the movie that is now cut by the American side, we're in a lot of trouble."

"I know. I know. It doesn't look good." I was sitting in my guest house at the time. My kids, boy and girl twins named Dylan and Kaylie, were five years old by then. I'd typically join them for dinner and help Jennifer with their bedtime routine. After the kids were asleep, I'd head out to my guest house office and make calls to China. "The fact is, we are all simply trying to make the best movie possible. There's no anti-China motivation or anything. That's what is crazy!" I exclaimed.

"Doesn't matter. China Film Group is already pissed about the SEC investigation. They will see this as Americans cutting out crucial China footage. Think of all the time the Shanghai government put into creating their skyline with us. Now a lot of it isn't even in the film! It's a loss-of-face thing."

"I get it, but I can't tell Rian Johnson to put more footage in the movie just because China wants it in there. If it doesn't make the film better, then we shouldn't be imposing crap like that. We'll be out of business fast. We're not in the China infomercial game!" I was frustrated. I grabbed a beer out of the mini-fridge and popped it open, putting my feet on the desk. I popped on a Dodgers game.

"You need to come up with something. Dan will freak out if we don't get some of that footage in there."

"What if we make two cuts of the movie? One will be the cut Rian wants, the other takes the footage we want and puts it in the film for China's audience?" I suggested. "We could make the China cut a good five to ten minutes longer that way. We could get all the great skyline shots of Shanghai in there and more. Lots of Xu Qing's footage too, since some of it didn't make this latest cut!"

"Can you do that?" Billy asked.

"I don't see why not. What would Rian care? He gets his cut for the world. We get our cut for China."

"The government may force us to do that anyway."

"I know. So, let us be the one that suggests it first. Puts us on offense."

"Let me ask Dan to see if he's good with the plan."

"Perfect. Talk when I get up in the morning." I hung up, smiling.

23.

US AGAINST THE WORLD

ON JUNE 19. 2012, a *Los Angeles Times* headline read, "A more Sino-centric version of 'Looper' will be released in China."

Yes, we had decided to extend the China cut of the film by several minutes, allowing for both Shanghai and Xu Qing to get more screen time. However, the goal was to keep the initiative quiet. We already had Kevin Feige mentioning our sometimes "heavy-handed" way of showcasing China. News like this going public didn't exactly curb such a belief.

It also caught the attention of Chinese authorities, who until then, weren't aware of the two cuts of the film. On the surface, this may not have seemed like that big of a big deal. However, when one realizes how much "face" means to the Chinese, a look under the hood at our plan with *Looper* gave new cause for concern. The news, unfortunately, beat us to the punch. Our lobbying team was ready to pitch the "two-cut" idea to the government at the time but hadn't yet. Those executives knew how to massage it well to get the buy-in. But with an article already printed, we were on our heels.

Think about it from the Chinese perspective. Here's a film that they bent over backwards for in terms of providing amazing access and support during shooting. Our production team then got the absolute best footage of one of their most prized cities. Additionally, the Chinese worked tirelessly with our filmmaking team to construct a city skyline that was both realistic and impressive, symbolic of the city's prowess far into the future. Then there's the great actress Xu Qing. When Hollywood cast her in this major production, it was a source of great pride for the Chinese. For them to hear that both Shanghai and Xu Qing were possibly being cut from the global film was insulting. However, when you add to that the notion that the filmmaking team didn't believe the film's China relevancy was interesting or important enough in the story to make the final cut, it's downright embarrassing.

"China, your contributions to the film are only for your local audience to see. The rest of the world is simply not interested," I joked to Jennifer one evening over a glass of wine. "That's essentially what we are saying."

"And now the *Los Angeles Times* put it on the front page?" she asked.

"Yes. It's not good!"

Little did any of us know how the new *Looper* strategy and the simultaneous ongoing SEC investigation of Hollywood studios would combine to create even greater challenges for us. And they popped up in various ways that no one could have predicted. For one, that amazing *World War Z* opportunity disappeared. Paramount's president of production, Tall Exec, was dodging me over the next steps. Highly unusual for him to disengage like that. Our friendship dated almost as far back as my mailroom days, and our kids attended preschool together. Our deep history and family closeness resulted in multiple Rolodex cards. I knew a lot about him. So, it got frustrating that he was avoiding me. We really wanted this deal, and he was the key to closing it.

Fortunately, our sons also played on the same tee-ball team. I approached him during pre-game batting practice one Saturday morning.

"Tall Exec, you've been dodging me," I said. He looked as if he knew I was going to get in his grill that day. "No returned calls. No responses to emails. Totally ghosted. What gives? Don't you owe your son's greatest-youth-basketball-coach-ever a response?"

He laughed.

"I know. I apologize."

"So what's the real story?"

"This SEC investigation. It's fucked everything up. I've been told by counsel I can't speak to anyone related to a Chinese entity or working for a Chinese entity," he explained. "That, unfortunately, means you. At least when I'm in the office, I guess."

"I'm glad tee-ball games are okay. then."

We both glanced at the field. My son, Dylan, was batting. Tall Exec's son was on deck.

"Your son has a terrible stance."

"You think? Looks like he's trying to take a dump!" I laughed.

"Look. I'm sorry. It's not cool to freeze you out, but this SEC thing is serious. You guys might even be in the middle of it, I hear."

"Well, if we are, that would be news to me," I responded. It was surprising to hear him possibly implicate us, but it did confirm what I sensed around town: that DMG's possible involvement was a topic behind closed doors, with those discussions accusing DMG of being guilty. I found it interesting that during the peak of our company's high-profile success, my phone sheet still wasn't full of incoming calls. And when I made outgoing calls, the response time seemed longer than usual.

"It doesn't matter. The reality is everyone thinks your company is involved, and everyone sees you as the face of the company here in Hollywood. I'm one thousand percent sure you have never given an envelope of cash to a government official, but you're the DMG guy here, so by association, you are guilty too," he explained. He was beyond serious.

"I can tell you, looking you straight in the eyes and reiterating how long we've known each other, and how long our families have known each other, I have never seen our company do anything that would be an FCPA violation, especially in terms of what is legal and allowed regulatory-wise in China," I argued.

"Doesn't matter. Guilty until proven innocent. That's your reality." He was blunt. "Look, I'd tell you to go take one of those offers you've gotten over the years, but I'm willing to bet you haven't had an incoming call about a new job opportunity since this whole thing started." He looked me straight in the eyes. "Have you?"

Oh shit. He was right. I couldn't even respond.

"Your real friends out there will tell you the same thing. Ask any of the guys at our monthly cigar night. They know what their general counsels are saying. They are privy to that stuff, and you, my friend, are right in the crosshairs. Don't fool yourself. And all of Marvel knows too, and I guarantee Disney is working to get you guys out of *Iron Man 3* on a daily basis." He paused a second, realizing the terrible news he was giving me. "You're a dead man walking—for now. But remember, you're one of the most well-liked, respected, and honest guys in town. If you need anything, those people in big jobs who have been your friends as long as I have will come through. You will be better than fine. Guaranteed. You just may have to see them at tee-ball games to get them talking, though."

We both laughed a bit. A moment of consolation.

"I sensed all of this. I've gotten the hints. It's depressing."

"Don't worry. Right now, it's all an orange-jump-suit, perp-walk, and cuffed-and-stuffed type of fear. It's new and unknown to everyone. People will come back around when the SEC backs off. You will come out the back stronger, and all those opportunities you had before will be there in an even bigger way. I promise."

"I know. I believe you. I hope."

He sensed I was super depressed. I looked towards his kid.

"You will be fine."

His attention turned. He laughed, attempting to break the mood for the better.

"Look at my son's ridiculous batting stance!"

"Hah! It ain't that bad. I'd take him as a batter over Dylan any day," I responded.

"Don't become a baseball scout!"

We laughed and watched a few unsuccessful swings by both our sons.

"So, is our involvement in *World War Z* dead?"

"Yes. Dead. The fat lady has sung."

To hear that out loud was depressing and super disappointing.

A second nasty side effect emerged from both the SEC issue and the two-cut strategy for *Looper*. It arrived during the casting of the Dr. Wu role for *Iron Man 3*. To get the benefits of overwhelming government support, the role obviously had to go to a Chinese actor. He had to be a mainland Chinese too, not Taiwan or Hong Kong, with a Chinese passport (not an American-born Chinese individual or someone who married a foreigner). The role also required someone with the acting chops to share screen time with Robert Downey Jr., one of the most iconic and versatile actors in modern-day Hollywood.

That combination was unfortunately hard to find. And particularly hard to find with male actors, since very few spoke English. In general, females have an easier time speaking English and many of them do. Most male actors don't even try.

After searching under every stone and auditioning dozens of actors, similar to our search for a Chinese strongman, we found our guy — Chen Dao Ming. He was perfect for the role, and we were super excited to cast him. However, around that same time, the *Looper* two-film-cuts strategy started generating more and more noise which created controversy in

China. Much of the press was criticizing the move made by DMG. Additionally, China Film Group and their bosses at the SARFT continued to be insulted by the SEC's accusations. The untimely investigation of Han Sanping seemed completely uncalled for in their opinion. Retaliation was high on the agenda.

Press coverage in both countries that focused on the SEC and two-film-cuts matters gained steam for weeks after we cast Dr. Wu. Both items soon became water-cooler topics for anyone interested in the movie business or the bilateral relationship. Artists in China were particularly aware of the controversies as they were impossible to ignore. Chen Dao Ming was one of them, and how he reacted was anyone's guess.

With production approaching quickly, we had to get a deal done with his agent immediately. Kevin Feige wanted Chen on set early, but Chen needed to acclimate himself and get comfortable with the role. Kevin did not want Chen holding up production by not knowing his lines, or making Robert feel he was working with an incompetent actor.

Chen's agent agreed to a deal and started coordinating travel for his client with our team. Then, abruptly, he went dark. All communication ceased.

"What's the status of Chen's travel? Is he confirmed for the flight?" I asked my Beijing-based colleague Max Epstein one night.

"No," Max responded tersely.

"What? He needs to be in Wilmington in a couple of days!"

"I know. I know."

"What does his agent say?"

"The guy went completely silent on us for days. Then I finally got a hold of him earlier today."

"And?"

"He can't find Chen. He's not responding to emails, calls, anything," Max explained. "I'm not sure what to do at this point, nor is his agent."

"This isn't good. Do you think I need to let Feige know?" Alerting Feige was the last thing I wanted to do. We'd spent a week getting Marvel to approve Chen. We had no other options.

"Unfortunately, I do."

I hung up. That was not the news I wanted to hear. After mulling my next move, I shot an email to Feige.

Marvel was furious the next day as the news of our vanished actor circulated. Not only did we lose trust with Marvel creative over this embarrassing mishap, but I also lost the ability to argue for some additional China relevancy in the film. And we still needed more.

Thankfully a few weeks later, we found another great actor, Wang Xueqi, to play the role. Though he wasn't our first choice, nor was he China's biggest star, Wang did have lots of strong attributes, leading us to believe he could be our Rod Tidwell—an overachieving, past-his-prime actor with the ability to deliver a stellar performance. Wang could, in essence, "show us the money."

Wang was best described as a Chinese Gene Hackman who was versatile, extremely skilled, and super well known. But Wang's lack of availability and an American worker visa caused a delay in production. That was costly and lost us even more goodwill with Marvel. On the positive side though, Congressman Adam Schiff (D-CA) did personally jump in to help get Wang's worker visa expedited as quickly as possible. The Congressman understood the importance of what we were all doing. He saw film diplomacy resulting from our bilateral collaboration as a positive.

As for Chen Dao Ming, he did eventually pop back up. It turns out he fled to New York City. Why? Once he'd gotten the role, Chinese journalists had bombarded him with criticism asking why would he take such a small role in an American movie? A Western form of propaganda? Especially when the US government was accusing China of crimes? Pundits saw it as kowtowing to Hollywood studios and the Americans. They also feared his role would be greatly diminished by the final cut, a.k.a. the *Looper* issue, or it would even be fully cut from the film's final version.

It turned out later that such a dire prediction for Dr. Wu's role was almost spot on!

Wang was a joy to work with. We recorded a lot of behind-the-scenes footage of him intending to showcase China's collaboration with Hollywood. The macro of what we tried to capture was crucial. For instance, we needed background material to use for promoting and marketing the film both to consumers and government officials. Both entities wanted to know what it was like being on the set of a big Hollywood production. More importantly, both wanted to witness Wang, DMG, and China as major players in the film. Capturing moments of enthusiasm and excitement around anything China-related on set was a priority and often scripted. At times, it almost felt like we were shooting footage for an infomercial.

Dan and I alerted our behind-the-scenes team, as well as Marvel's, as to the specifics that were needed. We requested that artists on camera should be seen in various film production environments including the wardrobe department, hair and makeup department, rehearsals, on various stages, in various locations, and in post-production facilities. The goal, once again, was to display China and Marvel's involvement in the film, and the actors' and crews' excitement to have China be a part of what could be one of the most successful movies in history.

That initiative played out stressfully during our days on set. Still, it was successful. On camera, we interviewed Robert Downey Jr., Sir Ben Kingsley, Gwyneth Paltrow, Samuel L. Jackson, Guy Pearce, Shane Black, and Kevin Feige. Questions ranged from "What will China add to the film?" or "How is the first time working with a respected Chinese actor?" or "What excites you about shooting this in China?" to "What do you think you will learn from this Chinese experience?" and "What do you want to say to your Chinese audience?" You get the picture.

Then we had each do what are commonly referred to as "Shout-Outs." As an example, imagine Robert Downey Jr. saying on camera something like, "Hey China, we are here on the *Iron Man 3* set...," or, "See you next time, China...," or, "Hey China, I'm Robert Downey Jr., and I am really looking forward to filming on location in China very soon."

All that explained why Feige mentioned certain creative ideas as "heavy-handed." Our behind-the-scenes footage, or exploits as he saw them, only compounded the belief that we intended to force China into every nook and cranny of *Iron Man 3* if given the chance. I'm not a Communist Party sympathizer, but when I think back about some of the items we pressed for, solely to help gain support from the Chinese, I can see how someone could assume that I was.

Bottom line, if we wanted to open the market, we had to play it a certain way. I like to look at things as glass-half-full. We were bridging cultures and we were going to make millions, if not billions. We were also forging a much stronger bond with China through such a high-profile endeavor. The world would be a better place as a result, and that was what I kept telling myself. It allowed me to sleep at night. I sincerely believed it.

We did have our share of critics, though. And lots of them. I was alerted by a studio executive to the following post on the *Los Angeles Times* media blog:

Adrian Spradlin *at 11:14 p.m., June 12, 2012*

DMG's Dan Mintz, and his co-conspirator Chris Fenton who lives in LA, are the biggest Turncoat/Benedicts of our time...In the name of profit, they will sell out America, our democracy, and our values...What's next? Hollywood glorifying the merits of Communism/Autocracy/Centralized Planning/Rule BY Law? Or will it be the deficit of democracy and how human, environmental, labor, and civil rights are all bad?

McCarthy was right. It's just that he was wrong about the threat coming from the Soviets, it's the CCP that penetrated Hollywood...

Things that make you go hmmm...and a dagger through my heart as well. I was speechless.

Two weeks later my friend, Congressman Tom Rooney (R-FL) and I discussed the importance of *Iron Man 3* via email. I described it as such:

Marvel's IRON MAN 3 is a joint venture with China's DMG on a single US major studio film, resulting in at least $10M to $20M of funding coming from the Chinese to the US, thusly creating an emboldened US GDP increase (though fractional) along with the creation of jobs on US soil (as most of the production occurs in the US, rather than in China). What I'm facilitating between the two countries is very patriotic. I'm proud of that fact.

As far as third-party validation goes, I got an interesting email from one of the top US-China transactional attorneys, Stephen Saltzman at Loeb & Loeb:

On my last trip to Shanghai and Beijing your name came up several times, as execs from both US and Chinese companies alike were applauding your role in the Iron Man 3 deal, and in general the job you're doing for DMG. I can remember back to the two of us having lunch at the GHR (Beverly Hill's Grand Havana Room) and discussing the strong man competition you were working on...before everyone started looking at the Chinese marketplace... so my heartfelt congratulations.

To say what we were doing was complicated, patriotic, pro-communist, conflicted, complicit, or controversial was inaccurate. It was, in fact, all of the above.

That summer, China pushed a nationalistic agenda by threatening to retake the Senkaku Islands back from Japan, adding one more challenge to our docket. I witnessed firsthand the power China's Propaganda Ministry had over its people. That vital arm of the Communist Party simply flipped an anti-Japanese switch, and the entire populace suddenly despised anything Japanese—way more than usual. The immediacy of the impact was startling. Numerous Honda, Mazda, Nissan, and Toyota facilities had to shut down due to violent protests. In Beijing, I saw angry protestors congregating in front of the Japanese embassy, and newspapers showed Japanese model cars being overturned in the streets of Shanghai. In other cities, Japanese cars were lit on fire, burning out of control while mobs shouted anti-Japanese chants. For the first time in ten years, Japanese car sales dropped year-over-year in the world's largest car market, and other Japanese goods and services suffered similar fates.

The US sided with its longtime ally, Japan, which only muddied the bilateral relationship further and created a pile-on effect with the ongoing SEC investigation. This was terrible for the movie business as the government took on a new form of retaliation—box-office revenue mitigation!

First, China decided to stop all day-and-date releases of Hollywood films. That meant no Hollywood film could be released in China on the same day as its North American release, only significantly later—a step that promoted the proliferation of pirated DVDs. It also made the films stale by the time they were released, severely dampening box-office returns. Second, the government dated the release of similar movies on the same date. As a result, that summer saw *Spider-Man* and *Batman* released on the same day, as well as *The Lorax* and *Ice Age*. When similar films are shown too close to each other, they cannibalize the other's box office, thus achieving the government's unspoken goal.

With our film *Looper* needing a release date in the next couple of months, the pressure was mounting. The challenges steadily increased. Sometimes direct bullets hit us. Other times strays. It didn't matter. None of it continued to bode well for us.

In an attempt to calm the mounting animosity between the two countries, I again reached out to Congressman Tom Rooney. I wanted to help lawmakers and regulators understand the China market better. Perhaps through a better understanding, the tension would abate. Much of the scrutiny placed on Hollywood studios was a result of confusion in DC. I was convinced the SEC needed a tutorial on how the film distribution system worked in China, and I planned to figure out a way to do just that.

Congressman Rooney connected me with a Washington, DC-based nonprofit called the US-Asia Institute (USAI). It was one of the most valuable introductions I've experienced during my career. The USAI has brought delegations of House and Senate members, as well as their senior staff, to China since 1979. Each delegation is co-hosted by the National People's Congress and the Chinese People's Institute of Foreign Affairs. No angle or biased agenda is influenced on any trip or participant. The trips are simply platforms for diplomacy with learning, people-to-people contact, and gaining an understanding of each side's respective point of view. At the least, the five forces of diplomacy I often refer to—national security, politics, human rights, culture, and commerce—are openly discussed. At best, participants see how far apart the superpowers are with the first three, but how we can possibly work together on the final two and agree to do so.

I immediately signed up DMG to host two large delegations late that summer in Beijing. One was comprised of chiefs of staff for various Congressional members and another for legislative directors. For each delegation, we walked them through a four-hour tutorial at DMG's Beijing headquarters, covering how the movie business and overall media industry worked in China. Who are the private companies involved? Who are the American companies working in China? Who are the state-owned enterprises? Who are the regulators? Who are the government entities? And how does the overall ecosystem work? We covered it all.

At the end of the presentation and office walkthrough, we would lead each delegation up a flight of stairs to the rooftop of our building, thirty stories in the sky. There, the door would open to a sight they couldn't believe: a basketball court. Dan referred to it as "the highest basketball court in all of Beijing," and he was probably right. That court and the game played on it symbolized common ground. Everyone plays basketball, right? We play it, and so do you. See, we aren't that different over here in China!

Colleagues would hand out balls for delegates to shoot around as photos were taken. We would tell each delegation about how basketball was the first wide-reaching cultural interaction between the US and China, leading to significant commerce. Yes, there was ping pong, but the monetization of that sport never truly materialized. Basketball, on the other hand, through Michael Jordan's first visits, and the resulting proliferation of all things NBA and Nike throughout the nation, became the ultimate trailblazer in the bilateral exchange of culture and commerce.

"Movies will be next!" Dan would always add.

"Film Diplomacy!" I'd call it.

When the members of each delegation left, it felt as if we'd connected with them and gotten everyone thinking differently about China. More importantly, attendees were much more educated on how the system worked. The hope was that they would go back to Washington with a much deeper knowledge of China and apply it to sensible and more relevant laws, policies, and regulations. And taking it one step further, perhaps it would even help the Hollywood ecosystem get out from under the dark cloud of the ongoing SEC investigation!

Since those two delegations, I've been a regular on Capitol Hill and have continued hosting Congressional members and their senior staff in China. Most recently was a trip with three House members in late 2019. To this day, the diplomacy resulting from every trip is invaluable.

Back in Los Angeles after those two August 2012 delegations, I sent the following note to the DMG Beijing-based executives, most of them Chinese, who helped me host and present:

> During my 12-hour flight back to LA I couldn't stop thinking about the wonderful team effort you all put forth to host some of the most influential people in Washington, DC. On behalf of DMG, China, and the US, I thank you all. You helped create a wonderful event for both delegations, and as a result, I believe we made the world a better place by helping to bridge a gap across the Pacific. We are experts in culture. We are successful in commerce. Let's continue to focus on both, solidifying the bilateral relationship for generations to come.

24.

POURING GASOLINE ON A FIRE

NOT TO SOUND like a broken record, but the challenges we faced by the end of that summer continued to increase both for *Iron Man 3* and *Looper*. Beyond the issues already discussed, critics in China pummeled *Looper*, asking the government to revoke its co-production status. If that happened, the monetization potential would crash, and we would be screwed.

The same thing was happening on *Iron Man 3*, with the government feeling pressure from the Chinese public and the local filmmaking community to also revoke its co-production status. Aside from just ongoing dislike and tension between the two countries, *Iron Man 3*'s issues were compounded by two other items that arose late that summer. First, the film's director, Shane Black, while at San Diego Comic-Con, told reporters when asked about the upcoming China portion of production: "It's weird because we're not going to China." Of course, that quote was carried widely and feverishly in China immediately. We were then lambasted as liars and opportunists who were selling the film as a bilateral collaboration that it simply was not.

Shane was accurate when he said he wasn't going to China. However, talking about it publicly was never supposed to happen. We didn't intend to trick anyone, especially the Chinese government.

But at the same time, we wanted to alert officials of the specifics more gently and strategically later. Just blurting it out to reporters created massive headwinds.

Variety put out an article detailing the turmoil in China over fake co-productions on August 27, 2012. Both *Looper* and *Iron Man 3* were the focus. Part of it read:

China tightens co-productions policy
Government cracks down on abuse of system
By Clifford Coonan

BEIJING -- Chinese co-productions must be genuine co-productions, with significant Chinese input, the head of the country's biz regulator said, as the government cracks down on people using the rules to gain easy access to the booming market.

Zhang Peiming, the deputy bureau chief of the State Administration of Radio, Film and Television, told local media that all of the requirements had to be met, such as having one third of the coin from China, the main cast has to be from China, and part of the movie must be shot in China.

"Some so-called co-production movies just do superficial changes, with little investment from China, and use very few Chinese elements, and call it a co-production. These co-productions get around the quota system, and take domestic investment away and threaten Chinese movies," Zhang said.

Immediately following that article, a senior executive at a major studio, whom I'll keep nameless, sent out an email to staff essentially citing *Looper* and *Iron Man 3* as "bolt-on" co-productions. An obviously between-the-lines order for staff to avoid doing business with DMG. The executive ended the email stating, "I am pleased to report that none of our projects are these sorts of false co-productions."

The second issue, and compounding the first, was that Robert Downey Jr. got injured during production in the US, so filming had to shut down temporarily. That lost time meant a rush towards the finish in order to make the May 2013 worldwide release date. Now Robert would not have time to shoot anything in China. It also meant no first unit crew or talent there either. Thus, Shane Black was accurate. He just wasn't strategic.

Both issues were big fat problems. We had lots of pressure to change course, come up with a solution, or blow it all up. The Chinese government was riding us daily to fix the loss of "face." The film was so high-profile that anything going awry was exceptionally public and embarrassing for them. The Chinese press also continued to fan the flames. China's diminished role in the movie, the tiny role for such an iconic Chinese actor, and the overall manipulation of the system for the benefit of making more money for Hollywood were three of the destructive themes relayed widely.

"Can't you keep Doctor Wu meeting Tony Stark in Shanghai?" I asked Kevin. "Even if Robert doesn't go to Shanghai, we can still shoot a second unit with Wang on location to make it seem as if Tony's there."

"It doesn't make sense. It has to take place in Bern, Switzerland," he responded calmly. He wasn't feeling the pressure I was feeling. Movie pressure, maybe, but not intensity on a geopolitical level.

"No offense, but Bern doesn't make sense to me."

"Chris, I want you to get what you need, but I can't be flexible here. When we added Doctor Wu, he had to have a legitimate place in the Marvel Universe that was consistent with the other stories, timelines, and characters. If it's not, our fanbase will call us out on it, and they are the most important part of all this. They are what got us here in the first place."

"But what does Bern have to do with anything?" I asked. "That, I don't understand."

"I won't get into the weeds, but for simplicity's sake, we need to understand where Doctor Wu came from in the Universe, and what he was doing throughout time, even though we may never see that storyline anywhere but in our minds."

"Okay."

"So Wu is a scientist, working on various change-the-world-for-the-better inventions. On the eve of the millennium, he meets Tony Stark in Bern. Then the *Iron Man* movie happens, and we see Yinsen in a cave during the film's opening, helping people in Afghanistan survive shrapnel from Tony Stark's weapons. Yinsen helps Tony too. Around this time, the RT comes into play. Tony leaves, and while *Iron Man* is playing out, Wu visits Yinsen who is his good friend and sees his plight. He needs a device that can help save his people, so Wu goes back to China to develop it. *Iron Man* happens and then *Iron Man 2* happens, and all this time Wu is working on this device and staying in touch with Yinsen. Yinsen is then killed. But Wu keeps working on it. Then *Iron Man 3* happens and Tony Stark remembers Wu from Bern and recalls that Yinsen said Wu was working on a device to help keep shrapnel from converging on a human's heart. When Tony realizes he can live as himself, meaning without the RT and without the crutch of being Iron Man, he decides to remove the RT, but he can only do it if Wu has perfected the device, and if Wu can do the surgery himself. Both answers are yes, and at the end of *Iron Man 3*, Tony has the surgery. Wu performs it successfully, and Tony throws the RT into the ocean in the final scene. It's pretty monumental. Tony Stark is finally comfortable with himself from that point on. He doesn't need to be Iron Man. He doesn't have to be Iron Man. Instead, that is the moment Tony embraces his own true identity as a flawed human. He is finally comfortable in his own skin. Your boy Wu is right there at the end with him too. He's a crucial character. And then, credits roll. *The End*."

"Wow!" I exclaimed. "That's why you run Marvel and make the most successful movies in the world, I guess."

He laughed.

"We'll figure out how to get you something in China. Let me work on it."

25.

WORST-CASE SCENARIO

JUST BEFORE SUNSET on September 4, 2012, a woman rang the call box of the gate surrounding our home. I happened to be walking outside at the time, so I walked over to her. She held a couple of brown packages.

"Are you Chris Fenton?" she asked.

"Yes, I am." I reached over the gate to grab what she had. She handed me something to sign and left. "Thank you," I yelled to her back.

"Presents?" my son Dylan asked, standing back by our front door. "Are they for us?"

"I don't think so."

"Kaylie, Daddy got some presents!" Dylan shouted into the house.

"Don't get her all excited. It's just work stuff," I laughed.

I opened the first package, noticing the contents came in an official government envelope. I skimmed the letter inside. My blood pressure surged. Instead of walking back inside, I had to sit on the stairs. I was just subpoenaed by the SEC—personally!

"What's in there?" Dylan asked innocently.

"D, please go back inside. Daddy needs to read these by himself."

I opened the other package hastily. It was a subpoena for DMG. Holy shit!

I walked into the house. A daze overcame me. Jennifer walked up to me.

"Dylan said you got some presents?" she asked.

Seeing the expression on my face, she knew something was wrong. I handed her the letters.

"Oh my God. What does this mean?" she asked, skimming through them.

I grabbed my phone, calling Dan. I was pissed. The SEC investigation had suddenly become super personal.

"Hey. It's me," I said, shaking.

Jennifer continued to skim through them, her law degree coming in very handy.

"You'll never believe what just got delivered to my house."

"What?"

"Subpoenas for me and you from the SEC. We are under investigation for FCPA violations relating to Hollywood studios and the film business in China."

"What the fuck? Seriously?"

"Yes. I'm not kidding."

"Come over now. And call that attorney you just did that Beverly Hills Bar Association panel with. She's focused on this stuff. We'll need her."

"Will do. Heading to you now," I responded, hanging up the phone.

I walked over to Jennifer. She looked scared but also pissed— Tiger-Mom/Tiger-Wife demeanor coming alive.

"How are you involved in this? I don't understand! How dare they!"

"I don't have any idea how I'm personally involved. It makes no sense. I would have to be giving envelopes of cash personally to Chinese officials, and I don't know any of them. I don't even interact with them." I hugged her hard. "We'll be ok. I promise. I'm heading over to Dan's and calling the attorneys on the way over."

"Dan better get us out of this shit situation. He's the one going around town bragging about all his guanxi with government officials in magazine articles and everything. He put a target on his back, and now it's on us!" She went full Tiger-Wife, or as I like to say, zero-to-sixty! "He'd better fix this!"

"He will," I responded, heading out the door.

26.

BITTERSWEET BUT STILL NUMBER ONE

A TWEET WENT OUT the following day from China expert Kevin Ma, stating:

"*Looper* has been pulled from its September 28 release date in China. Originally a China-US co-production. Status pulled."

Seriously? I was under investigation by the SEC while attacks on both *Looper* and *Iron Man 3* continued to barrage us on both sides of the Pacific. It was nuts. I felt as if everyone, and I mean everyone, was rooting against DMG. It felt so personal at that point too. I couldn't just let it bounce off of me, especially since it had dragged my wife and family into it.

"Chen, you've got to help me, please!" I begged Chris Chen, Executive Vice President at Endgame, one of our partners on *Looper*. "CFG & SARFT are putting major pressure on DMG to have a 'Chinese Element' pictured on the artwork along with the 'big Hollywood stars.' We need our Chinese actress there next to Bruce [Willis] and JGL [Joseph Gordon-Levitt]. We are scrambling to make this happen. Please help!"

"Seriously? We're crushed on time. What are they saying? If we don't, then what?"

"I'm not in those government meetings. I'm not sure what alternatives, if any, the government is giving us. All I can say is that my colleagues in Beijing are receiving massive pressure to make it look like China has a real presence in the film — globally."

"It does, though!"

"It doesn't globally. You guys have a cut with very little China going to the worldwide market. It's a loss of face, and they are asking us to address it somehow."

"China is a central part of the plot. It didn't even exist in the film before you guys came along."

"It's not what's in there. It's what they know is *not* in there, and when the press outed the two-cut strategy, they just assumed lots of China got cut. Obviously, this pressure is coming from officials higher up than even SARFT. The negative political climate towards the US and Hollywood movies right now is beyond bad," I explained. "FYI, Hollywood films made sixty million of the sixty-one-million-dollar total at the box office last week in China. That's not good if you're trying to build a local business! The local film industry is up in arms. The timing couldn't be worse!"

"I'll do what I can. You know I will."

"I appreciate it, Chen. Thank you," I said, hanging up.

And Chen did come through. Our Chinese actress, Xu Qing, made it onto the global poster, and it was just what we needed to get CFG and SARFT to finally sign off on a release date! Finally, some good news!

I was able to issue the following confirmation to all the journalists asking about the situation:

DMG Entertainment, Endgame's producing and financing partner on Looper, confirmed that the film will receive a very wide day-and-date release in China on September 28, a historic launch period due to the week-long Chinese holiday that starts the same day.

Robert Cain, a top media blogger and someone whom Hollywood paid great attention to when it came to news and opinion regarding China's vibrant, yet volatile, film industry, sent me an immediate congratulations via email. Robert and I had gotten to know each other rather well over the years. I respected his expertise, and we would swap information often about all things China. It was nice to get accolades from him, so I responded quickly from my hotel in Palo Alto:

I know. I'm pinching myself. Looper is such an awesome story. Not only is it the first Hollywood film to get a day-and-date in a very long time, but, FOR THE FIRST TIME IN HISTORY, it's a Hollywood/International film garnering a release during the October National holiday. Considering the geo-political issues on the macro side, and the sensitivities going on with respect to the cross-Pacific film biz on the micro side, it's obviously a feat we are very proud of.

I was in Palo Alto for two reasons. One, to give a keynote address to Stanford's business school focused on the media business between the US and China. And two, to discuss in private with the former US Ambassador to China, Jon Huntsman, his thoughts on the SEC's investigation. It was a crazy weekend to be up at Stanford too because it happened to also be the opening weekend for *Looper*. Additionally, Zhang Xun and Meng Yang from the China Film Co-Production Corporation were both in attendance at the Stanford event and speaking on my panel. The topic — *Looper*, and quite frankly, how *Looper* shouldn't be a co-production. The CFCC happened to be overruled on their *Looper* opinion by the higher-ups at SARFT, so they were not happy. Even worse, they were pissed that DMG went over their heads to SARFT to get it approved. You can imagine how uncomfortable that panel discussion was.

"Did you see Zhang and Yang yet?" Dan asked, calling early on the day of my speech.

"Yeah, at dinner last night. It was tricky. They were there with one interpreter. Lots of sensitivities around *Looper*. They kept leaving the table to take calls from 'Beijing.' When they'd get back, they'd again reiterate the political firestorm around *Looper*. After each call, they would tell me a new way to discuss *Looper* for today's panel. 'Co-pro-duction' is the toxic word of the year. They forbid me to use that term. They are specifically nervous about the Q&A section for our panel tomorrow. We decided on the term 'international cooperation effort with financing from a China entity (DMG),' or more simply, a 'joint venture,'" I explained, rolling my eyes.

"They are that uptight about a co-pro label? What the fuck!"

"If the word 'co-pro' comes up, I obviously need to deflect. They made that abundantly clear several times. It's the one English word they know well and cringe whenever they hear it referring to *Looper*," I added. "It's so insane!"

"Agree. Everyone's so damn uptight around this film in China. But who cares? We got it done! Talk later."

I took a deep breath in and let it out, attempting to savor a some-what non-chaotic, slightly successful moment — which doesn't happen often when it comes to China.

Things got better the next day when *Looper* opened number one in China. Journalists picked up my Stanford keynote and ran headlines such as, "Chris Fenton Discusses the Bilateral US-China Film Relation-ship." Reaction to both the success of *Looper*'s opening, as well as the diplomatic explanation of what it fostered bilaterally, was exhilarating.

Such a historic achievement gave me great fodder to use a few days later when lecturing at the US Naval Academy. That lecture followed with meetings in DC. During the trip, I sent an email to Daniel Postaer. He had recently moved on from DMG after eight very successful years, but we were still super close. He was my partner in crime for much of the *Looper* process, World's Strongest Man, Michael Phelps, the begin-nings of *Iron Man 3*, and everything in between. I loved that guy!

Looper opening baby! All started with you, (Chris) Chen, and me!! Lectured three classes at USNA - really amazing. they drove me up from DC for the day. In DC for 5 days for insane China-related WTO / Trade issue meetings. Incredible experience. House/Senate Chief of Staff's, SEC, Appointed Treasury Dept officials, DOJ, IMF, Library of Congress, etc. Still in shock about it all (got to eat at the Capitol Club too - as a registered Democrat!).... Off to Miami tomorrow for IM3. Jennifer is not psyched about all the travel, and ripping mad about the whole SEC problem, but we've got a happy healthy family and I'm helping to change the world!... CF

ps. Huntsman was cool. Dig that cat. Met with him last Friday (not sure if he'll be running again though). Couldn't help me with SEC, so will keep searching for the magic fix....

Freshly energized by my time in DC, I reached out to a buddy I'll refer to as "the Brit," who at the time was a top dog at the Motion Picture Association of America. My thought was to join forces with the MPAA in order to help end the SEC investigation hanging over Hollywood and, of course, hanging over us. I figured if we could swap notes and combine lobbying and education efforts, the plan might actually work.

"China has been challenging lately," I started off our call. "Stacking films of similar genres on the same release date, killing the day-and-date releases, rejecting any sort of US-China co-productions, filling quota slots with non-Hollywood titles, and so on. I'm not going to lie. These past eight months have been brutal."

"Couldn't agree with you more, Chris," he responded in his cheery British accent. "Lots resulting from the overall negative US-China rhetoric bouncing back and forth across the Pacific. That Japanese dispute didn't help either. It's obvious this isn't the friendliest bilateral relationship currently."

"Not at all." I grabbed a stress ball off of my desk. "What do you think of the SEC situation?"

"That's certainly not helping. A real slap to the face of Han Sanping and China Film Group. Now Big Brother is coming to protect its own. Face has been lost."

"We're in agreement. DMG certainly supports the SEC and its agenda. A level playing field is a must, and ridding the market of bad seeds is a good thing. But this blanket investigation is smothering Hollywood's gains in the market."

"Agreed," he said, taking a deep breath. "And the timing of the investigation was terrible." The Brit paused a moment. "By the way, I have a colleague from legal joining the call."

"Hello, Chris," an unfamiliar voice said.

"Hello," I responded, slightly surprised to have someone else on the call. "And yes, I agree the timing wasn't ideal, especially after Biden and Xi announced a new deal too. And to have it hit the press via the *New York Times* during Beijing's proudest film moment, their own international film festival, was yet another massive loss of face," I added, squeezing the stress ball. "It was an embarrassment to SARFT and CFG, and now we see the retaliation."

"Agree. Makes the Chinese feel that the US believes everyone is corrupt," the Brit said.

"Since you're seeing Chairman [Chris] Dodd this week, do you think you could suggest a delegation visit to China in the coming months, but instead of members of Congress, SEC officials? The USAI could organize it with our counterparts at the National People's Congress. After such an educational visit, we believe the SEC may switch their focus away from a blanket inquiry and move it, instead, towards an investigation that's more targeted."

"Not to interrupt here guys, but I think that's a terrible idea," the Brit's colleague interjected.

"Why is that?" I asked, squeezing my stress ball with greater force.

"It would completely work against our member studios and embolden their investigation. The SEC is not your friend. When you're under investigation, it's guilty until proven innocent. Understand? And besides, the SEC going to China will only reiterate their belief that everyone in China is corrupt. You know that, and I know that. Do we want the SEC to know that?" he explained combatively.

"I disagree with that statement. In fact, it's quite offensive." I was irritated. "I'm surprised you're a lobbyist given such a hardline stance."

"Listen, we are advising all our member studios not to talk to the SEC unless they have to. I realize you may plan to sit with them voluntarily, but that is ill-advised. Additionally, I highly recommend you stop hosting Congressional delegation trips to China while the investigation is pending."

"We'll agree to disagree there. I'm not letting the bilateral exchange of culture and commerce come to a screeching halt over a misguided SEC investigation, and I intend to do anything I can to solve the issue. If we cut off people-to-people exchanges between the two superpower countries, I'd argue we are consciously starting a new cold war. This time with bigger implications than any cold war in the past," I ranted passionately.

"I'd say this conversation is over," he said sternly.

"Brit, you agree?" I asked.

"We all need to cool off a bit," the Brit affirmed.

"Well then, thank you both for your time," I said, hanging up. I put my head down on my desk, feeling defeated. That did not go well. I liked and respected the Brit, but his colleague was another story. Not cool.

I heard a knock at the door. I was in my guest house office.

"Come in," I said.

The door opened. It was Jennifer. She was a happy sight considering the mood that call had just put me in. A smile formed on my face.

"You okay?" she asked, walking towards me.

"Yes, but trying to find a solution to this SEC situation. I came up a little short on a call with the Asia division of the MPAA just now. Everyone is running scared."

"I figured. I could hear the gist as I walked out here." She sat down on a chair facing my desk. I got up to grab her a glass of wine. "Now that you're back in town, we need to talk about this SEC situation. It's keeping me up at night," she admitted.

"I know. It keeps me up at night too." I handed her a full glass. "We have attorneys representing us personally and others representing the company. But it doesn't feel right. Feels like we're being hung out there."

"I feel the same way," she said, grabbing my hand in support. "How do you feel about it overall? You know, the thirty-thousand-foot view?"

"I'm a true patriot of the United States, and I feel that I have been thrust into a position, with a tremendous platform where I can help open the biggest economy in the world to one of the few US exports the Chinese consumer wants. I can also help educate the SEC, moving them from a blanket inquiry and towards a more focused approach. All it would take is a simple Chinese-Film-Industry-101 type of presentation. There are obviously misconceptions I can easily help clarify," I responded, almost as if I had rehearsed such an answer. "I'm ninety-nine percent behind fighting this thing tooth and nail."

"Yeah, but what about the other one percent? Be honest, do you know what people on the ground in China have been doing at DMG? You're ninety-nine percent certain they have done things right, but what about the other one percent?" She took a sip of her wine. "I fully support your fight, but think about what's at stake."

"The reputation I've built throughout my career continues to deteriorate, as some of the guys at my monthly cigar night mentioned. Some, I know, are aware I'm part of the investigation. Some don't, but they suspect it. Crazy thing is, they can't even come clean with me about it, and they can't even ask because everyone's scared. That's what's so fucked. Guys like Tall Exec are told they can't talk to me. These are friends of mine. Friends for a long time and this SEC thing forbids us to have a normal relationship. I need to track buddies down at tee-ball games just to talk to them now?" I was spinning. Jennifer put her hands firmly on my shoulders, showing support. "At least my involvement hasn't been mentioned publicly. At least it's not out there for everyone to know."

"But what if that happens?"

"It hurts us all and decimates my career." I poured a new glass for myself.

"What does the mean for your future? What about mine?"

"Toast. We're both screwed. And what's worse, we are victims of something we had nothing to do with. I'm not bribing officials. I don't even know them. I don't even speak their language. And quite frankly, I honestly believe no one at DMG is bribing officials either. Like I said — I'm ninety-nine percent certain."

"You're probably right. But what if people at DMG are guilty of bribing, or of corruption?"

"That's what I'm scared of," I admitted, taking a sip.

"Specifically, why do you think the SEC is investigating us? Why are they investigating DMG?" she asked, starting to go zero-to-sixty into Tiger-Wife mode.

"Honey, please. Stay cool." I grabbed her hand, calming her down. "I don't know why. Maybe it's because someone in the organization is guilty, but I don't think that's the case. I truly believe that. There's a part of me that thinks they are investigating us because we are successful in China and that in and of itself is suspicious because the market is hard to navigate. And DMG does it well. There is envy out there from so many who can't get stuff done. I'm sure people have targeted us. Or maybe the US government is upset that we are kowtowing to the Chinese — which we are not!" I stopped myself. "Though sometimes I think we are." I paused again, gathering my thoughts. "We are opening the market, dammit! Sometimes you need to placate the host in order to be a good guest. I wouldn't call it pandering. It's good business." I clutched her hand tighter and sighed. "I don't know. I'm confused. And I'm sorry you're a part of this mess."

"It's not your fault." She pulled back, looking into my eyes. "You know you'll have to meet with the SEC. And I guarantee you'll have to handle the meeting yourself. No one from China is going to come here to fight this battle. Don't expect help from them. It's you and only you."

"I'm afraid you're right."

"I am," she said. She was calm and suddenly at peace about it. "But you realize you've been here before. More than once. First, it was getting fired at William Morris, and then it was Lehman Brothers going bankrupt. You have learned to be resilient. And we've learned how to bounce back together."

"That is so true. Thank you." I toasted her. "Cheers. I can handle it. I'm certain."

"I know you can, and we will together."

"Us against the world."

"Indeed."

27.

COLLABORATION ON DISTANT LANDS

WE CAREFULLY WORDED a press release with both Marvel and Disney that went public on December 4, 2012. It had to please both sides of the Pacific, while also mitigating any criticism from either the hardcore Marvel fans or critics from the Chinese side. We also all knew the SEC would be watching. Far from an easy task, especially since trust between both countries had been waning consistently on a macro level, resulting in the internal trust breaking down between us, Marvel, and Disney. I sent an email before the press release to a few colleagues expressing my frustration:

> So hard to get any help now from anyone. It's a China issue. No one trusts shit out of the country. No one. No company. No official. Nothing is trusted. I'm battling that...CF

The release landed shortly thereafter:

Leading Chinese Actor Wang Xueqi Cast in Marvel's Iron Man 3 as Dr. Wu
Third Installment in Blockbuster Franchise to Start Filming in China on December 10th

"This is a very exciting time for DMG Entertainment, Marvel Studios, and the millions of Iron Man fans around China who have been eagerly waiting for this moment," said DMG's CEO, Dan Mintz. "Uniting the best of the United States and China to produce world-leading entertainment on *Iron Man 3* is truly a unique experience and marks the first time a franchise movie of this size has been shot in China."

Iron Man 3 continues the story with a new chapter that will deliver more heart-pounding action than ever before. Marvel's *Iron Man 3* will find Tony Stark with his back against the wall, facing his most fearsome foes yet.

With a film career that has spanned over 25 years in China's film industry, Wang Xueqi is well known for award winning performances in many films including *The Founding of a Party*.

In terms of the above *Iron Man 3* press release, we did receive enormous pressure to include one particular film of Wang's for his list of credits. And keep in mind, Wang had done dozens, if not hundreds of films, over his career. The film was titled *The Founding of a Party*, a government-funded tentpole movie portraying the birth of the Communist Party in China (CCP). Every big Chinese actor and actress played a role in it, and every production company and studio in the market, DMG included, fought to be a part of the team that made it. Lots of goodwill with the CCP was at stake in the making of that film, and the Chinese government was particularly proud of the result. To see journalists reporting on Wang's casting in the massive global *Iron*

Man franchise shortly after his role in China's patriotic *The Founding of a Party* brought lots of pride to every government official.

Of course, it was only a matter of a few minutes before the first, diving-one-layer-deeper question popped up on my email. It came from a *Daily Variety* reporter:

> Hey chris - writing up this story on Wang Xueqi. Can you tell me how much this casting could help re coproduction status, or getting the film into china, period?

Just one second to breathe. Please!

I also started getting calls about China's most famous actress, Fan Bingbing. Rumors were swirling that she was playing a role in the movie—a guarantee for winning more support from both the government and consumers at the time. The rumors were fortunately true, but we couldn't confirm them at that point. Her deal wasn't done, and political issues were preventing us from making the news public.

I had to hop a flight for Beijing anyway. We were starting the Chinese portion of the production. Being unreachable for fourteen hours was the best part of Air China's lack of wi-fi, especially at that point!

And on one side note, just before boarding, we did get this email from a top executive at IMG Sports:

> It's been a few years since we've worked together on World's Strongest Man in China but I remember our association fondly and successfully. I hope this note finds you well. We would like to bring World's Strongest Man back to China in 2013 and wondered if you could help us with a site. The specs have not changed much, we still need room and board plus a few small extras for a fairly large group. We're pretty loose as to the timeframe we use to produce the show and almost any period of about ten days works for us.

I look forward to hearing from you and hope we can work together once again.

Best regards...."

It all goes full circle...I guess we were doing something right.

The Beijing shoot for *Iron Man 3* was so crucial. Not only did we have to get good footage for the global cut of the movie, but we also had to make it known that we were there. The film's production in China was indeed happening, despite what Shane Black said. People needed to know that. There were cameras and crew on the ground. And we had some of Marvel's decision-makers there. We also had a fantastic young Marvel executive, Brad Winderbaum, directing the Chinese production.

We also had our Chinese actors, Fan Bingbing and Wang Xueqi. Both had massive star power, which made the Chinese production so much more meaningful. Additionally, we had the top half of the Iron Man suit and the extremely skilled stuntman who wore it. That costume gave us the ability to show that Iron Man was actually in China. Maybe it wasn't Tony Stark, a.k.a. Robert Downey Jr., but it was Iron Man, at least from the waist up.

I clearly remember the Beijing production because of another reason, the Sandy Hook Elementary School massacre. It's often difficult to get news from the West on the CCTV networks in China, or at least news stories that aren't completely angled with Communist Party propaganda. Even in nice hotels, the feeds of CNN International, BBC, and others are partially censored. When one of those networks airs something that isn't deemed appropriate for the Chinese audience or is something that could be construed as anti-Chinese, the television you're watching simply goes dark. Abrupt darkness without warning.

And then when the offensive story is over, the screen goes back to the original programming as if nothing happened.

However, when it came to the coverage of the Sandy Hook massacre, there was no blocking of the news whatsoever. Even CCTV was covering the event themselves and lending opinions constantly. Why? Because the overarching theme was that the United States is akin to the Wild West. A dysfunctional democratic country plagued with gun-toting cowboys and murderers. Newscasters issued warnings to Chinese citizens who wanted to visit or vacation in the US: America is violent. Be careful. There are guns everywhere. Look at what they did to their children.

Watching the coverage through the eyes of Chinese opinion was both fascinating and alarming. It made me self-reflect quite a bit. As a deeply patriotic American, it was always hard for me to ever digest spin in China. It felt like blatant propaganda so often. But the reality with the Sandy Hook coverage was different. Some of what the reporters were saying did resonate. Let's face it, what happened that day in Connecticut was beyond tragic and absolutely evil. How we prevent something like that in the future is anyone's guess, but I did hope that some kind of constructive plan would come out of it. Wishful thinking, I suppose, but I still hoped.

Brad Winderbaum assembled a skeleton team under Feige's supervision to capture what we needed from China. His crew of a dozen combined with DMG's much larger team to get the job done. Even though it was technically a "second unit," meaning no lead or supporting actors or even the director, there were still some pretty complicated scenes. A few of them involved outdoor set pieces, which in the middle of December in Beijing, will always be a challenge. We faced bitter cold weather and extreme wind during the shoot. And on the day that involved a large convoy of black Audis carrying "Tony Stark" through the heart of Beijing, it actually snowed—or maybe it was smog-flakes. Hard to tell the difference.

"It looks like we are shooting a scene from *Gorky Park*. Cold, windy, snowing, gray, everything you'd expect in a darkly lit, brooding KGB spy flick," Dan explained to Brad as we were lining up the motorcade shot.

We were standing on a busy corner of central Beijing, across the street from CCTV headquarters, an impressive building, creating a fantastic backdrop.

"You can't even see the buildings in the background. We should delay shooting a couple of days!" Dan argued.

"We don't have time. It looks fine. We'll deal with the coloring in post," Brad responded, referring to the post-production film finishing process. Though he was quite intimidated by Dan, Brad was so busy getting things set up, he didn't have time to feel insecure.

"Marvel movies are blue-sky in tone. This has none of that!" Dan pleaded.

"We'll fix it in post. Don't worry." Brad continued to sort through camera lenses.

"The government will be pissed. They want to show off the city. This makes Beijing look like a smoggy and cold mess!" Dan was getting frustrated. He looked at me, asking silently for help. His eyes said, "Fucking do something!"

"Brad, let's please switch to an interior shot today. We can check with China Film Group to see if we can get access to the soundstages early. Break for lunch now. Start up in a few hours." I suggested, putting on a second layer of gloves. It was extremely cold.

"We don't have time. I need to get this production done and get out of here. I've got my orders."

"I've got my orders too. I need to make sure this film gets released, and we can get our money back from this market!" Dan demanded. I strategically put my hand on his shoulder, carefully leading him away from Brad.

"Crane ready?" Brad asked.

"Yes," a Chinese cameraman responded.

"Okay," the assistant director shouted. "Roll sound. Roll camera. Background!"

Extras started roaming the streets. A few random cars drove into the frame.

"Action!" Brad yelled.

Dan and I watched the line of black Audis start their roll down the busy road. Dan was right, it did look like *Gorky Park*, or at least how I remembered that movie from the old Cold War spy days of the Soviet Union.

"Let's get out of here. This is a disaster," Dan said.

"You're being too pessimistic. It actually looks pretty cool."

"Not for what China wants. It looks terrible." He shook his head. "Let's grab something to eat."

Overall, the shoot went okay. Or as my wife would say "fine," which any husband knows isn't a resoundingly good way to describe something. Though we didn't win the battle over the outdoor shots, we did get lucky with Wang Xueqi's scene with "Iron Man" as schoolchildren gathered around. The scene as described in the script: "Wang shakes hands with our hero, Iron Man, and wishes him luck in saving the world. The children rally around and cheer on Iron Man as he lifts into the sky. All is done in front of an iconic Chinese backdrop."

The kids were super energetic and fun to work with. Wang played his role perfectly. The skies were deep blue with no smog whatsoever. The sun was bright and lit up the backdrop of one of the last remaining gates of the massive wall that, at one time, surrounded ancient Beijing, an iconic Chinese backdrop indeed. The same city gate defended by a top-notch local three-on-three basketball team: the eventual winners of our Battle of the Nine Gates event years before.

At the end of shooting that day, we took a photo to leak to the press. In it was Wang, Iron Man, at least from the waist up, and the ancient Chinese gate. To make it look like a shot from production, we added into the frame the top part of one of the production cameras. Additionally, we put everything a little off-center. We wanted the image to look like someone snuck a photo from the set — the reality of which was close to impossible because of massive security fencing surrounding the area. Marvel took secrecy very seriously. They wanted no public access to their sets, and the China portion was no exception.

When the leaked production photo went to journalists, it was immediately posted. Even in the US, the staged photo received lots of coverage. Most importantly, the photo served its purpose. Our intended audience in China saw that part of *Iron Man 3* was being shot in Beijing. It was the truth too. Wang worked hard in those days. So did Fan Bingbing. We had Chinese crews, we had Chinese backdrops, and we used Chinese soundstages. Whether Robert Downey Jr. was actually in the suit or not during the shooting in China didn't much matter.

And no one thought to ask.

28.

THE END OF
THE SECOND ACT:
ROCK BOTTOM

"**D**ID YOU SEE the *New York Times* this morning?" Jennifer asked. She handed me a coffee. I had been in our guest house taking calls and had come into the house for a quick bite of breakfast.

"I haven't yet. What does it say?" I grabbed a seat by the kids.

"Long article, but there's a good portion dedicated to *Iron Man 3*." She began reading out loud:

"Questions about how Chinese forces are shaping American movies are now playing out in the making of *Iron Man 3*, which is set for release on May 3.

"Disney and its Marvel unit want *Iron Man 3* to gain co-production status, partly because the previous two *Iron Man* movies performed well in China. To work toward that distinction, Disney and Marvel made a deal last year for Beijing-based DMG Entertainment to join in producing and financing the film.

"But they have taken a middle-of-the-road approach that appears intended to limit Chinese meddling in the creative process. A finished script was not submitted for approval and the companies have not yet made an application for official designation as a co-production. Rather, they are trying to show a heightened sense of cooperation in hopes the government will approve the status once that application is formally made in the spring.

"The producers made a presentation to censors early in the process, describing broad strokes of the story, the history of other Marvel and Disney movies, and plans to integrate Chinese characters into the movie.

"That won a conceptual sign-off for the film, which is being directed by Shane Black. Next, bureaucrats were invited to the set and were able to meet the star, Robert Downey Jr.

"That's the most relevant portion, but there's more," she said.

"I guess that's not terrible. Pretty accurate too." I started eating a PowerBar. "It does reiterate how much ass-kissing we do with China, though. I'm sure the anti-China hawks hate that stuff. Fanboys probably not too happy about it either."

"That all you're eating?"

"Yeah, not hungry." I grabbed a gummy bear vitamin off of my son's plate.

"Hey!" Dylan shouted.

"What were the calls this morning?" Jennifer asked, giving Dylan another gummy. He didn't even notice. The kids were engrossed in *Yo Gabba Gabba!*, a children's television series that must have been created during a writer's bad acid trip.

"Well, the first call was one of our SEC defense attorneys calling to say that this guy at the SEC, FED [a symbolic nickname], is on a rampage again. He's still waiting for tons of requested items from China. It's super frustrating. He has all our LA stuff, but China has been slow to move," I explained. "He's convinced we are guilty as all hell, and the team in Beijing is not helping our cause. I'm right smack in the middle of the firing line as a result!"

"I hate starting the morning talking about this. It always makes me super upset. I wish it would just go away." She shook her head, walking towards the sink. "It's so unfair, and you are dealing with the brunt of it. It's killing you and your reputation, and it's eating away at me." She walked back towards me, her eyes red and on the verge of tears. She's usually such a Tiger-Mom or Tiger-Wife. Seeing her well up illustrated the severity of the situation. Her concern and fear ran deep. Far deeper than I thought.

"I know. I'm dealing with it. I'll figure it out somehow." I paused, feeling another rush of depression and anxiety coming on. "I still think about that conversation I had with Tall Exec at Dylan's tee-ball game. I took his cue and had similar conversations with some of the guys at cigar night. It's all true. I'm not interested in leaving DMG. I believe in what we do. But still, not a single incoming call about any sort of new opportunity since this all went down. Even if I wanted to give up on all this and walk away, I'd have nowhere to go. I'm poison in this town. Absolute poison." I took a big gulp of coffee. "Until the SEC situation goes away, I truly am dead-man-walking. Just like Tall Exec said."

"Let's change subjects. We've been through tough times and we'll get through it." Jen forced herself to recover. "Dylan, what's the movie Daddy is doing?"

"*Iron Man 3!*"

"Kaylie, who is Daddy working with?"

"Robert Downey!"

"So cute! I love you little buggers," I said, kissing them both on their heads.

"It's more fun talking about what you really do day-to-day, right?" she asked.

"For sure. I need to focus on that. I guess."

"You do. For your own sanity. Even though making movies with China is about as insane as it gets."

We both laughed.

"Trying to schedule an early screening of the film for SARFT and CFG. It's supposed to happen next week in Beijing. Tough to coordinate, and some of the post-production still needs to get done."

"Why do you have to screen it so early?" she asked, refilling my coffee.

"Need to see if they have any changes. Censorship issues. That kind of stuff," I responded. "Dan is going to freak when he sees the cut. He'll know CFG & SARFT will have issues. Big issues."

"With what?" She sat down between Dylan and me. Kaylie was still deeply engrossed in the television show.

"Well for one, the operating scene is a mess. You're not supposed know this, but our Chinese guy takes the RT out of Tony Stark's body. And Shanghai is now Bern. Yes, fucking Switzerland, not China. Then one of our big Beijing set pieces, a motorcade of Audis transporting Tony Stark, takes place on a terribly cold, snowy, and smoggy day. It won't match the colors of the rest of the film. Like Dan said, it looks like a scene in *Gorky Park*."

"What's *Gorky Park*?" Dylan asked, giggling.

"Yeah buddy, sounds funny, but it's a movie title from back during the Cold War."

Dylan moved on to the television again. Too long a description for him, apparently.

"What else?" Jennifer asked rhetorically.

"The establishing shots of Beijing all are smoggy too. There's a background plate, so it looks like the scene is in a certain location. But it's the Hong Kong skyline instead of Beijing. It's so obvious too! I'm also irritated because Marvel owed screen time to advertising partners Yili Milk and TCL Electronics as part of a deal they made for *Avengers*. So, as a result, their brand integration exec forced us to have Fan Bingbing and Doctor Wu stand in front of a TCL television, drinking Yili milk — for like sixty straight seconds! It's so fucking random, and it makes absolutely no sense in the film either!" I took another swig of coffee. "Guaranteed Chinese critics say we forced an infomercial on them, especially since the footage won't be in the global cut of the film. [After viewing *Iron Man 3*'s China cut, a critic for China's *People's Daily* said, "The Chinese portion of the film is just terrible. It's a pointless commercial with a lot of plot holes," validating my assumption.] And the worst part of it all, the movie is long, but the plot is complicated, so some material is uncuttable. That means, for us, the worst-case scenario."

"What's that?"

"Our Chinese actor is barely in the film, or at least barely in the US cut of the film. His scenes are almost all gone!"

"Wang *Sushi*?" Kaylie asked.

"Yes, Wang *Sushi*!" I laughed. Kaylie timed her humor nicely for a six-year-old.

"Seriously? Two cuts of the film again? Repeating the *Looper* mess?" Jennifer asked. "That won't go well with the Chinese critics and press."

"No, it won't. My guess is it will kill our hopes for co-production approval too, but I need to worry about this screening first," I explained, concerned. "We'll need a plan to somehow appease the Chinese government given all that isn't working in our favor right now."

"Daddy, just tell them to put more *Sushi* in the film!" Dylan interrupted.

"Exactly, Dylan. More Chinese pandering." Jennifer laughed.

"Do you really think the ass-kissing is that blatant?" I asked.

"Pretty much so," she responded. "You're feeding the beast."

I laughed uncomfortably. She wasn't wrong.

"It's just how the rules are played there. We need to get the government on board. We fail at that, we can't monetize any of this," I explained.

"I get it, but you realize you're fully feeding the beast." She was so matter-of-fact, it startled me. "Don't fool yourself."

She started clearing plates from the table.

"If that's the case, then 'feeding the dragon' is probably a better term," I suggested.

We both laughed.

"And when you feed the dragon, it appreciates the sacrifice. You win the dragon over. It protects the villagers, right?" I asked. "That's what we're doing, and it's working. The perfect quid pro quo."

"Yeah, but every time you feed the dragon it grows stronger. It becomes more influential. It will only want more and more until you can't stop it."

"If that happens, we'll change course," I explained.

"I think you may be past that point," she said, walking into the kitchen.

I didn't react. I couldn't. I let what she said sink in, as it was awfully tough to digest. Was she right? I didn't know for sure. That said, it was a painfully enlightening moment. My blissful ignorance had vanished. Blindfolds fully removed as we faced the dragon from that moment forward.

On February 6, 2013, I was driving to Universal Studios to see some footage of another movie we were doing called *47 Ronin*, starring Keanu Reeves. The big-budget film was generated from an ancient Japanese legend. It told the story of forty-seven outlawed samurai who attempt to overthrow an evil emperor. The thematic story was rampant with honor, nobility, truth, and duty.

My car phone rang. It was David Galluzzi, the chief counsel for Marvel. He had been an ally and friend through the roller coaster of the past twenty months.

"David, how are you?"

"Good, you?"

"Can't complain. No fires to put out today, at least so far!"

"Well, I got one for you now," he said calmly. "I apologize."

"Figured as much. My blood pressure rises when I see your name pop up on my phone."

He laughed uncomfortably.

"You sitting?"

"Driving. And it's a road with lots of padding in case I want to purposely crash. Give me the news."

"There is no Doctor Wu in the final cut of the movie. China cut, yes. Global cut, no."

"Come on!" I pulled over. "You serious?"

"Unfortunately, I am. I'm sorry."

"Congrats on officially giving us none of the minimum requirements we asked for in our original deal," I said sarcastically.

David went on to explain, "The thought here now is this: Marvel's attempt to tinker with the film to incorporate Chinese relevancy was extremely tough to pull off. Very little got accomplished. So, perhaps we don't make it a big part of the agenda, at least publicly moving forward. We should instead spin the *Iron Man 3* process differently. We play into how that last *New York Times* article described it, something like activating China relevancy around the film. Perhaps even adding material for a China cut, inventive marketing, promotion and distribution strategies, that kind of thing. That's the stuff that really makes sense to us at this point." He paused a beat. "There must be a way to do that kind of thing to get government support because it's not going to come from the global cut of the movie. It's simply not."

"This kills any shot at a co-production approval for us. That means no day-and-date release. Our ability to monetize this film becomes virtually impossible. You know that, right?"

"I do, and I'm sorry," he admitted. "Let's talk later after you have time to digest."

"I'll need to report this to the team in Beijing first. I'll get back to you after."

"Understood."

I hung up, putting my head down on the steering wheel. Not the news I wanted to hear.

29.

THE THIRD ACT: INSPIRATION, STRATEGY, AND HOPE

"**T**HIS IS CHRIS," I said, picking up the phone.

"I have J.C. Spink for you," an assistant's voice responded.

"Where you at?" J.C. asked, popping on.

"Just getting home."

"Meet me at Jones in fifteen minutes," he demanded, as if my wife and two young children didn't expect my presence home that evening. With all the back and forth to China and elsewhere over that past year, I made it a goal to be at home at night when I was in Los Angeles. I had clocked as many as 140,000 miles in years past, and this one was on that same track. Being with my family was a priority whenever possible.

"Why? What's up?"

"I haven't heard from you much, and I'm reading all the headlines involving my good buddy. Figured you may need to talk."

He was right. I did need to talk, and he was the right person to talk to.

After all, J.C. was the guy who was quoted in that 2003 *New Yorker* article I mentioned earlier saying, "You come in [to Hollywood] with the thousand people in your group who will all kill to get ahead. Twenty years later, only twenty people are left standing, and they're running the town. You all screwed each other over plenty, so you kind of hate each other, but, at the same time, you're in this crazy dysfunctional family where you have to coexist." As startling as he was with that frank description, most in Hollywood agreed with it. And though the quote wasn't completely relevant to my current challenges, J.C. had an uncanny way of observing what others couldn't to explain complexities in simple and direct ways. For me, I always knew I'd pick up a piece of advice or wisdom from J.C. whenever we spoke. I always viewed our time together as time well spent.

I turned the car around, knowing Jennifer would understand.

Jones, or more specifically, Jones Hollywood, was a stalwart, non-descript yet ultra-cool Hollywood hangout disguised as an Italian restaurant with pretty decent food. What started in the early nineties as one of the hardest places to get beyond the velvet rope became a spot that almost every Hollywood player in my generation felt was a place of consistent hipness. Even better, it aged well along with all of us. Like many of us who had bouts of career and personal reinvention, so did Jones. After rare lulls in hipness through the years, the restaurant would always find a second wind, coming back alive with a vengeance, reinvigorated and attracting all the right customers again with great food, epic drinks, and an exclusive, yet cozy, atmosphere.

J.C. always loved the place and would practically take up residence there, sitting regularly at one of the restaurant's darkly lit booths under the massive collection of whiskey bottles lining a shelf just below the ceiling. He loved the place so much, he rented a home right behind it for many years.

The main room was always so dark that no matter the time of day, it took a few minutes to let your eyes adjust before you could find your guest. I walked through the heavy, windowless door to where I knew the hostess stood by memory.

"J.C. Spink," I announced in the darkness.

"Follow me," a voice responded. Her shadow led me down the front row of booths to the main room's far corner.

"I put on 'Hungry Like the Wolf,'" J.C. announced, referring to Hollywood's best jukebox. The song filled the room, energizing the atmosphere. "Figured you could use a little Duran Duran."

"Nice call," I responded, sitting down.

We caught up on several things, shooting the shit about Hollywood gossip, sports, random items from the 1980s, and, of course, J.C.'s exploits with various "girlfriends" since the last time we had covered the subject. Fortunately, at that period of his life, J.C. had settled down nicely with a woman named Kim. This development didn't generate as many entertaining and often sordid anecdotes, but it did make me feel better that J.C., being in a somewhat steady relationship, wasn't resorting to his harder-partying ways—a regrettably realistic concern, and one that J.C. wasn't shy of talking about himself.

"So, what's really bothering you?" J.C. finally asked.

"Where to start? For one, the SEC is unjustifiably investigating me personally, as well as DMG. That's like orange jumpsuit, *Shawshank Redemption* kind of shit. It's causing Jennifer and I some serious bouts of insomnia and stress."

"Are you guilty of anything?"

"Absolutely not! I wouldn't even know how to approach a government official in China. I don't know any of them. That's all done by our lobbying team."

"Are they guilty of anything?"

"I'm ninety-nine percent certain they aren't, but I don't know for sure. I do know we host officials for various events and have a close relationship with many of them as a company, but we also have lots of business with the entities those officials oversee. Everything I'm aware of and have seen is a hundred percent the way business is done legally in China. I believe that most, if not all, of the studios are doing it by the book there too," I explained, eating some of Jones's great pizza. "Bottom line is, we're all guilty until proven innocent, and that blows.

Even worse, everyone at the studios knows we are caught up in it too, so we are dead-man-walking for any new business right now. The taint of this thing is poisoning me personally too. It's terrible, and I can't help but feel depressed about it and cannot sleep a wink. Jennifer's feeling my pain also. It's wearing on her. That makes me extra sad."

I took a big gulp of wine. I hung my head. J.C. seemed a bit speechless.

"The SEC dragged me into this mess! That's what is killing me. And the shrapnel has hit Jennifer too! We have our own, personal attorneys representing us now, separate from the company's. This is not just about DMG anymore. It's crushing us as people—mentally, emotionally, and reputationally, and we are one hundred percent innocent. We have nothing to do with FCPA violations, and I wouldn't even know how to do something like that if I wanted to," I explained, starting to spin. "It's completely fucked. Even with the present business we have, it feels like our partners are constantly trying to get out of the deals. Yes, that includes Disney and Marvel. I know they'd get out if they could. And for me, I haven't had a new opportunity come across my desk since this all started."

"Shit, it's like you've got a big-ass herpes sore on your lip!"

I started a reluctant grin.

"Dude, it's not funny. I'm being serious."

"I know you are, but there has to be some humor in this," he said, devouring a slice.

"There isn't, unfortunately. Not in this case, and you know I'm rainbows and unicorns and the first guy to try to find comedy in anything."

"You need to make the argument, then. Take your attorneys out of it. Humanize your side and the other side and deal directly with whoever is creating this problem," he suggested, digging into a bowl of pasta. "The reality, too, is you have no fucking choice. You told me about Tall Exec and those other cigar night conversations—you are poison in town. People love you, Fentoni, but the SEC is single-handedly destroying your career. They think DMG is guilty, so they think you are guilty. It's terrible, but you need to fix it. Look, I know you have nothing to do with any of the stuff they've roped you into, but it doesn't matter. You have to act. You've got to get aggressive."

"I know, but I'm honestly scared."

"Remember when you told me about that huge, muscle-bound kid at the Catholic school in your hometown who wanted to beat you up when you started dating his ex-girlfriend?"

I nodded.

"You told me you went to a party at one of his friend's houses, fucking ballsy and a bit stupid I'd have to say, but you went. Even stupider, you brought his ex who was then your girlfriend—again, what the fuck were you thinking? But you told me when you walked in, there he was, staring you down. The whole party stopped. Duran Duran, if you guys were even cool enough to listen to them, went silent on the stereo. Your girl wanted to leave. And what did you do? You walked right up to the guy and said something like 'I know this is a party for your friends, your school, and at your friend's home. I'm asking for your permission if I can be here. But if you want me gone, I'll leave.'" J.C. sipped his drink. "And you told me he was so shocked you went up to him directly, as were his buddies and everyone else at the party, he felt he had to allow you to stay. He even felt some respect for you—respect for a stupidly overconfident move! But it worked. You humanized the situation. And you went right at the guy. Boom!"

"You remember that story well."

"Fuck yeah, I do. It's ballsy. I love that!" He took another swig. "Now who is the person running point at the SEC?"

"A guy named FED."

"Then go see him. Walk straight up to him and do the same damn thing you did back in high school. Then, explain to him what the real story is. Humanize the issue. Write the back of his Rolodex card out before you meet him. Know everything about him. Find some common ground. Make that connection. Then answer his questions and show your sincerity and honesty." He grabbed a handful of calamari. "Right now, all you are is a name on a page. He's going after an object. A statistic. He's got no point of reference or emotional connection to you."

"Love that you bring up my Rolodex. Classic."

"Fuck yeah. One of the great things I've learned from you. I do it too now."

"Our attorneys will be adamantly against me sitting directly with FED. Not how it's done. My attorneys will freak over it too."

"Who the fuck cares?! You've always been someone to address things directly and head-on. Take them out of the middle and just do it," he suggested, washing down his food with some bourbon.

"So that's solved, what else? What are you going to do about the press? Why is Cieply attacking you?" he asked, referring to Michael Cieply at the *New York Times*.

"He's not. He's just covering the story like everyone else. Both in China and the US. It's an angle that sells papers. We are either China's pawn or manipulating things for co-production status. No in-between. In the US, the press is making it out to seem like we are pandering to China just to make a buck. Communist sympathizer shit. In China, they are making it out like we are trying to trick everyone. The film community thinks we are getting unfair and unwarranted advantages from the government. And the government thinks we pulled one over on them because we promised one thing and are delivering something different," I took another big swig from a new glass of wine. "Then there's the SEC investigation. That's fun to write about, and it gets lots of online clicks and sells papers too."

"Are Disney and Marvel helpful?"

"No."

"So, it's Marvel in one corner and Mao in the other. A battle royale?" he asked.

"All of it is embarrassing to Marvel. And to Disney. They are wondering how they can just get out of this mess, for sure. The extra dollars aren't worth it to them at this point. Too much hassle and the stuff we need in the film for a co-production isn't there. It's a pain in the ass, tough to fit logically into the Marvel Universe. The production timeline is super tight. And, let's face it, some of it seems overly pandering to China. I mean, Feige has been cool through it all, but I know he probably wishes he never agreed to any of it at this point," I explained. "So, yes. Technically you could say it is Marvel versus Mao, and I'm caught smack in the middle of the crossfire."

"Do you believe in what you are doing?"

"Of course I do!"

"Why?"

"If we pull this off, *Iron Man 3* will be the biggest movie ever for Hollywood in China. And, come June, Marvel will be Disney's biggest brand in the market...A global brand too. Immune to issues that flare up between the US and China. Hell, I've already seen the black market for Marvel merchandise disappear. The government has essentially paved the way for Marvel to monetize the market. They don't do that for just anyone. Disney has so much to gain from this too. If we get this done, Marvel will be the most valuable American-made IP for movies in China for sure, and for generations too. Guaranteed. Possibly even consumer products. And, of course, we have lots to gain. From *Iron Man 3* alone, we can make a bundle financially. We'll be the leaders in fostering the bilateral cultural and commercial exchange. In such a position, we'll make billions. We'll be able to take DMG public. It will be insane," I responded. "But honestly, what makes all of this even more important to me is not money-related."

"What is it, then?"

"*Iron Man 3* is bringing the US and China closer together." I took another swig. "Look, the press loves covering the drama of the sausage making. That's for sure. It's the bane of my existence. But some are starting to talk about the benefits of the collaboration too. And leaders of both countries are starting to mention it also. We pull this off, it creates a better bilateral relationship between the superpowers and ultimately makes the world a better place."

"So, you do believe in what you are doing?"

"Fuck yes!"

"Then go say it publicly!" he said, happily grabbing another bourbon from the waitress. "Who can you use as a mouthpiece on this? Cieply?"

"I love him, but I don't think so." I grabbed another glass of Sangiovese and took a big sip. Definitely going to be a taxi night. "To do it right, I'd need someone who would write what I want, but it has to be because they believe it too. It can't look like a plant. It has to be real. Truthful. From the heart. And accurate."

"Well, you can't get a journalist to buy into that unless they know their shit. They have to know the US-China space as well as you—maybe even better. Who is that?"

"Agree. It can't come from a journalist. They'll think I'm spinning a story anyway. I need someone who believes in what I believe. They need to feel good about writing it."

"So, who? Think boy. Think!"

"There's a blogger named Robert Cain that everybody in Hollywood who's dealing with China reads. He's super-educated in this space. A true expert. He's probably the right guy."

"Do you know him?"

"Yes. Pretty well too. Definitely a mutual respect between the two of us."

"Can you get him to believe in what you believe?"

"I think he already does."

"Can you tell him the story you want to be written, and will he see it as the truth and something he'll want to put out as his own opinion? You need him to say the same things you just told me, but for it to resonate, he needs to own it."

"I'm confident he sees it the same way as me. He knows we won't qualify for a co-production now. He has been watching this process the whole time. He understands the Chinese point of view," I explained, finishing my last piece of pizza. "That said, I know he sees the importance of making *Iron Man 3* successful."

"He should write an article saying, 'why the fuck should anyone care about co-production status,' or whatever. The important thing is that the two countries are working together. That's what is important."

"Totally agree. I'm thinking the headline should summarize, 'Will *Iron Man 3* get approval for a co-production at this point? Actually, who the fuck cares!' or something like that, but a bit more tactful," I laughed. "The important thing is that the US and China are collaborating on a massive tentpole movie. The exchange of culture and commerce between the two nations on something like this is beneficial to both superpowers and also the whole fucking world!"

"Now you're talking!"

"And for Hollywood, there's the ticking clock. We either get this done ASAP, or China picks up the pace and does it themselves. We need to get their consumers hooked on our content, or their own film industry will do it with their own stuff, basically knocking Hollywood out of the market forever."

"There you go! Now go get it done!" J.C. exclaimed. "Think of this dinner as the beginning of your third act. Your low point is now behind you," he added, referring to the three-act structure of a motion picture screenplay.

"Love that metaphor, and I definitely love you! I so needed this! Thank you."

"Hungry Like the Wolf! You're the wolf! Make it happen!"

We both finished our drinks and headed out. I was totally invigorated. A smart, aggressive plan was in place. Time to implement it.

30.

JUST DO IT

THE SUNLIGHT OF February 28, 2013 finally started to peek above the horizon of the Los Angeles Basin as I jogged past the clubhouse of Wilshire Country Club. My 5:00 a.m. runs were commonplace since I hadn't had a good night's sleep in weeks. Jennifer wouldn't let me hit the city's streets until the clock crept past 4:59 a.m. for safety concerns. So, most early mornings I'd make China calls, watching Bloomberg Asia in my home office until that time.

That day was particularly stressful, and my eyes were fully open for the day at 1:00 a.m. Two and a half hours of sleep? Not terrible. Could've used more, though. My jog that day was more of a five-mile sprint. Anxiety coursed through every part of my body. I needed desperately to run it off—flight or fight was kicking in. And that morning I was going to meet with the SEC to fight!

I arrived thirty minutes early to a stark white, ground-floor lobby of a discreet building in the mid-Wilshire corridor of Los Angeles where I would meet Big Gun and Pit Bull (both nicknames), DMG's attorneys from one of the priciest law firms in the country. Though a rather large building, it was surely one that you never would've noticed, especially if you weren't looking for it.

Though I wanted to see FED, the SEC's lead investigator, and his team alone to establish person-to-person, human contact, Big Gun and Pit Bull were strongly against it. Even the personal attorneys for Jennifer and me agreed that some legal counsel was necessary.

"Meeting with the SEC is no casual matter. We need to be here to keep you from saying things that can damage our case," they explained upon arrival.

"How can I damage our case, if I did nothing wrong? I'm happy to answer any questions they have. And as transparently as I possibly can."

"It's not as easy as that."

We chatted for a bit more and headed up to the main floor of the Los Angeles bureau of the SEC. The space wasn't very impressive. In fact, it was quite the opposite. There wasn't even someone at reception, as I recall. We had to ring a bell.

"At least they aren't spending taxpayer dollars recklessly," I said.

Big Gun and Pit Bull both chuckled.

A young employee brought us to a small conference room. Though nicer than the Marvel studios conference room where I had fallen off the broken chair, it still wasn't much to brag about. A small coffee pot sat in the corner along with a pitcher of water. A stack of cheap Styrofoam cups stood next to them.

While I was pouring a coffee, FED walked in. Two associates joined him. FED looked to be roughly my age with a slight, yet possibly athletic frame. If anything, he could have been a long-distance runner. He had a nice head of hair and a bit of a big-swinging-dick swagger. His facial expression was all business, and his two associates looked as if they were there simply to take notes and nod.

"Thank you for coming in. Definitely a good gesture, considering the circumstances," he said, sitting down. "Let's please begin. What do you have for us?"

"As discussed, our client thought it would be a good idea to meet face to face. Make a direct connection and answer any questions you may have. He'd also like to give you a bit of an overview of the film business in China," Big Gun explained, almost sounding a bit nervous.

Such a trait seemed unusual given his confidence in most meetings, especially since he was charging $880 per hour to represent us. That said, he knew his stuff. I was pretty confident I was in good hands with him, even though I would've rather done the meeting solo. Things get so stilted when legal teams are around.

"That's all fine and dandy, but you guys owe me a lot of requested material from Beijing. This better not be a waste of time."

"Look, I get we still owe you things from the China side, but I do think there are some misunderstandings here. I think some of it can get cleared up, if I can share with you a quick tutorial on the current state of the film business in China and how it operates," I interrupted, very respectfully. FED's face already wore signs of frustration. I became instantly aware that this was not going to be a friendly meeting.

"I'm a bit confused as to what the purpose of this meeting is. I thought you'd be giving me what I requested. Instead, you came in here to spin me on things I already know about," he huffed. "Am I missing the point here?"

"Yeah. I would like to clear up some misconceptions you might have regarding China," I argued. "And, quite frankly, I wanted to put a face with the name on your investigation. I'd like you to know me a bit."

"Not relevant to me. I know China, and frankly, you and I are very different people. Why would humanizing this make a difference?"

"Well for one, we are both fathers," I said, attempting to break the ice. "I have two five-year-olds. You have a four-year-old. That counts for something, right?"

"Great, you did some research. You should've spent that time getting me requested documents from Beijing."

"Look, FED. Let me please, at least, walk you through some things. I brought in some presentation material too. I just don't think this investigation is completely accurate. Yes, I believe in taking down the bad seeds, but to just blanket the entire industry with an investigation seems wrong."

Big Gun and Pit Bull looked concerned as to where I was going.

"I simply don't believe US studios would put line items in their budgets for officials like Han Sanping. I don't think they would have even put his name on global movie posters if they intended to bribe him or did bribe him. It makes no sense. If you bribe someone, you do it quietly. You don't display it on all the marketing materials for the world to see."

"Han Sanping is a government official. If someone pays him for access to a market, that's something we want to investigate," he explained. "Truthfully, I see this all as a terrible case of pandering to the Chinese by money-hungry Hollywood executives. My gut is that you all will do anything to get access to China's market. It's about money, and it's always going to be about money. China is not our friend, and we should stop this kind of begging and cheating to get to their consumers."

"That attitude, with all due respect, is not good for the country. We have an amazing export here in Hollywood called movies. It's one of the big three American exports we have that the Chinese want. Think about it: real estate, our college education system, and entertainment — which includes Hollywood and our sports industry — are our biggest commodities! For films, China will soon be the biggest marketplace in the world. We are making progress getting Hollywood movies into that market, but if the SEC slows the process down, the Chinese will catch up to us. They will find their own filmmakers to make high-quality, Mandarin-language movies that cater, in a much more relevant way, to their own consumers. If they do that, Hollywood will be shut out. The clock is ticking with regards to monetizing one of our greatest US exports. If that clock expires, the opportunity is lost. The bilateral exchange of the commerce of Hollywood films ends." I took a sip of my coffee, attempting to read him. Nothing. Just a blank and annoyed stare. "If Hollywood's commercial exchange ends, so does the cultural exchange. That exchange fosters a stronger bond with China, the only other global superpower. Without it, the bond breaks down. Is that what you want? To be shut out of the market on the commerce side and to have no cultural exchange? Without those two items, we start a new cold war. Why? Because we already don't agree with them on the other three diplomatic forces—national security, human rights, and politics. It would be a complete breakdown of the five forces of diplomacy. No common ground. No collaboration. No communication. Simply, a new cold war that never, ever ends."

"Nice speech, but also a nice deflection." He paused, attempting to read me too.

"You have to admit. There is some confusion about our laws in China."

"There isn't. It's black and white." FED stated firmly.

"Well, how about during my last Beijing trip when a colleague asked, 'Why is it okay for Congressmen running for president to fly to Las Vegas to meet with Sheldon Adelson so he can cut them checks for millions for their presidential campaigns? That seems like bribery. Doesn't Sheldon want something for those checks?' Of course, I scratch my head on that and say, 'Because it's revealed publicly.' And they respond, 'So was Han Sanping's credit on Sony's movie. It was on the one-sheet.' I paused a moment, attempting to read FED. His associates looked at him for a response. I continued, "I simply don't know how to respond to that stuff. I don't know why Sheldon, or, for that matter, any big donor giving money to an elected official is fine either. And I live in the US! You know those big donors are asking for something in return. They don't just do that for charity's sake. How am I supposed to explain the difference?"

(As a side note—a more recent exchange, related to "Phase One" of the US-China trade deal, between hosts David Faber and Jim Cramer on CNBC's December 17, 2019 broadcast of *Squawk on the Street* offered an example of the confusion around this "what is bribery versus legal financial support for elected officials" issue:

Cramer: …that is one of the things the president was counting on…was that Xi (Jinping) would bless Sheldon Adelson of the Las Vegas Sands. You know that? I used to call it Macau Sands. That's a deal point that the president wants. He wants good news for Las Vegas Sands.

Faber: Because he's [Adelson] such a huge supporter [of President Trump] — Adelson?

Awkward pause.

Cramer: Yeah. That happens.

Faber: I'm just pointing that out.

I understood back in 2013 that Sheldon and others were playing by the rules/laws set forth by US regulators. That was clear due to the public nature of it all. However, when American business journalists seemed disjointed when discussing the topic on the air, it highlighted a lack of clarity. It proved why my Chinese colleagues asked the questions, and why I had to shed light on the issue to FED.)

"The studios are sucking up to China's Communist Party, and some are breaking laws doing it. It's black and white to me. There should be no confusion," He countered. FED's associates looked perplexed, as if they knew he hadn't answered my question. "You want us to back off, then feel free to whistle-blow on some of those 'bad seeds' or hand us over some damning evidence on Han Sanping and his cronies at China Film Group. Without that, we keep this investigation going." He was frustrated.

"Okay. Everyone, let's please just step back," Big Gun intervened, politely. "I'll talk to my client about this whistleblower idea you just threw out there. We'll get back to you on that one. In the meantime, let's please allow Chris to give a quick tutorial. I do think it will be helpful."

"Fine. Go ahead," FED said reluctantly.

I walked him through the business, from the Standing Committee down to the people at China Film Group. I explained revenue splits in the quota system and buyouts. I walked FED through co-productions, from marketing and promotion to scope of distribution to release dates, from films like *Looper* to *Iron Man 3*. And I recited facts from the market size in the early days, to now, and into the future. It was a good hour of material. My attorneys thought it went well, and FED's associates took plenty of notes. FED, however, did not. He was clearly bothered by it all. I wasn't getting through to him. It seemed like a completely lost cause.

And then fate intervened.

"*Beep, Beep, Beep, Beep, Beep,*" an alarm rang. "This is the fire alarm. Everyone in the building, please evacuate down the stairs to your designated evacuation area outside. This is not a test," a recording said over a loudspeaker. It continued to repeat.

"Saved by the bell. Unbelievable." FED said sarcastically. "Follow us."

We all followed FED. It was a bit awkward. If given the chance, he probably would've left us in that conference room to die in the fire. Instead, he begrudgingly had to lead us to safety. He couldn't force us to take our belongings either. That meant we'd still have to go back to the conference room afterwards. Quite ironic and unfortunate for him. Not only did he have to save us, but he was also stuck with us too.

"How'd you like living in South Beach?" I asked.

As we slowly moved down the crowded stairwell, the flood of people around us made it impossible for him to avoid me.

"I'm from Florida originally myself."

"Didn't like it. Too hot." He was blunt.

"You like living in Glendale? I trained up there for six months at the ATF Citizens Academy. I had a blast doing it. An amazing federal program," I said, referring to a twelve-week program for civilians that the Bureau of Alcohol, Tobacco, Firearms and Explosives sponsors each year.

"Yeah, those guys do a lot more than just track firearms."

"Nice part of Los Angeles too—Glendale. Sprucing up that downtown area."

"It's okay. Affordable," he responded bluntly.

I was trying to make conversation any way I could.

"Saw that blog post about your experience on paternity leave. Pretty cool how you took it and enjoyed it and even wrote about it. Lots of guys don't, they're too chauvinistic. Their loss. The kid experience is only once or twice in a lifetime, right? Your job offers you the ability to spend more time with your newborn, you should embrace it."

"Yeah, too bad for those chauvinistic guys, I guess. I'm glad I did it." He was clearly bothered by the small talk. "You obviously did your homework." He paused a second. "I'll give you one—I once had a buddy named Chris Fenton. How 'bout them apples?"

"That's good. Well done. Chris must have been a super cool guy."

"He was okay."

"By the way, I read your anti-Wall Street bailout blog."

He turned to look at me and stopped walking. People behind us on the stairs had to stop their descent too.

"What about it?"

"I agree with it. I'm a believer in capitalism and free markets. Let failure happen to those who deserve it. It prevents speculative risk-taking down the road. Cleanses the markets," I responded.

I caught his attention. We started walking again.

"The bailouts rewarded those who should've failed. Makes the banks think they are too big to fail, so it promotes the same terrible speculation all over again," I added.

"Amen! I'm with you there," he responded, looking me straight in the eyes. "Probably easy for you rich Hollywood guys flush with Chinese money to take that position, though. Letting the markets fail. No bailouts." He looked away, continuing down the stairs. "Wouldn't have hurt you much. Crushes everybody else, though."

We finally made it to an exit door. When we walked outside, I grabbed his shoulder gently. I turned him towards me, looking him straight in the eyes.

"FED, with all due respect, you are one hundred percent wrong. My wife and I lost everything in 2008 when Lehman went under. Every dollar in our retirement accounts and portfolios went *poof!*"

"Ah, the one bank allowed to go under got you good. I'm sorry. But did you have gambles you shouldn't have had?"

"If you call UBS structured notes aligned with the indexes a gamble, then I guess so. Personally, I was told they were conservative investment vehicles," I responded a tad sarcastically.

"Wow. I am sorry. Really sorry. Those shouldn't have done that."

"Yup! I can't even begin to tell you how traumatizing that experience was for my wife and me. I remember where I was standing when I got the phone call from my broker, and I remember my wife's exact face when I told her. And, I'm still not over it. Nor is she. We're still pissed and feel super victimized. It deeply affected the way I view the world now."

"And you're still anti-bailout?"

"Of course I am."

We found a quiet corner. Big Gun and Pit Bull started to walk over, but I waved them off.

"Those terrible times will happen again on Wall Street. But next time, it will be even worse. Without failure and punishment, no lessons are learned, and the same behavior continues."

"Agree. You and I see eye-to-eye on that. I'm concerned about the moral hazard we created. No one was punished for taking risks. Everyone was bailed out."

"Middle class wasn't. They lost homes. Jobs. Everything." I shook my head. "No one on Wall Street went to jail. A total shame."

"Madoff did."

"He ripped off the rich and powerful. That's the only reason. If he ripped off Scandinavian pension funds, farmers, or subprime middle-class borrowers, you and I both know he'd still be living large on Park Avenue and Worth Avenue."

"You're probably right." He took a beat, gathering his thoughts. "Listen, you guys need to get us what we asked for. That's key. Get your Beijing people to cooperate. How it plays from there...well...it could be easy. If you truly have nothing to hide."

"We have nothing to hide," I said confidently.

"Good, then. I'm trying to catch the bad guys."

"I'm not one of those."

"You don't seem like it," he said. "Just get me what I need."

"Please know this investigation is crushing our business. Yes, we have *Iron Man 3*, but that's because we're already deep into it. If Disney and Marvel had their way, they'd kick us to the curb. Everyone who matters knows we are under investigation."

"I get it."

"And for China, this whole investigation is super embarrassing and insulting. Causing a loss of face to the world's only other super-power is not a positive."

"I'll agree to disagree that China is a superpower. I do think they are corrupt over there too. Not everyone, but some of them. But point well taken."

People already started walking towards the stairwell again. Looked like the "all clear" was given.

"And don't worry. You'll always have a job. The US studios aren't going to give up on China because of the SEC. And the Chinese won't stop loving Hollywood because of the SEC either," he added.

"I hope you're right."

"I am. You'll be fine," he responded. "Look. Everyone is heading back in. Let's go."

He walked ahead rather briskly. I followed.

A hand grabbed my shoulder from behind. It was Big Gun.

"What did you guys talk about?" he asked.

"I think we bonded. At least a little. We covered a bunch of areas. Some related to the SEC issue. Some not. It seemed to go okay. Felt beneficial."

"What should we cover when we get back to the conference room?" Pit Bull asked.

"I think we're good. Let's just grab our things and go. We have some work to do still. But the human connection may have helped our cause today. At least I hope," I replied. "I need Beijing to cooperate. We need to get FED the documents he requested. Then maybe, just maybe, this dark cloud comes to an eventual end."

I could only hope.

"Hello, this is Robert," a voice said.

"Robert Cain, this is Chris Fenton."

"Hey, Chris. How are you? I've been reading lots about *Iron Man 3*. Almost there!"

"It is. Thank goodness too. The press on both sides of the Pacific has been super tough on us. The governments also. Usually, it's just the Chinese government you have to worry about, but in this case, we have the SEC all over our backs too!"

"Yeah, it's pretty terrible," he said. "You guys are doing something very historic and positive for the bilateral relationship. In my opinion, everyone should be supporting your efforts on *Iron Man 3*. So much to gain for all sides."

"That's actually why I'm calling. I have a question for you."

"Ask away."

"Do you truly believe *Iron Man 3* is an important project? And if it succeeds, it fulfills a higher calling beyond just making a few bucks for the players involved?"

"Absolutely!" He didn't blink. "The commerce is just a positive side effect."

"Thought that's how you felt. Love that!" I took a breath. "So, I was wondering if I could ask you to write an op-ed for your blog. With *Iron Man 3* as the subject?"

"Maybe," he responded. "What's the angle of the piece?"

"Will *Iron Man 3* get China co-production status, and does it really matter?"

"Interesting hook. I have heard lots of conflicting news about the co-production status," he responded. "What is the story on that?"

"It doesn't matter. Am I allowed to say that?"

"It depends."

"The US and China are collaborating on a massive global film. That's what matters. That is happening." I said with conviction. "What label the film receives is not as important. Journalists should stop caring because the bilateral benefits are already set. They are for sure real, and we all win."

"I love that. And it's true. Hmmm." He took a moment, gathering his thoughts. "No matter what, the bilateral cultural and commercial exchange that *Iron Man 3* fosters is positive, regardless of the box-office results or the designation it receives in China. That's good for the world," he said, thinking out loud. "The world's two superpowers glued closer together by Iron Man himself."

"Through Film Diplomacy. An extremely beneficial Marvel and Mao Effect on the bilateral relationship."

"Exactly," he agreed. "I can run something like that. Let's write it together."

"I'd love to, but only on background and off-the-record. At least for now. Dan is happy to chat with you directly about it too, but the goal is to have Marvel, Disney, CFG, and SARFT all read your piece, thinking, 'Wow, that's a great article with the perfect angle and so darn timely! How lucky are we!'" I let that sink in. "After the movie opens, it won't matter. We're happy to let everyone know. But until then, mum's the word. Make sense?"

"Definitely."

"And do you think you can get the *Wall Street Journal* to pick up your piece after the fact? Perhaps add their own color to it? They tend to like your blog posts." I asked in hopes of planting a seed.

"I think that could work."

"Your blog would hit the important niche audience. The *Wall Street Journal* can then take your op-ed, add color and more detail, then blast it globally." I waited for a beat. "Pipe dream, or doable?"

"Doable. They just need to think it's newsworthy."

"The *Journal* has been covering *Iron Man 3* very closely. I think you just need to post the piece. Assuming you write what I think you'll write, my gut tells me that they'll think it's newsworthy."

"Please send me what you've got. It needs to be strong with a point of view that really resonates. I'll tweak it in my voice, thoughts, opinion, and so on. It needs to sound like me, not Chris Fenton. But we do see this all pretty much the same way. Cool?"

"Done. Emailing now! Despite all the noise, obstacles, and critics, I truly believe we are making the world a better place. We are keeping the superpowers bonded through two of the five forces of diplomacy — the exchange of culture and commerce. On behalf of DMG, China, the US, Disney, Marvel, my family, and all the fans of the IRON MAN franchise, thank you."

Robert's op-ed posted on his blog, *China Film Biz*, March 7, 2013:

Will 'Iron Man 3' Get China Co-Pro Status, and Does it Really Matter? Most of the Co-Pro Benefits Have Come Already

Throughout the piece, Robert detailed with great precision the most important aspects of what we discussed. But, as any good journalist should, he covered a handful of additional items and also offered a few slight critiques. Neither of us wanted it to look like a press release, and it didn't read like one.

I particularly loved how it ended. His strong complimentary description of benefits due to Disney and Marvel for their successful execution of such an innovative strategy, subtly, in almost a behind-the-back kind of way, praised DMG's efforts. A smile stretched from ear to ear when I finished his piece:

> For Disney and Marvel theatrical revenue is only a small part of a bigger picture that includes their interests in the Shanghai theme park and their consumer products business in China, both of which I expect will benefit nicely from the exposure and interest they've generated in the Iron Man franchise. This is exactly the sort of hustle and outside-the-box thinking that are required to ride the China wave. If Disney keeps up this level of focus and commitment to the market, this could be the year they win bragging rights as the top-grossing U.S. studio in China.

The *Wall Street Journal* followed Cain's blog post with its own version the very next day:

'Iron Man 3' Blasts Away at
China Co-Production Myth
Mar 8, 2013

Written by senior staff writer Laurie Burkitt, the article reiterated much of what was important in Robert's piece. However, having such praise blasted out to the world from the *Journal* made it especially satisfying. And her additional commentary only reinforced the magic of what we were starting to actually accomplish:

> The creators of Iron Man hope to win everyone over, so they've avoided over-playing any China plot for an easy entry into the market, said Mr. Cain. At the same time, producers have kept

things friendly with China by shooting scenes in the country and featuring Chinese stars Wang Xueqi and Fan Bingbing next to Hollywood stars Robert Downey Jr. and Gwyneth Paltrow.

The film is already getting big play in China, where officials have allowed studios to promote the film for the past year. Typically foreign studios are only allowed to promote their films in China a few weeks prior to the their [*sic*] release, Mr. Cain said, noting that "Iron Man 3" may even be released in China first [before the rest of the world].

31.

THE TIDE IS TURNING

"**SPOKE TO THE** gang at Marvel. They love Cain's piece and the article in the *Journal*! They think the gods have intervened! Little do they know, the gods had lots of help," I craftily said to Mike Chambers, the head of DMG's corporate communications, on the night of March 8. "Marvel's publicist even said, and I quote, 'Even though it caught us off guard, the Robert Cain blog happened to be exactly how we would've wanted to say it ourselves. We were very lucky.'"

"Indeed. Brilliant!"

"Then they tried to take credit for the *Wall Street Journal* piece. Whatever. The bottom line is our highly constructive messaging strategy worked. It relieved some pressure. And journalists now are pursuing a more positive narrative around everything."

"Agree," Mike said with a sigh of relief.

"All it took was my epic wife giving me a pep talk and then some brainstorming with the great J.C. Spink. I'm feeling the tide turn!"

"Everyone raves about Jennifer. Need to meet her and this J.C. guy someday when I come through LA."

"I'll make that happen," I said. "And Cain really delivered too. Love that guy. He believes in what we are doing and wanted to support it. He is with us a hundred percent."

"His op-ed was right on the mark. Burkitt's [the *Wall Street Journal* reporter] piece helped too. Very well respected, and she knows her stuff." He paused a beat. "And by the way, Billy [Neo — Beijing-based DMG VP] told you that the China cut passed censorship, right? I heard only one change is needed."

"Yeah. Amazing news! Billy emailed me last night," I responded. "Now we need to be ahead of the news regarding the two film cuts. No reporters are asking as of now. But if they do, and if they think it's a story…will we be okay to disclose this with *Looper*-like spin?"

"Don't know. I need to ask the team and Dan. Not sure how they are alerting CFG."

"Let's hope it's a non-story, but in this climate, you never know," I said. "Let's also keep the positive vibes out there that this turn of good news continues!"

"Your lips to God's ears!"

"No kidding."

"I got good news. Raining and pouring, baby," I said to Andy Anderson, our jack-of-all-trades executive in Beijing. "Can you connect Chambers with us?"

"Good news? Say it isn't so!" Andy responded, sarcastically. "Hang on. Mike is right next to me."

A moment passed.

"I'm here," Mike said. "What's up?"

"Guys, I just got word from Robert's [Downey Jr.] people that he's in. He's going to come to Beijing for the premiere!"

"Holy shit! That's insanely great news!" Andy exclaimed.

"No kidding! On a roll!" Mike added. "But what's the catch?"

"Hah, yeah! Too many years working in China, Mike. There's always a catch," I said, knowing there was one. "His schedule isn't optimal. That's the catch."

"Okay. Meaning what?"

"He needs to come to Beijing four weeks before the movie opens. We won't even have a finished cut of the film to show then."

I waited for that to settle in.

"Even worse, I'll have to miss my wife's thirty-fifth birthday!" I added, half-joking.

"Oh, and we're also out of coffee!" Andy laughed, quoting a line from *Airplane*.

"I'd rather the Communist Party be pissed at me than my wife. I haven't told Jennifer yet. Dreading that."

"Well, not sure how you play that one out, I feel for you, but we'll make the early premiere work," Andy responded, laughing.

"That's the spirit! I mean, do we even want attendees spending two-plus hours watching the movie if we have Robert there in person? We should take full advantage of that!"

"Agree," Mike said. "What about the additional 'shout-outs' to complement the *Iron Man 3* promotion on the Chinese New Year CCTV Gala show?"

"What did you tell me to tell them?" I asked, testing.

"Just as the *Wall Street Journal* article mentioned, the Gala is the most-watched television program in China every year. Hundreds of millions tune in. It's the greatest promotional platform in China for absolutely anything. The government has never allowed anything American on the show, especially a Hollywood blockbuster film. The opportunity is both historic and an absolute must. It's China's Super Bowl, and we must continue the promotional momentum from it," Mike responded.

"Well, good thing I told Robert's reps the same thing. I pitched the new shout-outs. He and Wang together on camera."

"And?"

"He'll do it! Robert is in!"

"Boy, do I love that guy," Andy said with an obvious smile on his face you could feel across the world.

"No kidding. That guy is beyond awesome!"

"He sure knows what he needs to do to make his brand successful. The guy is not only a great actor, but he's also a true businessman. We are very fortunate."

"I'm loving this. Please get us the rest of the specifics. We'll get to work," Mike said.

"I'll get you the scripts for Robert. They mainly have him thanking the Chinese for their support, revealing that he's coming to Beijing, and an obvious calling-to-action to see the film in May. Super simple," added Andy.

"Indeed!" I was about to hang up. "Oh, and one other thing. The United States Congress invited us, along with Disney and Marvel, to screen the film at the Capitol Visitor Center in Washington DC for members of the House and Senate!"

"Holy shit!"

"That's incredible. What's the essence of the event?" Mike asked.

"'An educational and cultural evening in Washington DC to tell the unique story of the co-production of *Iron Man 3*. This film is a prime example of how US-China collaboration can facilitate the implementation of the 2012 agreement reached at the highest levels of the US and Chinese leadership to significantly increase Chinese market access for US movies,' is how they phrased it on the invitation."

"Crazy how many eyes are watching us," Mike responded. "Such an amazing story. And think of how much headbutting both sides have been doing to each other through this!"

"Totally agree. I told J.C. it has been Marvel versus Mao for more than a year, with us caught right in the crossfire."

"No shit. So true," Mike agreed.

"We still have lots of work to do to get to our Hollywood ending on this," Andy added.

"Yup. No celebrating until opening day. When we break records! Until then, let's keep our heads down and get the work done," I recommended.

"Amen."

I hung up. I smiled, picking up a miniature Iron Man on my desk.

"Maybe this will all work out...Iron Man may save the day after all!"

"First off, thank you, thank you, thank you."

"What for?" Brad Winderbaum asked over the phone.

"For getting Doctor Wu back in the global cut of the movie. Even if it's a tiny little role, it's something. It saved our asses!"

"Anything for you, Chris!" He laughed, knowing I'd been on the short end of many sticks over the past year. "So, what do you need Kevin [Feige] to say? Hope it's not too aggressive!"

"'It was an amazing experience working with the tremendously talented actor Wang Xueqi. Marvel is thrilled to have his Chinese fans see their favorite male star in his first Marvel film, and we are very excited to introduce him to the international audience. We hope to use him in other Marvel films, and we definitely expect Hollywood to utilize his talents as a leading man for many years to come,'" I read over the phone. I waited for a beat. "What do you think?"

"What's the quote for Fan Bingbing?"

"'It was exciting to have Fan Bingbing partake in our *IM3* China efforts. What an amazing talent! Marvel definitely hopes to use her in future Marvel films, and we definitely expect Hollywood to chase her for the biggest roles in the best films long into the future.'"

"Those are pretty hardcore," he responded. "You need those quotes to be from Kevin?"

"Yeah. We need this for both marketing and promotional purposes, as well as the government. The quotes will be used quite a bit for the Beijing premiere. I'm leaving next week for it."

"Hmmm."

"Look, I know you have Kevin's ear, so I figured I'd run this by you first," I explained. "These shout-outs for *Iron Man 3*'s Chinese stars are a smart and necessary way of being both respectful and diplomatic to the massive fanbases and China as a whole. Like I mentioned to Galluzzi, the NBA does the same thing when praising Chinese pro basketball players and their local basketball industry. China has tremendous pride in their local heroes, both athletes and celebrities. There is honor in their local cultural industries too. Whether it's the CBA or their own local film industry, this plays into that. The NBA receives goodwill in return, and so will we. Goodwill equals *big* revenues."

"Understood. And what are the other talking points you mentioned the other day?"

"One, *Iron Man 3* is a collaboration between the US and global studio entities, Disney and Marvel respectively, and the Chinese studio entity DMG. This means China has creative, financial, and physical production involvement, as well as a handle in marketing and distribution. Two, Wang Xueqi will be seen around the world as Doctor Wu, but a China cut includes footage with a special appearance by Fan Bingbing that no one else in the world will be able to see. We expect people to fly in from other parts of the world to see these scenes. And three, even though we initially pushed for co-production status, strict time constraints forced us to shorten the production schedule, which hindered us from meeting some key requirements for co-pro approval. We are now focused on collaborating with our vital Chinese partners to make the best movie possible for the global audience."

"A lot to digest. Not promising anything. Email them to me. I'll talk to the PR team and Kevin," Brad said, pausing for a quick beat to gather his thoughts. "You guys are really impressive...gutsy too. I have no idea how you can stomach some of the stuff you have to do to please China."

That was Brad's way of saying we were feeding the dragon. No doubt about that.

"The game has its rules, and we're just following them. If we play it right, it's good for everyone." I responded. "Thank you for running it up the flagpole."

Brad was about to hang up.

"Oh, and one other thing."

"What?" he asked.

"The Iron Man glove that Robert wore at Comic-Con."

"Yeah?"

"Can we have it? I'd like to take it with me when I go next week."

"Why?"

"Some government officials want to put it on, apparently. Take pictures with it. That kind of stuff."

"We already shipped you a life-size Iron Man statue for that. Now you want the glove?" He waited for an answer. "You're kidding, right?"

"I'm not. Please see what you can do."

"You guys are nuts," he said, laughing.

"I guess we are," I responded, hanging up.

We definitely were. We had to be crazy to get the job done.

32.

CRESCENDO

"**I'M SO SORRY** I'm missing your thirty-fifth birthday."

"Chris, it's ok. We'll celebrate it when you get back," Jennifer said.

I grabbed my bags from the trunk of our car, placing them on the curb.

"It still makes me sad. You've been so amazing during this whole experience." I hugged her tightly. "To miss such a big day. It doesn't feel right."

"You are going to China to make history, again. How many people get to do that once? Think about that. And you get to do it over and over. Take pride in that."

She was my rock.

"I'm so proud of you. And so are the kids," she added, not skipping a beat. "You worked your ass off to get here. Overcame some serious challenges. Feel good about it. Soak it in."

"I appreciate it. I really do. I'm going to miss you guys so much."

"We will too. But we know all that you've had to do to get here, so we'll be cheering for you from across the ocean." She kissed me. Then she looked me straight in the eyes. "Probing journalists, insecure Disney China execs, SEC investigation, Chinese government influence, Downey getting hurt and shutting down production, Shane Black's comments at Comic-Con, co-production or not, terrible weather for

246

Beijing production, Chinese actors getting cut from the footage, forced infomercials, two film cuts…"

"I know. It's insane we are here. Alive and kicking."

"Enjoy the moment!"

"I will. Promise." I hugged her again tightly, my eyes welling up a bit. "I'm heading off to China for that country's biggest premiere with the biggest star ever! It's surreal."

"It truly is. Be proud."

"I'm so happy my parents will be there to see it. I wish you could too!"

"Someone needs to hold down the fort while you're gone."

Our embrace ended. She looked at me.

I love her so much.

"I got to go."

"You do."

"I love you and I'm proud of you. Have an amazing, magical, wonderful, exciting, fresh, fun, successful, safe, happy, healthy, awesome, awesome, awesome week while I'm gone," I said, stating a slightly altered version of something we say to each other every day.

"I love you and I'm proud of you. Have an amazing, magical, wonderful, exciting, fresh, fun, successful, safe, happy, healthy, awesome, awesome, awesome week while I'm holding down the fort," she repeated to me.

"Wish me luck."

"Good luck and safe travels."

"And I wish you luck," I said, grabbing my bags. "See you really soon."

"Go make some history!"

"We will!"

The initial *Iron Man 3* press event in the ballroom of Beijing's Grand Hyatt went better than we could have hoped. Robert Downey Jr. was the ultimate showman. Adoring fans and fawning Chinese journalists were entertained beyond their wildest imaginations. He stepped up, and the feedback from all those who attended was super encouraging. Strong, positive buzz exploded around the film as a result. And we were just getting started!

I ran back to my room and changed out of my suit. I needed to check on preparations at the Forbidden City, the location of the premiere that night. *Iron Man 3*'s premiere was only hours away. I rushed downstairs to catch my car. Not a moment to waste, especially given Beijing traffic.

"Get the red carpet ready. Robert will be here in five minutes. It's game time."

33.

THE CLIMAX: ROLL SOUND. ROLL CAMERA. MARKER. ACTION!

APRIL 6, 2013, THE RED CARPET BEGINS
BEIJING, CHINA

THREE BLACK AUDIS arrived. The few qualified security personnel on-site were helping to move hundreds of curious onlookers standing in the way as the cars crawled forward. Andy Anderson and I ran over to greet Robert and his team. Billy Neo joined.

I peered into the first Audi. The windows were so tinted you couldn't see inside.

"Middle Car. He's in the middle," Dave said.

We darted to the middle car. I tapped on a rear window. It rolled down. Robert was looking right at me.

"Ready to go?" he asked.

"Ready if you are."

"Great. Let's do this."

Dave came over with his security detail and opened the door for Robert. Robert got out looking like the movie star he is.

An explosion of crowd noise erupted. Screams. Yelling. Insanity. Everyone there started to rush towards the entrance of the red carpet.

"Wow! This is quite a party!" Robert yelled, looking around. "What a setting! Look at this!"

"Robert, please remember the safety protocol we're following tonight," Dave stressed.

"Yeah. Yeah. Yeah. I got ya." Robert didn't look the least bit concerned. "This is China, baby! How bad can it be?!"

He ran over to the frenzied crowd and started shaking hands. People went nuts, shouting his name, pushing and shoving, climbing over the barricades, shoving anything they could to have him sign, taking selfies, shooting photos, you name it. It was pandemonium.

While watching him closely, I attempted to instruct a few of our *Reservoir Dogs*-black-suit-wearing farmers to work as shields. Suddenly, a shadow dropped from above.

"Guys, what the fuck did I tell you about the trees? You need to remove those people. Now!" Dave shouted.

The "shadow" was an overly passionate fan who jumped down into the crowd below to get a closer look at Robert. His falling body took out at least three people. It caused several others to fall over in the commotion. It was hard to tell if everyone was okay, but no one seemed to care.

"Hey. Hey. Hey. Everyone, please be civil. There's plenty of me to go around," Robert quipped.

"Kirby, please get some guys over here to clear the trees," I demanded respectfully. "We don't need Dave pulling the plug again."

"Agree. I'm trying." The sweat on his forehead was so abundant it looked as if he had somehow gone for a dip in the frozen moat surrounding the Forbidden City.

"Guys, if this starts to get out of control, we will need to do a human shield," Dave shouted. "Andy, do you have someone who can help organize a few of our farmer friends to join?"

"On it, Dave."

"Billy, where do you want Robert to go?" Robert's publicist, Allison Garman, shouted.

That night Billy was working as our red-carpet coordinator.

"We need to move this along."

"I need him to interact with most of these people. Super important that the press witnesses that," Billy shouted back.

"That will take too long."

"I'm loving this!" Robert said. "Not a problem! I'm here as long as you need me. These fans are great!"

"They are loving you too!" I yelled.

"What a rush!" Robert yelled. "I love you, China!"

Over the course of thirty minutes, he worked his way through the fan portion of the red carpet. Next step: the press portion. There was a small gap between the two segments, and it lacked proper security fencing and barricades. The awkward layout of the area made it an impossible problem to solve.

"Guys, get over here. Let's build a human shield around Robert," Dave shouted.

I joined Billy, Andy, Kirby, Dave, Allison, five farmers, and two of Dave's direct detail in forming a human wall around Robert. We had to get him roughly fifty yards to the press line. It seemed straightforward, except for the massive crowd starting to encroach on us on all sides.

"This is pretty crazy, guys!" Robert shouted, watching this all happen around him. He wasn't at all concerned, though.

"Hang in there, Robert. Just need to get you a little way further," I said.

"Holy shit!" Dave yelled.

A shadow fell from a tree. The object landed squarely on both Dave and Kirby, knocking Kirby over. Dave, however, being built like a Jason Statham-esque brick truck didn't even flinch. He grabbed the shadow off of Kirby. He ripped the shadow towards his terrifying face of fury and stared squarely into the shadow's eyes.

The shadow was a stick-thin Downey-crazed Chinese man.

"*Robert!*" the man yelled in a Chinese accent.

"Get the fuck out of here!" Dave yelled back, throwing him through the air and into a deep trench behind the red carpet.

Andy and I looked at each other, scared that Dave may have just killed a Chinese fan. I ran over to check. The guy appeared to hit the bottom of the pit. He bounced, literally bounced back on his feet. The extremely slender, injured man then dashed away. I looked around at the crowd. Not a single person noticed. Not one. All eyes were on Robert.

"That could've been bad," I said to Andy as we finally ushered Robert to the press line.

"That was fucking crazy!"

"Boys, that was one bizarre way to pep me up for some press interviews! Throwing people at me from trees! Well done!" Robert yelled, running straight towards the shouting reporters.

"He's pumped up!" I said.

"Yeah, he's killing it. This is so great!" Billy said, running along with Allison to catch up with Robert.

I hurried over to join also. All the big Chinese platforms, broadcast networks, press outlets—you name it—were there. And Robert, being the consummate showman, made sure he gave time for every single one of them. I watched Robert do his thing for a good forty-five minutes.

Intermittently I forced myself between overzealous photographers, journalists, and fans who encroached too closely upon him at times. Dave was on his game though, orchestrating the most competent of our hapless, overdressed farmers to work, almost seamlessly, with his own men. Fans were right behind us and all around us.

The massive physicality and tremendously large quantity of farmers were a big reason why we could continue with the event, given the constant security breaches by the ravenous crowd. Dave smartly placed them together, interlocking arms, creating a wall. Like posts placed only inches from each other on a fence, with each post being a good six to seven feet tall. The farmers got more secure with their role as the night wore on. Some got so good at handling unruly fans, I noticed the few competent Chinese security personnel scouting them as new employees. Too bad for the herds of sheep back home. Some of those guys were destined for the big city life very soon!

"Billy, look at the time," I yelled, pointing to my watch.

"I know." He looked towards Allison. "Time to shake hands with government officials and take pictures with DMG's founders and the Disney executives. We also need Robert photographed by the *Iron Man* Audi and the Audi executives."

Allison was supportive of it all. Robert was having fun, so she was happy too.

"Final item before the show starts will be the big celebrity group shot. Robert with all the Chinese stars who are doing the show with him. That will be on front pages everywhere!"

"Okay. Lead the way."

"Robert, follow me!" I placed my hand on his shoulder. "Sorry, everyone. We need to take Robert to the next section," I said to the journalists clamoring for more.

"I'll follow you. I'm dying to see what's behind those massive gates!" Robert shouted while fist-bumping the outstretched hands of a few remaining journalists.

We walked Robert to the gates. Andy and several other colleagues opened them, creating the ultimate reveal.

"Check that out, Robert!" Andy exclaimed.

"Oh my! You guys really know how to throw a party!" Robert proclaimed, looking up at the enormous ancient temple. It danced majestically in the spectacular lighting Kirby had perfected earlier. The stage, now defined by brilliant runway lights along its floor which were complemented by a magical mix of lights from above, was a showman's dream. Vivid colors of red first, then green, then yellow, then purple, then pink, and then mixtures of them all, alternated along the walls of China's famous temple.

"I need to get up on that stage—now!" Robert exclaimed. He was licking his chops.

"Just a few more items before the show starts," I said. "This way, please."

We led him to the receiving line of government officials. DMG's founders, Dan, Peter, and Bing, were there to make formal introductions. The awaiting officials beamed with excitement. Most had no idea whom Robert was, but each person was well aware of his massive global celebrity power. Their collective pride at Robert being in their country was clearly evident. Hollywood had put China on the world's stage that night.

"The stage and setting are really spectacular. I've done many of these over the years, but this is the greatest I've ever seen," Allison whispered to me as we walked briskly to the greeting line.

You name the government entity and they were all there. CFG, SARFT, Ministry of Propaganda, the Film Bureau, Beijing Municipal Government, various CCP members, CCTV networks, all of them. Everyone who mattered was at this premiere.

In Jamie Bryan's *Fast Company* article, he quoted a top agent at Creative Artists Agency: "Let's put it this way...the Chinese market is driven by relationships, and the relationships that Dan and his firm don't have are probably the only ones you don't need."

Nothing exemplified that quote more than the scene inside of the Forbidden City that evening. Everyone who mattered was in attendance. Those who didn't weren't.

I stepped back in amazement, watching the next thirty minutes from afar. I wanted to soak it all in, similar to how I remembered Jennifer and I did at our wedding reception, stepping back into a quiet corner of the hotel ballroom. Those few moments as spectators, rather than participants, created a very special memory for us both. Though it also etched a hard-to-forget visual of J.C. removing his shirt to maximize his dance groove to OutKast's song "Hey Ya!"

I also found my parents, who had flown in for the event. It was so great for them to see it all. They were amazing sports about it too. The frenzy around all of the planning and execution left me very little time to spend with them. They completely understood.

Kyle Ching, the executive overseeing our army of photographers, walked up to say hello. He looked exhausted yet energized.

"Kyle, please make sure we get several fantastic photos showing the massive size and scope of this event. Not sure how to get it in a single picture, but we need to," I said.

"Not a problem. Guys are posted there. There. And there." He pointed. "We have every lens possible too."

"Photos will circle the globe tonight, so they need to be epic!"

"Roger that."

"A picture speaks a thousand words. Your guys shoot this right, we'll have ones that speak a billion."

"Mom and Dad proud?" he asked my parents.

"Yes, we are," my mom responded.

"So cute!" he said. "Sorry we had Chris tied up so much. You get any time together?"

"Barely. I was able to take them to Xi He Ya Ju in Ritan Park."

"Great spot. Amazing food," my dad said. "By the way, what's with all the basketball players on the red carpet?"

Kyle and I laughed.

"Those are farmers from the burbs," Kyle responded. "Just big guys who typically herd sheep, but tonight they're helping keep the crowds in line. What made you think they were basketball players?"

"For one, they are tall!" my dad responded. "And China seems pretty basketball-crazy overall."

"Ha! DMG helped create that love for basketball," Kyle said. "We've done lots of basketball stuff over the years."

"Yeah, well now it's going to be all Marvel, all the time," I joked.

"Don't forget Mao," Kyle said. "He ain't going anywhere!"

We all laughed.

"So true. And it took a while to get Marvel and Mao on the same page," I said. "Exhausting."

"Yeah, a serious street brawl at times," Kyle agreed. "But look around us tonight. Marvel and Mao are allies!"

"Yup! Once enemies, now united!" I exclaimed. "I'd say we've been *feeding the dragon* pretty darn nicely to this point...so now it's finally time for the dragon to feed us in return."

"That's for sure. Lots of goodwill. I think we paid our dues and then some," Kyle said.

"Billions on the line...maybe even trillions, if we're successful and others follow our lead!"

"It's an amazing accomplishment," my dad said.

"You all should be very proud of yourselves," my mom added.

"Let's wait till this film breaks all the records first," Kyle warned.

"No kidding. From your lips to God's ears!" I agreed.

"Gotta run," Kyle said.

"Me too." I looked at my parents. "I'll see you after the show."

"Sounds good."

I ran back to Robert and the team. He had just completed the receiving line introductions, photos, and all the schmoozing. Though exhausted, he plugged along as if he had the energy of a teenager hopped up on Red Bulls. We guided Robert and his entourage back-stage, putting him beneath the stage at his mark. He stood on a platform that would elevate him to stage level. He changed into some traditional Chinese clothing and gathered his thoughts for a beat. Shortly there-after, he gave me a thumbs up.

"It's *go* time," Kirby said, barking Mandarin into his headset. "Is he ready?"

I nodded.

Kirby barked again. Gave the thumbs up.

"Break a leg, Robert. Teleprompter on stage right and left and behind the crowd on left, middle, and right. You can't miss them." I said.

"Rock and Roll!" He grinned.

"Have fun!" I yelled as the platform elevated from underneath the stage.

Watching from below, I saw him ascend into the spotlight. The crowd went nuts!

"*Ni Hao!*"

Thunderous applause. He waited for a beat for it to settle.

"I'd like to thank the state for allowing this unprecedented access to the Forbidden City. Would you look at this? *Wow!*"

Applause.

Robert continued, "I'd like to thank our sponsors Audi and TCL for taking such good care of us. I'd like to thank my friends at DMG for ushering in a new era of international entertainment partnerships. Lastly, I am happy with your various artist impressions on the Iron Man suits."

Applause.

"Importing culture to China is like bringing sand to the beach. I'm a longtime student of your spiritual principles, traditional Eastern medicine, martial arts, and a huge fan of your movies. While I'm humbled to be here as a traveling salesman and tourist, I must admit, back home my nickname is 'Box Office Emperor.'"

Massive applause.

"All kidding aside, I'm astounded to be in this most glorious setting of the Forbidden City! I wonder what it must have been like in its day. One can only wonder." After a long and appropriate pause, Robert then announced to the crowd, "Without further ado, let this amazing *Iron Man 3* variety show of sorts begin!"

Everyone went crazy. And then for the full ninety minutes of the show, the crowd remained on its feet, loving every minute of it. The nationally broadcasted *Iron Man 3* premiere entertained everyone at home watching too. It delivered both as an amazing spectacle and a powerful promotional vehicle for the movie—a ten out of ten in every category.

When it came to a final close, Robert, still incredibly energized from the massive amounts of on-stage adrenaline, walked off stage. The crowd roared behind him. Kyle and his team of cameramen rushed to catch his final words.

Dan was the first to greet Robert as he descended towards us. The thunderous applause still deafening. Every camera light blasted on him, capturing his backstage arrival from multiple angles.

"So, Robert, what did you think of that?" I shouted.

In the mayhem, my parents, fortunately, found us all. They walked behind me, sharing in the moment too.

"DMG knows how to throw one heck of a party! That was insanely fun!" Robert shouted directly into our main camera.

He turned to Dan, putting his arms around him.

"Wow! All I can say is wow!"

Dan and I caught each other's eyes.

"Good job!" he yelled to me.

I nodded.

The two of them then walked towards a row of Audis waiting to whisk Robert and his entourage off. Dan, Peter, and Bing shook hands with Robert one final time and waved him off.

"Chris, you guys really do know how to throw a party," my father whispered.

"No kidding. We are so proud of you," my mom added, giving me a big hug.

I grinned ear to ear.

"Cut! That's a wrap!" I announced to the team.

A few of us ran to a quiet spot. My parents joined me along with Mike Chambers. We had to get exclusive photos and details of the premiere out immediately to international journalists. The first call I made was to Nancy Tartaglione at *Deadline Hollywood*. Earlier she had promised to do something very special for the event. Like Robert Cain and Laurie Burkitt of the *Wall Street Journal*, Nancy also believed deeply in our cause. The exchange of culture and commerce between the US and China *Iron Man 3* fostered was crucially important in her opinion too. Tonight's event symbolized such a vital collaboration, and she wanted to cover the spectacle of it.

"Nancy? Yeah, it's me, Chris. Yeah, Chinese phone. Okay, you got the details via email, but I'm here with Mike Chambers now, and we will get you exclusive photos from the event so you can run something first."

"Okay, I'm ready," she responded. "Please send away, I'll get something online ASAP."

'Iron Man 3' Gala Is First Of Its Kind In Beijing: Photos
By Nancy Tartaglione

> A red carpet gala was held for Iron Man 3 this weekend in Beijing's Taimiao Temple in the Forbidden City. Robert Downey Jr. attended the event in what was the first time a Hollywood film has ever been celebrated inside the imperial temple....

That was how the article started, and it only got better from there.

"We're so glad we could be here," my dad said. "Truly something special."

"Super proud of you," my mom added.

Before I could respond, a text popped up on my phone. I took a glance.

"Just saw *Deadline*. Congrats dude! It all came together. Marvel and Mao getting along pretty nicely! Hungry Like the Wolf!.... J.C."

I smiled, looking back at my parents.

"Thank you both for coming. It really meant a lot to me."

"Wouldn't have missed it," my mom responded.

"I guess you're no longer on vacation anymore, right?" my dad joked, referring to those unsettling days after my firing from William Morris.

"Hah, yeah. No one ever goes down in history for what they did on vacation!"

I pulled out my phone again. Texted Jennifer.

"April 7th here in Beijing. Happy 35th Birthday! Love you so much!!"

"Thank you!" she texted back. "J.C. just forwarded me Nancy's article. Amazing! Congrats! So proud!!!! Love you lots!"

I smiled, soaking up the moment. What a night!

Jennifer couldn't have been more amazing about it all, either. Here was a woman who stood by me through a significant firing, the decimation of our life's savings, a 24/7 US-China schedule, a brutally intrusive and stressful SEC investigation, multiple bouts of negative press, the tarnishing of my hard-earned reputation, the spillover damage to our standing in the community — you get the picture. I could go on and on. She could've left me multiple times. She could've just given up on me. But she never did. She always stood by my side. She was my rock, and I couldn't have gotten past so many rocky times without her. I love her so damn much.

"Thank you. Can't wait to celebrate with you, Kaylie and Dylan when I get back!"

My parents, colleagues, and I walked off towards the brightly lit stage to get some photos together. It had been a long journey to get to that moment, and we all wanted to memorialize it. Such moments don't happen often, and with China, you never know how long they will last before the next challenge rears its angry dragon head.

34.

FINAL TOUCHES

I ARRIVED BACK IN Los Angeles invigorated, yet wary that we still had some work to do. The days leading up to the film's release in China, as well as globally, still held some challenges. For one, we hadn't gotten an official release date from the Chinese government, which was worrisome. We hoped for a release date on a national holiday weekend, typically a time when non-Chinese movies are banned from release. But that particular weekend had another film, *So Young*, scheduled for release also, and it was from an extremely popular Chinese filmmaker, Zhao "Vicki" Wei. Both critics and fans were arguing that *Iron Man 3* could damage *So Young*'s box-office revenues if it were to open the same weekend. Such a result would be a hard blow to the pride of China's local film industry.

To overcome the *So Young* and national holiday challenges, we had to move into overdrive on our lobbying efforts. We pushed both SARFT and CFG with all we could muster, leaving nothing behind with persistence, messaging, relevancy, and hard facts. Our talking points were clear, rehearsed, and reiterated constantly, making sure the dragon fully appreciated the extravagant feast we served. Ten that I remember well were:

1) A Chinese entity, DMG, was involved creatively with the film.

2) A Chinese entity, DMG, was involved as a production company on the film.

3) A Chinese entity, DMG, co-financed the film.

4) A Chinese entity, DMG, is marketing the film.

5) A Chinese entity, DMG, is distributing the film.

6) Chinese stars, Wang Xueqi and Fan Bingbing, were involved in the film.

7) A portion of the film was shot in China and utilized Chinese crew.

8) The film's plot and creative incorporates Chinese relevancy and references.

9) The value and excitement of incorporating China relevancy into the film was announced one year ago to much fanfare.

10) The Forbidden City *Iron Man 3* gala showcased the full extent of China's pride in *Iron Man 3*, and it was heavily attended by both SARFT and CFG.

Pushing these crucial points became even more relevant on April 11. That happened to be the day Quentin Tarantino's film, *Django Unchained*, was abruptly pulled from movie theaters one hour into the very first showings of the film. I mentioned this story earlier because it was a significant event. The completely shocking action by the government entities overseeing the movie business sent shivers down the spines of everyone in Hollywood, Marvel and Disney included.

Quentin's problem only inspired the press to cover any rumor or hint around *Iron Man 3*'s release, or possible cancelation, more ravenously. Was it going to be April 26? Or May 3? Or some other date? Or would it get blocked? Did it get banned? Both confusion and hearsay ran rampant, creating great fodder for public consumption.

For our marketing team, it fostered quite a challenge too. The reality they had to deal with involved marketing a film with no specific call-to-action since no release date existed. The best they could do was to create posters and advertisements simply saying *Iron Man 3* — "coming soon." Not the best way to prep an audience to buy tickets.

After an incredible amount of nail-biting, last-minute lobbying efforts, and public relations narratives supporting our cause, good news finally came. SARFT and CFG approved an official release date for May 1. We received word of it on April 26, not exactly a large cushion of lead time. The mad scramble to change posters, outdoor ads, commercials, and other forms of marketing with the new date started a frenzy and continued 24/7 until May 1.

35.

HISTORY MAKING

"**G**UYS. PLEASE BE quiet," I said to Dylan and Kaylie the morning of April 30, which was close to midnight on May 1 in China. I was driving them to school early that day. "Daddy has to call China."

"*Iron Man* day!" Kaylie shouted.

"Robert Downey makes lots of money today," Dylan added. He was, and still is, very much the Fenton family's version of Alex P. Keaton from the great 1980s sitcom *Family Ties*. For a kid, he's rather obsessed with the idea of making money, and lots of it.

"Shhhh. Please," I said, laughing.

"Kyle Ching! It's Fenton. What's the word?"

"Hey man. It looks great so far. I'm at the theaters in U-town. Midnight screenings are all sold out!" he responded.

"Yes! Love that!"

"In Beijing, forty-six theaters with seventy screenings. Only two have available tickets. Shanghai is even better with sixty-three theaters and eighty-two screenings. Only four theaters have tickets left. Chengdu had twenty-seven theaters and thirty-eight screenings. All *sold out!*"

"Boom!" I shouted. "Please keep me posted. Taking the kids to school, but any other tidbits, please let me know. I need to keep the press informed."

"You got it! And I'll take lots of pictures."

We hung up.

"Daddy is happy today!" Dylan announced.

I laughed. Indeed, I was. With all the things that can go wrong on an opening day—so far, so good!

"Making another call," I announced, calling Andy Anderson.

"Andy, what's the word on your end?" I asked.

"Two thousand midnight screenings, a record! We will definitely break records for midnight screenings and box-office revenue. Unclear what that will be yet. Another record will be tomorrow. Thirty thousand screenings are booked nationwide starting at 9:00 a.m.!"

"Yeah, baby!" I yelled. "What do you think of that, Dylan and Kaylie?"

They both give me a big thumbs up in my rearview mirror.

"Hey, Kaylie. Hi Dylan!" Andy shouted. "IMAX will have a new record tonight for sure also," he added.

"By the way, Robert was on Jon Stewart last night. He said, and I quote, 'China was mind-blowing! I had a ball!'" I said.

"That's so cool," Andy said. "All the *Transformers 3* records should fall this weekend. Fingers crossed. Let's talk later."

"Please keep me posted. Let's hope the Marvel and Mao Effect is in full force!"

"I like that. The Marvel and Mao Effect?"

"Yeah. Thought of it last night. Marvel and Mao. Once enemies, now united!"

We hung up.

"Daddy, when do you start *Iron Man 4*?" Dylan asked.

I laughed out loud. Good question.

I dialed another call.

"Billy, what do you have for me?" I asked Billy Neo.

"Here's what I have for confirmed bookings, and all of these should be records. First, we have six thousand screens. Six thousand! That's more than thirty percent of all the screens in the country."

"Insane! Five years ago, there weren't even five thousand screens in the whole *country*!"

"Midnight screenings — twenty-five hundred. Opening-day screenings look now to be thirty-three thousand."

"Yeah, baby!"

"If those all hold. All records!"

"Please keep me posted. Talk later."

"Will do!"

"What do you guys think?" I asked the kids.

"Today is a happy day for Daddy!" Kaylie responded.

Dylan gave me a thumbs up from the backseat.

"You are both correct!"

"Did you sleep at all last night?" Jennifer asked, handing me a new cup of coffee. I sat at our breakfast table on the morning of May 1, which was the end of the day May 1 in China. I was staring at my computer, handling emails with reporters, Marvel, Disney, DMG — the gamut.

I turned my attention to her.

"Not at all."

"But it's a good kind of insomnia, right?"

"It is," I responded. "Thank you again for being so supportive through all this."

My phone rang. It was Andy.

"Tell me something good?"

"Fenton, you won't believe this, but we destroyed every record out there!"

"Let me have it. What are the numbers?"

"Okay, the final tally for day one is twenty-one-point-five *million dollars*! That breaks every record ever in this country, and it should be the largest single-day box office for Disney in any market other than the US!"

"Incredible! Absolutely incredible."

"How's the coverage in the US?" he asked.

"About to be awesome!" I responded excitedly. "I just emailed your box-office numbers to *Hollywood Reporter*. Those record-breakers should be online in a matter of seconds."

Jennifer walked behind me to catch a view of my computer screen. She wanted to witness what we had all worked so hard for over the past two years.

I refreshed my browser.

"There it is!" I shouted.

"What does it say?"

"*Iron Man 3* Smashes China's Opening-Day Box Office Record!"

"Yeah, baby! Off to celebrate! Talk later." Andy responded gleefully.

I stood up to give Jennifer the biggest kiss.

"We did it!" I said, hugging her tightly. "Wow!"

Two text alarms beeped. I looked at my phone.

"Who is it?" she asked.

"Louis D'Esposito and Kevin Feige from Marvel."

"What did they say?"

"'All here are very excited about the China opening, and it is a testament to all your hard work. Thank you. It's much appreciated. Best…Louis,'" I responded, reading his text verbatim.

"And Feige?"

"Just one word—'AMAZING!'"

She smiled, knowing just how much that simple text meant to me. What a journey!

When it comes to Hollywood, days like May 1, 2013, rarely happen. With all the things that can go wrong in making a movie, it's hard to believe *good* movies can even be made. Compound that with the wild-cards of fickle audiences, missteps with marketing, poor distribution dates, and, in many cases, just terrible luck, it's almost impossible to believe that any movie, if actually *good*, can be *successful* also. The odds are massively stacked against both, and that's without adding China into the mix. A sports bookie would treat such as a three-game—*good*, *successful*, and *China* — parlay bet with an impossible chance of success. The upside, if a miracle did happen, would be an enormous payout.

Our three-game parlay bet did win, though. A massive payout was imminent.

I got to do that morning what few in Hollywood ever get to do. I took congratulatory emails, calls, and texts from peers, colleagues, friends, and family all attuned to the extremely rare success experienced by all of us involved with *Iron Man 3*. I sat at my breakfast table and soaked in those laudatory moments with Jennifer by my side, never once taking it for granted. We worked our butts off to get to that magical moment, and for much of that time, it seemed it would never actually happen.

It did though. It really did.

In my gleeful daze throughout that triumphant day, there were two conversations I remember most. Both for different reasons. The first was a congratulatory call from J.C. He was extremely proud of me for what I had accomplished. He knew how tough a slog it was. He then ended the conversation saying:

> You created a bond between Marvel and Mao. You got it done
> despite the overwhelming obstacles. You were truly Hungry Like
> the Wolf. Now enjoy the rewards.

J.C. always had a Duran Duran reference at the ready. I loved him for that. And even better was his point. Friendships and relationships, whether Marvel and Mao or J.C. and I, were key in his mind for any sort of success in Hollywood and life itself. And to him, success grows as those relationships bond further.

I'll go one more step, though. The Marvel and Mao friendship won't just help those two. As their bond develops, so will the benefits globally. Why? Because the Marvel and Mao relationship evolved beyond just a transaction, just like a strong friendship that goes deeper than just business. The relationship bonded culturally too. It grew into a friendship forged with emotional, creative, empathetic, and humanistic ties. Thanks to *Iron Man 3*. And as that bond grows, so, too, will the bond grow between the US and China. Ultimately, that stronger bilateral relationship will benefit the whole world.

I then spoke with Dan. We recapped many of the trials and tribulations of the past two years with a handful of laughs. It was now finally comfortable to do that. At the time of many of those challenges, it hadn't been. In fact, during many moments, things had felt so hopeless that finding any humor was a lost cause.

As the call came to a close, Dan congratulated me. He told me it was a job well done, and that we conquered so much against so many obstacles. Never should we doubt ourselves again.

Just before hanging up he asked, "Now that *Iron Man 3* is done, what's next?"

We both laughed, but I knew he was serious. What was next? What challenge can we top that is even bigger? Even better?

I didn't have an answer for him then, but it wasn't long before I did. However, as I learned from Marvel, one never discloses any secrets to a story's sequel prematurely.

It is time to fade to black. At least for now....

36.

THE AFTERMATH: TYING UP LOOSE ENDS

OVER THE NEXT few weeks, *Iron Man 3* grossed a staggering $125 million in China, representing more than 10 percent of the film's worldwide gross. *Iron Man 3*'s worldwide box office of $1.2 billion was the fifth highest in history. Since *Iron Man 3*, Marvel has had six films gross more than $180 million in China, with *Avengers: Endgame* being the most successful, grossing a whopping $610 million.

A month after *Iron Man 3*'s historic China run, I delivered a keynote at *The Wrap*'s Grill Conference: "Was *Iron Man 3* a Movie or a Treaty with China?"

Weeks later I gave a presentation to the United States Congress: "Film Diplomacy: A Win-Win for US-China Relations—The *Iron Man 3* Story."

Iron Man 3's monumental success enabled DMG to go public on China's Shenzhen Exchange in 2014. Shortly thereafter, DMG's market cap surpassed $8 billion.

On November 24, 2014, WikiLeaks revealed our involvement in the SEC investigation publicly after hackers breached the computer system at Sony Studios.

On September 2, 2015, the SEC finally concluded its investigation on us. No enforcement action was recommended.

My long, successful run with DMG ended March 2018. Applying the wisdom gained from those trailblazing years towards improving the US-China relationship became the priority mission of my career.

Jennifer continues to be the love of my life. My rock. My escape. And my salvation.

Dylan and Kaylie continue to grow up quickly. As parents, Jennifer and I are dedicated to raising them the best we possibly can. As a professional working between the US and China, I'm dedicated to leaving them a world where the two superpowers get along.

And I still have my Rolodexes.

J.C. Spink passed away on April 18, 2017.

At his standing-room-only memorial on May 4, 2017, I gave one of the six eulogies. I told our Duran Duran story, and the room filled with laughter. J.C., wearing the extremely comfortable pajamas heaven provides, grinned ear to ear.

Hungry Like the Wolf.

Rest in peace.

37.

THE AFTERWARD: TO PONDER

CONRAD HOTEL, HONG KONG
AUGUST 29, 2019, 11:48 P.M.

THE DISTINCT, PEPPERY odor of tear gas wafts through the salty, nighttime air. Sitting on my hotel balcony overlooking the twinkling lights of Victoria Harbour in Hong Kong, I find it impossible to sleep. Down below, the riot police and cement barricades line the street. Last week, protestors took over Hong Kong International—yes, one of the world's busiest airports—halting all flights in and out. Earlier this week the citizens came out 1.7 million strong, boiling over with frustration about a law put in motion by their leader, Carrie Lam, the chief executive of Hong Kong.

Earlier today, behind closed doors, Ms. Lam told a small delegation of us—including Congressman Alan Lowenthal (D-CA), Congresswoman Dina Titus (D-NV), and Congresswoman Ann Kirkpatrick (D-AZ)—that she made an uncalculated error in proposing a bill allowing extradition to China. She underestimated the cultural impact on the local Hong Kong populace, and her proposal ignited a tinderbox of growing discontent which began when the British rule of Hong Kong ended in 1997 and year-by-year has been building toward the eventual full takeover by China in 2047. God help us when that occurs. If we—US, China, or Hong Kong—make even the tiniest cultural miscalculations, the island could plunge into chaos, even war with China, which would mean its annihilation.

Meanwhile, back in the United States, President Trump continues to escalate tensions with China, tweeting his way deeper and deeper into a never-ending trade war, and even worse, a rapidly deteriorating bilateral relationship.

I check my phone. A new tweet from the president pops up.

"What happened overnight?" a member of Congress will inevitably ask me tomorrow during morning briefings.

"'Our great American companies are hereby ordered to immediately start looking for an alternative to China,'" I'll read from my phone.

"Can a president even order that?" someone will most likely ask. And we'll all shake our heads at the increased challenge of our diplomatic mission.

The US-China relationship is in tatters—no exaggeration. We hear it every day from the Chinese leadership. I, along with the aforesaid distinguished members of the US Congress, am part of a team tapped to help bridge the two superpowers back together. And our Chinese counterparts have also formed a team.

I slide open the balcony door and step back into the cool hotel room. I know I shouldn't be here, literally. It's a miracle, considering the masses of defiant protestors congregating in the airport. None of our team knew if the US Consulate would prohibit our visit, citing security concerns, or if our mainland Chinese hosts would cancel our border crossing to ensure we didn't side with protestors or make "face-losing" statements to the international press. Face-saving is critical to accomplishing anything in China. We are moving backwards, to put it lightly.

As a trustee of the USAI, I'm tasked with fostering dialogue and diplomacy between China's leaders and members of the United States Congress, an initiative, I mentioned earlier, I've been doing since 2012. The Institute has conducted similar missions long before my involvement, more than 140 of them over forty years, and long before I helped build an $8 billion media company in China, at a time when no one in media wanted to touch China with a ten-foot pole.

What we need to realize now is that there's no time to waste. While pundits and politicians in the US are fixated on criticizing China over issues like tariffs, the rights of Hong Kong, military encroachment, politics, human rights, technology transfers, labor conditions, censorship, and other critical banter, I'm thinking, quite literally, of movies, the NBA, art, tourism, classic muscle cars, pop songs, sneakers, ping pong tournaments, Strongman competitions, Michael, LeBron, and Kobe, pandas, and superheroes like Tony Stark & Dr. Wu. The exchange of commerce and culture is essential, and it's needed now more than ever.

Why? Because without it, a cold war between China and the US begins and, unfortunately, never ends. That's not a world any of us would want to live in.

Carrie Lam appreciates this message. Just today she asked that US leaders tone down negative rhetoric towards China and stressed the importance of continuing commerce and cultural exchange between all three parties. As Ms. Lam so bluntly stated, "We must continue forging those bonds." C.H. Tung, the very first chief executive of Hong Kong, emphasized the same sentiment over dinner this evening.

During the Beijing portion of our trip, everyone, from top foreign ministry officials to Standing Committee members of the National People's Congress, expressed shock and awe with the speed of deterioration in the bilateral relationship. The party line went, "The two countries have lost the ability to communicate to prevent conflict. Constructive dialogue has all but ceased." Yet what each side fails to acknowledge is that they both need the other. Without resolving the trade dispute, nurturing civility towards one another, and promoting proper channels of diplomacy, both sides lose.

Cultural and commercial exchange results in a collaborative form of diplomacy, engulfing the "souls" of both nations and allowing them to work as one. This kind of diplomacy brings unity, both emotionally and economically. The benefits start with the cultural businesses, as I detailed earlier, and the individuals, athletes, and artists directly involved in those cultural businesses. They develop into an upward chain reaction, eventually influencing each nation's leaders. To ignore or misunderstand these principles is to guarantee the failure of one's economic mission, product, service, business, or dream in China. Therefore, it is a mandate of the modern world to understand how cultural and commercial diplomacy works, and why it's an ingredient for success. Or alternatively said, without it, a component for geopolitical failure.

Cultural and commercial diplomacy has been referred to as "soft" power, but it's far from that. It can induce more change than presidential visits, parades, political speeches, or even military force. One could argue that Big Macs (commerce) and David Hasselhoff (culture) had more to do with the end of the Cold War than an arsenal of nuclear weapons.

This diplomacy is also good for business — really good! *Iron Man 3* is a perfect example. By simply understanding the mechanics from a thirty-thousand-foot level, billions of dollars can be made. I've witnessed it firsthand, and you have now read about it. I have also seen how cultural diplomacy can be fraught with danger. For every Tony Stark or Michael Jordan success story, there are thousands of failed attempts to bridge the gap. A multitude of factors can contribute to this, including bad actors, bad ideas, inexperience, social media mishaps, lack of confidence, hubris, ignorance, weak grit, and poor execution, just to name a few. Even worse, the price of crossing the culture gap in the wrong direction can be catastrophic — think Islamist gunmen killing editors of *Charlie Hebdo*, or the riots following a Danish cartoon of Muhammad with a bomb in his turban. Navigating these divides requires careful consideration and a guide.

You provided the consideration. My story, I hope, was your trusted guide. And, most importantly, I sincerely wish that it helps prevent another cold war between the world's two superpowers.

And through my own self-reflection, as I told my story, I see I have been complicit. I have been feeding the dragon, contributing to some of what the China hawks passionately protest. That said, my mission has remained steady: we either continue to coexist through the bond formed by the exchange of culture and commerce, or we consciously start a cold war between the world's two superpowers.

I hope you join my mission.

FIVE WEEKS LATER...
UNITED STATES OF AMERICA
OCTOBER 4, 2019

The NBA's Houston Rockets' GM, Daryl Morey, tweeted, "Fight for freedom. Stand with Hong Kong."

A storm of controversy resulted. China swiftly punished the NBA by taking its games off the air and off streamers. Consumers boycotted Rockets and NBA products. The US side "woke" to the idea of American capitalism pandering to China's Communist Party. It was a broom to a hornets' nest. Brooklyn Nets owner and Alibaba co-founder, Joseph Tsai, summarized his view of Morey's tweet, "Supporting a separatist movement in a Chinese territory is one of those third-rail issues, not only for the Chinese government, but also for all citizens in China."

Turned out his view differed from that of most Americans.

UNITED STATES OF AMERICA
OCTOBER 16, 2019

At the peak of the controversy, I appeared on *Bloomberg Businessweek*. I told host, Jason Kelly:

The NBA situation is obviously controversial to talk about. But it's also a fantastic moment in the commercial and cultural exchange between the US and China to have this conversation. The pillars — what I refer to as "Fenton's Five Forces" of diplomacy [a term Andy Campion, COO of Nike, recommended I emphasize more and also a tribute to "Porter's Five Forces" of business] — that keep the superpowers communicating and collaborating are also the pillars responsible for preventing a cold war. The first three — politics, human rights, and national security — we don't have an easy time agreeing with China on. We probably never will. That leaves us with the two others — commerce and culture. The NBA is one of the greatest cultural exchanges we have with China, and it's also a big commercial endeavor. Two pillars — two of Fenton's Five Forces — connecting the two superpowers. We lose those pillars, we lose that connection.

By not taking sides in the Hong Kong/China situation, the NBA keeps the ability to make billions in China. It also keeps two of the five pillars intact, helping the two superpowers avoid sliding into a dangerous modern-day cold war. But is the NBA's silence simply a subtle way to do China's dirty work? I once thought I knew the answer. Now, I'm not so sure. If anything, I'm definitely conflicted philosophically. To feed or not to feed the *dragon*, that is the true question — the moral, trillion-dollar dilemma facing Hollywood, the NBA, and American business.

However, deep in my heart I know we *must* continue to coexist through the bonds formed by the consistent bilateral exchange of culture and commerce. We *must* continue to feed the dragon. But we must do so without resorting to activities that marginalize the principles, ethics, interests, and beliefs of Americans. And no longer can we keep the conversation behind closed doors. Through open dialogue we will devise a more strategic, innovative, and intelligent implementation of China's often strong-armed requests, doing so without selling our souls as Americans.

I'm aware that this is no easy task, but I'm also 100 percent confident it can be done. All we have to do is speak openly, think differently, be true to who we are as Americans, and maintain the ardent desire to keep bilateral collaboration ongoing.

Not only is there big business to be had by doing so, but the fate of the world depends on it.

38.

POSTSCRIPT

I COMPLETED THIS BOOK in early January 2020. Three globally volatile and historic months have passed since, so I wanted to address a few items prior to printing.

1) Kobe Bryant tragically passed away. I witnessed his magic as one of the great ambassadors of bilateral cultural and commercial exchange. He bonded the superpowers through his charisma, his passion for both cultures, and his talent. He will truly be missed by his fans on both sides of the Pacific, but his template for bridging cultures will live on. May he rest in peace.

2) The virus, COVID-19, has spread across the world, disrupting the lives of everyone in China, the United States, and most other nations. Journalists, peers, and friends have asked my views on every aspect of this outbreak in terms of China. There are so many layers to the story and even more unknowns. Speculation is irresponsible, and diving into the micro will only create confusion. Therefore, I always go back to the important macro lessons of this book—what drives the decisions of the CCP.

First, the Chinese government wants their 1.4 billion people just-happy-enough that they don't revolt. Second, the CCP can achieve that by creating jobs and a larger middle class through strong economic growth. And third, they can foster populace contentment by orchestrating strategic public narratives through the Propaganda Ministry.

The COVID-19 outbreak severely damaged the Chinese government's ability to accomplish all three. Therefore, the CCP's biggest priority is to fix those. As witnessed, the CCP is suddenly insistent on getting people back to work, restarting factories, opening retail, forcing the People's Bank of China to take drastic actions, and forbidding investors from betting against an economic recovery. These all aid the second objective above.

With each of those cogs in China's economic engine falling into place, China's Propaganda Ministry needs to promote them to their populace. "China is back online!" is the key theme, and that occurs through symbolic means — pushing factories to billow smoke into the sky, encouraging cars on the road, or opening movie theaters across the country — or through tangible stimulus measures such as loosening credit, lowering reserve requirements, or providing large-scale fiscal stimulus. Getting the gears of their high-growth economy moving again quickly is a feat necessary in both practical and symbolic terms for maintaining the public's confidence.

But more needs to be done to keep the 1.4 billion Chinese content. The Chinese Communist Party also has to avoid blame for the outbreak of COVID-19 in the first place. And the potential of such blame landing squarely on the CCP lurks large. Internally, there have been many criticisms that Beijing acted too slowly and are largely to blame for the virus's spread. Externally, the message is the same. The world is blaming the Chinese for the global disruption created by COVID-19's spread, and the war of words is rapidly escalating — especially from the United States government. As a result, the narrative coming from Beijing is one of deflection and self-preservation. They are insisting COVID-19 came from the outside, and they are adamant that their efforts slowed the contagion so that the rest of the world had time to prepare.

I'm not agreeing with Beijing's rush to force its economy back online with the uncertainties of further COVID-19 spread so obvious, nor am I agreeing with their ongoing it-wasn't-us propaganda campaign. Instead, I'm simply reiterating the three lessons from above and throughout the book. Understanding China's point of view and motivations from the thirty-thousand-foot level helps us understand why they do the things that they do. Such awareness gives us the sound foundation needed to properly develop an effective and strategic response.

3) And that strategic American response is more crucial now than ever. I truly fear where the bilateral relationship is going. Once the COVID-19 crisis comes to pass, the US-China relationship could enter a Cold War phase. US leaders instigating disputes by labeling COVID-19 in derogatory ways or the CCP spreading misleading propaganda about COVID-19's origin is counterproductive. Not only that, it wastes valuable time and energy. Leaders should solely focus on ending the global crisis.

Post-crisis, and even though I'm growing more hawkish daily, I still must stress the importance of looking at China as a massive opportunity both politically and economically. China hawks should keep in mind that with every American product and service monetizing China's massive market, there is American influence that goes with it. Each time the Chinese watch a Hollywood movie, cheer during an NBA game, study at an American college, drive an American car, or run in a pair of Nike shoes, they are touched by the subtle soft power of ingenuity, initiative, democratic principles, and culture from Americans. And economically, the growing Sino-consumption of American products and services creates jobs and increases our nation's GDP.

I implore steadfast hawks to recognize this opportunity. The continued bilateral exchange of culture and commerce can benefit Americans greatly. And though we need to be more strategic and cognizant of underlying CCP agendas moving forward, that very mission is the underlying theme of my book, and it will always be what drives me personally. I sincerely believe the fate of the world depends on it.

Stay healthy and safe through these challenging times.

Godspeed....